Limitless Wrestling
The First Five Years

Michael J. Labbe

Limitless Wrestling: The First Five Years by: Michael J. Labbe
www.thewrestlinginsomniac.com
www.limitlesswrestling.com
© 2021 Michael J. Labbe
All rights reserved. No portion of this book may be reproduced in any form without permission from the publisher, except as permitted by U.S. copyright law. For permissions contact: LabbeMichaelJ@gmail.com
Cover design Michael J. Labbe
ISBN: 9798727486627
Imprint: Independently published

Introduction

Welcome to *Limitless Wrestling: The First Five Years*. In May 2020 during the first months of the pandemic I was working on a post for my blog *The Wrestling Insomniac* when I decided to make a spreadsheet showing the wins and losses of everyone that has wrestled in Limitless Wrestling. I was going to use this data for various posts that I was going to write over the summer leading up to Limitless' five-year anniversary. Instead I decided to compile this data into the book that you are holding. When I started out in my mind, I was thinking that this would be the Limitless Wrestling version of the old *Pro Wrestling Illustrated Almanac and Book of Facts*.

The rating period of this book covers the first five years of Limitless Wrestling from their debut in September 2015 at *Stage One* until the *2020 Vacationland Cup*. I was going to stop after the end of *The Road* Season 1, however after the announcement of the *Vacationland Cup* and the crowning of a new Limitless World Champion I knew that it had to be included. The win/loss records, the wrestler profiles, the show results and more only cover this time period. The full results for *The Road* Season 2 and Season 3, up until this goes to press, are included but are not part of the statistics.

I have done my best to include the most complete profile that I could of every wrestler that has competed in a Limitless ring, however that was not possible for all 303 competitors. I would like to thank everyone that I reached out too on Facebook, Email,

and Twitter answering my questions towards completing this book. I can't thank Randy Carver enough for being so open and accepting of this project. As you can see from the show reviews, I did use my blog for some reference as to what happened at the shows that I attended, and I listened to several podcasts that Randy had been on as well as the Limitless Wrestling podcast for further background.
I would like to thank Harry Aaron, Wrestlebrook Photo, Sunny D Photography, Jason Worthing and others for sharing their photos with me for this book.
Thank you to my friend Brandon Myers for his help in proofreading and editing this book.
This has been a passion project of mine for the past year and I thank you for taking the time to read it. I hope you enjoy it!

Michael J. Labbe

LIMITLESS
WRESTLING

Table of Contents

Randy Carver Jr.	1
The Numbers	6
Show Results	9
What Was Going To Happen	136
Alternate Show Posters	139
Bitter Rivals	145
Wrestler Profiles	153
Manager Profiles	348
Ring Announcer Profiles	354
Referee Profiles	357
The Limitless World Championship	365
Other Title Matches In Limitless Wrestling	375
Year End Awards	383
Top 10 Moments In Limitless History	392
More Limitless Wrestling Results	394
Epilogue	416

Randy Carver Jr.

A native of Lagrange, Maine Randy Carver grew up a fan of wrestling. He doesn't have a distinct memory of when he started watching he just always did. His first memory of Independent Wrestling was in September 2008 when he saw a poster with Doink the Clown for an NAWA: North Atlantic Wrestling Association show that had happened two days prior. His mother took him to the next NAWA show on October 11, 2008 in Brewer, Maine. Prior to seeing that poster he had no clue that Independent Wrestling existed.

He first dabbled in the world of pro wrestling in 2010 at the age of 13 when he started promoting backyard wrestling shows with his friends. He never wanted to be a wrestler himself, but he wanted to do every other aspect of the business. When he was 15, he got his first start in wrestling with the Brewer, Maine based IWE: Independent Wrestling Entertainment. He worked on the ring and helped set up the venues for the shows. A few months later the scheduled ring announcer wasn't able to attend the show and Randy volunteered to step in and perform the duties.

In 2014, Johnny Torres started booking for Paragon League Wrestling in Connecticut and he brought Carver down to be the ring announcer. By the end of 2014/early 2015 Randy was getting booked to ring announce in other states including in New York for Tier 1 Wrestling and a couple other promotions in Massachusetts. It's interesting to note that Randy didn't have his driver's license, so his mom drove him to these shows. The support that Randy gets from his family is evident to those that attend Limitless events with his mom and dad tearing tickets and working the merchandise table. It's interesting as they were not wrestling fans but became fans through Randy's fandom.

According to Randy the Maine wrestling scene was in a weird state; "There not too much going on and what was, was not the best environment or the best shows. Crowds were low, there were no real prominent promotions in the state."

Watching promotions in other states he started seeing how wrestling could be presented and how wrestling could be done differently. He grew tired of the culture of Maine wrestling and wanted to change it for the better. In November 2014, he started the ball rolling by talking with a close circle of people including the Maine State Posse, Ace Romero, Troy Nelson, and Xavier Bell. Initially the name of the promotion was going to be called Emerge Wrestling.

"I felt like Emerge defined what we were trying to do early on. We wanted to sort of rise from the ashes, so to speak, of a dwindling and defeated Maine wrestling scene to provide something worthwhile," Randy recalled. While researching the name, it was discovered that another promotion based in Indiana debuted as EMERGE Wrestling on January 10, 2015, so a different name had to be found.

"Limitless came up in conversation with the cliché phrase the possibilities are limitless, and it just hit me right there. I always wanted to build a platform that is useful for all types of wrestlers and attractive to all kinds of viewers. A wrestling smorgasbord, and that to me is the definition of a Limitless wrestling company."

Stage One was originally slated to take place at the Sea Dog in Bangor and two months prior to the event they contacted him stating they had double booked and needed to move him out a week, which was not going to work. When he initially started trying to book venues for shows Randy was just 17 years old and he had a lot of trouble trying to secure buildings. That all seemed to go away once he turned 18. He ended up running City Side Restaurant in Brewer, the venue where IWE ran their monthly shows. Trouble struck again, when this first show had a lot of talent cancel just a couple weeks prior to the show. Anthony

Greene, who would go on to be one of the top stars in Limitless, was not initially scheduled to appear on the card and was a late replacement.

For his second show, *Killin' & Thrillin'*, Randy moved operations to Orono and the American Legion Post 84. He never wanted to run in the same town as IWE and even tried to book the Legion for *Stage One*, but it was unavailable.

When the promotion started the attendance was low as Randy was battling the poor reputation of the Maine wrestling scene. However, that changed on his third event *Under Fire*, January 30, 2016 when 260 fans packed the American Legion to see Zack Sabre Jr. take on Chris Hero. This match helped jump start Limitless Wrestling in multiple ways, and they would continue to pack the Legion hall and build a following each month. The good word of Chris Hero also helped build Randy's reputation in booking other wrestlers that may have been leery of working with a promoter for the first time.

Over the years Randy moved Limitless to the Westbrook Armory and the Portland Club for a three-year run and then in the fall of 2019 he found a new home for Limitless at the AMVets Hall in Yarmouth until the pandemic brought Limitless back home to the

American Legion in Orono for The Road tapings. Along the way Limitless would pop up at festivals like La Kermesse Festival, the Hollis Pirate Festival, and even the Litchfield Fair.

When Randy started Limitless, he handed the ring announcing duties himself, however at the third show *Under Fire* he was sick with pneumonia and called in Rich Palladino to do the job. Rich Palladino or Ethan Scott have handled ring announcing duties since. Aside from his promoter duties and running almost all aspects of the shows Randy has provided commentary throughout the years and is the voice of The Road, Limitless Wrestling's weekly show on IWTV.

The Numbers

The rating period for this book and this section is from *Stage One* September 12, 2015 thru *The Road* Season 1 Episode 11 which aired October 7, 2020 and the *2020 Vacationland Cup*.

During this rating period 303 wrestlers have appeared at 43 events competing in 342 matches

Year by Year

2015
2 shows 15 matches 2 different venues

2016
8 shows 75 matches 3 different venues

2017
11 shows 93 matches 4 different venues

2018
8 shows 77 matches 4 different venues

2019
10 shows 81 matches 4 different venues

2020
3 shows 28 matches 1 venue
The Road Season 1, 11 episodes 48 matches

Most Consecutive Shows: 18 Xavier Bell
September 12, 2015 *Stage One* to July 21, 2017 *Nothing Gold Can Stay*

Most Total Wins: 30 Anthony Greene

Most Consecutive Wins: 14 Anthony Greene
September 12, 2015 *Stage One* to June 23, 2017 *La Kermesse Festival Night 1*
He also had a 12-match winning streak winning his final 12 matches in Limitless Wrestling

Most Total Losses: 17 Alexander Lee & DangerKid

Most Consecutive Losses: 10 Alexander Lee
July 23, 2016 *Hook, Line, & Sinker* to July 27, 2018 *Vacationland Cup*

Most Matches: Ace Romero 41 matches, DangerKid 40 matches

Most Matches between two opponents: 7 Anthony Green & JT Dunn

First Pin fall
September 12, 2015 *Stage One* City Side Restaurant Brewer
Fatal Four Way: The Influence: Mike Montero & Jason Devine defeated The M1nute Men: Devin Blaze & Tommy Trainwreck, The Cute n' Brute Connection: Owen Brody & BA Tatum and The Falcon Corps: Adam Falcon & Joe Quick

First Submission
January 30, 2016 *Under Fire* American Legion Post 84 Orono
"Fire Brand" Brian Fury submitted Xavier Bell

First No-Contest
October 29, 2016 *Who Watches the Watchmen?* The Field House at University of Maine Orono
Champ Mathews vs. Mark Moment

First Count-Out
November 03, 2017 *Hybrid Moments* Portland Club
Anthony Greene vs. JT Dunn double count-out

First Reverse Decision
January 24, 2020 *Flirtin' With Disaster* AMVets Hall Yarmouth
CJ Cruz vs. JT Dunn

First Disqualification
The Road Season 1 Episode 3 *Aired August 12, 2020* American Legion Post 84 Orono
Best of 5 Series Match 2: "Frisky" Frank Jaeger vs Alexander Lee

SHOW RESULTS

STAGE ONE
September 12, 2015 City Side Restaurant Brewer, Maine

- Fatal Four Way: The Influence: Mike Montero & Jason Devine defeated The M1nute Men: Devin Blaze & Tommy Trainwreck, The Cute n' Brute Connection: Owen Brody & BA Tatum and The Falcon Corps: Adam Falcon & Joe Quick
- "All Good" Anthony Greene defeated Good Hank Flanders
- Alexander Lee pinned "Cold Steel" Chuck O'Neil
- Scott Wild defeated "Fire Brand" Brian Fury
- Fatal Four Way: Brick Mastone defeated Isiah Kassidy, Xavier Bell, & "Top Shelf" Troy Nelson

- "Top Talent" Christian Casanova pinned "Mourning Star" Marcus Hall with Kenneth Banks
- Ace Romero pinned Alex Mason

Limitless' first show was supposed to take place at the Sea Dog in Bangor; however, a double booking caused the venue to be moved to City Side. As this was the first show everyone was making their Limitless debut. This show is the only appearances of Good Hank Flanders, Joe Quick, and Marcus Hall. At this show Xavier Bell started his ironman streak appearing at the first of 18 consecutive shows. Anthony Greene was a replacement for Verne Vicallo, also Mike Orlando and Steve Scott had the cancel day of the show.

150 plus people inside City Side for Stage One

Notes from Roy's Reviews on The Wrestling Insomniac blog: Good show and big breath of fresh air in the state of Maine. Good action the entire night. O'Neil vs. Lee was crazy. The best show in Maine in months and the best show I have ever seen at Cityside Restaurant. Notable Matches: Alexander Lee vs. Chuck O'Neil & Ace Romero vs. Alex Mason.

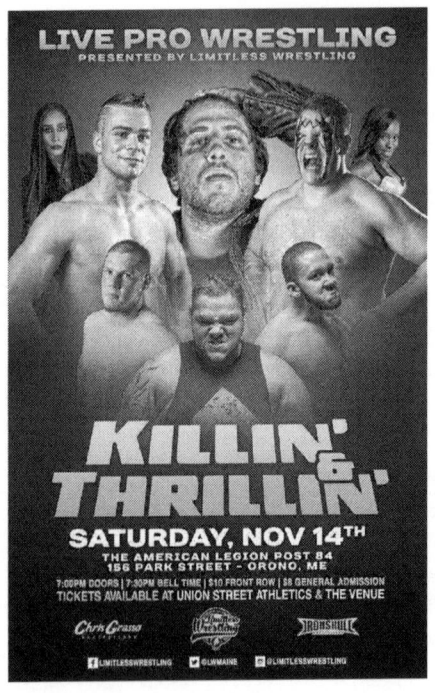

KILLIN' & THRILLIN'
November 25, 2015 American Legion Post 84 Orono, Maine

- "All Good" Anthony Greene pinned Flip Gordon
- Fatal Four Way: The Influence: Mike Montero & Jason Devine defeated Bash Brothers: "Cold Steel" Chuck O'Neil & Eric Spicely, Super Savages: Caveman & Mantequilla, and Da Hoodz: Davey Cash & Kris Pyro
- Brick Mastone pinned Max Smashmaster w/ a belly to belly suplex
- No DQ: "Dirt Dawg" Jeremy Leary pinned "Your Hero" Shane Marvel
- Tim Donst pinned "The Carnivore" Alex Mason

- Scramble Match: Xavier Bell defeated "Top Shelf" Troy Nelson, Alexander Lee, Christian Casanova, & Isiah Kassidy with a piledriver on Nelson
- Maximum Mecca pinned Sonya Strong
- Ace Romero pinned "White Delight" Scotty Wild

Show two would be the premier at the venue that would be home the Limitless for six consecutive shows. This show featured the debuts of Da Hoodz: Kris Pyro & Davey Cash, Eric Spicely, Flip Gordon, Jeremy Leary, Max Smashmaster, Maximum Mecca, Shane Marvel, Sonya Strong, Super Savages: Caveman & Mantequilla and Tim Donst. This show marks the only appearances to date of Tim Donst and Shane Marvel. This is also the first appearance of DangerKid but not as an in-ring performer. Kenneth Banks was originally going to wrestle Christian Casanova however pulled off the show and Casanova was added to the Scramble Match.

Notes from my blog The Wrestling Insomniac: Top to bottom this was one of the finest wrestling cards I have ever attended in Maine and the best since the 2012 Robbie Ellis Cup in Fairfield. Da Hoodz were the work horses of their match carrying it from beginning to end. For reasons unknown the Bash Brothers walked out before the finish signaling, they didn't need this. This was

Marvel's last match in New England before moving to Arizona. The main event was explosive and hard hitting as Ace Romero and Scotty Wild beat the tar out of each other. Romero can fly over the top rope in a way a man his size shouldn't be able to. You could see the welts and handprints on Wild's chest for the chops he received from Romero. Wild gave just as much as he received lighting up Romero with chops of his own. After his victory Romero announced he would be fighting AR Fox when Limitless returns in January. My buddy Mikey LaFreniere commented on the ride home that he thought this show was better than their first. I cannot stress enough that if you are a fan of wrestling you need to make the drive to Limitless it's well worth it.

"All Good" Anthony Greene locking up with my son Canaan. This is one of my favorite photos, it shows me that AG never lost his love and fandom of wrestling, and that he wants to spread that to all of his fans.

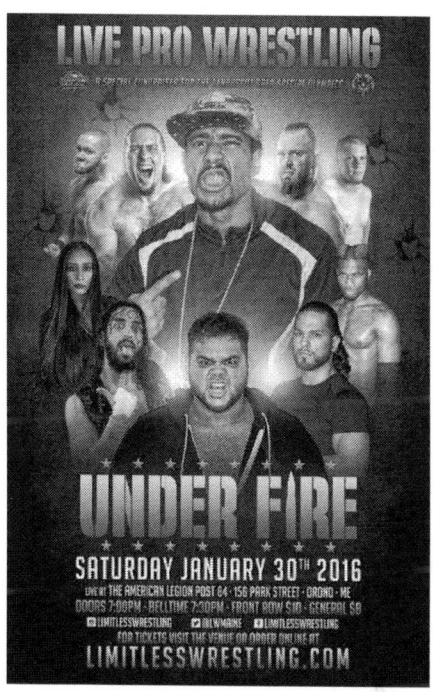

UNDER FIRE
January 30, 2016 American Legion Post 84 Orono, Maine

- Ace Romero pinned AR Fox
- Fatal Four Way Elimination Match: House of Glory Tag Team Champions: Private Party: Marq Quen & Isiah Kassidy defeated Cuban Rum Crisis: "Top Shelf" Troy Nelson & George, Alexander Lee & DangerKid, and Herbal Corps: Rembrandt Lewis & Adam Falcon last eliminating Cuban Rum Crisis
- House of Glory Elite Champion: Anthony Gangone defeated Sonya Strong
- "Fire Brand" Brian Fury submitted Xavier Bell

- The Influence: Mike Montero & Jason Devine defeated M1nute Men: Devin Blaze & Tommy Trainwreck
- Fatal Four Way: "White Delight" Scott Wild defeated Kris Pyro, Christian Casanova, & Ken Broadway
- Brick Mastone pinned "Carnivore" Alex Mason
- Zack Sabre Jr. pinned Chris Hero in 24 minutes 10 seconds

On a stormy winter night, 260 fans packed the American Legion hall for a match that legit has main evented around the world. This show featured the debuts of Anthony Gangone, AR Fox, Chris Hero, JGeorge, Ken Broadway, Marq Quen, Rembrandt Lewis, Rich Palladino, Zack Sabre Jr., and the in-ring debut of DangerKid. This show also featured the debuted of Private Party as a tag team, Isiah Kassidy made his Limitless Debut at *Stage One*. Ace and Fox were the original main event, however, was moved to the main event when Zack Sabre Jr. and Chris Hero was added last minute.

Xavier Bell with a Straight Jacket on Brian Fury

Notes from my blog The Wrestling Insomniac: The opening match was AR Fox vs. Ace Romero in a fast paced and hard-hitting match up. Fox nailed Romero with so many of his aerial moves including his ultra-impressive dive over the corner post to the floor. Ace got the win in one his best matches I have ever seen. Isiah Kassidy is young and is wicked good, can't wait to see more of him. House of Glory Elite Champion: Anthony Gangone successfully defended his championship against a very game Sonya Strong. This is only the second time I have seen Sonya and she is fantastic. Not only that but she is one tough lady. Gangone won with what looked a combination of a cobra clutch and cattle mutilation, the referee stopped the match after Sonya's had dropped 3 times.

The main event of the evening could be a main event on any card around the world as Zack Sabre Jr. wrestled Chris Hero in the greatest matches I have ever seen in person. Being in Maine I'm used to "names" coming in and going through the motions of a match and this was not the case at all. They seemed to hold nothing back battling in and out of the ring hitting each other some very stiff shots and painful looking holds. After 24 minutes and 10 seconds of competition Sabre scored the pin for the win. Both wrestlers received a much-deserved standing ovation for their efforts. This was the night I first met my pal Bradford who would be a regular at Limitless Wrestling becoming Bradford the Barber.

Sabre tying up Hero

Chris Hero hitting elbows with Bradford during his entrance

DON'T FEAR THE SLEEPER
March 19, 2016 American Legion Post 84 Orono, Maine

- Fatal Four Way: Da Hoodz: Davey Cash & Chris Pyro defeated The Influence: Mike Montero & Jason Devine, M1nute Men: Devin Blaze & Tommy Trainwreck and The Beaver Boys: Jon Silver & Alex Reynolds
- Xavier Bell pinned George Gatton
- Alexander Lee & Aiden Aggro defeated DangerKid & Wrecking Ball Legursky when Lee pinned DangerKid
- "White Delight" Scott Wild pinned "Prince of Queens" Brian Myers
- Sonya Strong defeated Mistress Belmont
- Johnny Torres defeated Alex Mason

- Four Way Elimination Match: "Dirt Dawg" Jeremy Leary w/ Skylar defeated Sasha Jenkins, Johnny Clash, & Big Daddy Cruz last elimination Jenkins.
- Team New England: Donovan Dijak, Ace Romero, & "All Good" Anthony Greene defeated Team Pazuzu: "Dirty Daddy" Chris Dickinson & EYFBO: Angel Ortiz & Mike Draztik

This show featured the debut of The Beaver Boys: Alex Reynolds & John Silver, Big Daddy Cruz, Brian Myers, "Dirty Daddy" Chris Dickinson, Angel Ortiz & Mike Draztik (now known as Santana & Ortiz), Donovan Dijak, George Gatton, Johnny Clash, Johnny Torres, Mistress Belmont, Aiden Aggro, Sasha Jenkins and Wrecking Ball Legursky. Skylar made her debut as the valet of Jeremy Leary. The original plan was to have Dickinson vs. Dijak; however, the match was changed to start the build for Dijak and Romero. On a personal note this is the show that Randy Carver likes the least, the draw wasn't good, he didn't think the majority of the matches clicked, and they had issues with the cameras. He felt the show was inadequate.

Notes from my blog The Wrestling Insomniac: The main event six-man tag was friggin awesome! Everyone in that match is really good, and you would be crazy to say you don't want to see any of them back. I think EYFBO should come back for one of the Fatal Four Ways matches. I would like to see Chris Dickinson vs. Ace Romero. Randy delivered once again with a kick ass show. He posted that he wasn't happy with the show and was going to make up for it in May, but in my opinion, you would be hard pressed to find anyone of the fans that attended that night who were unhappy with the show!

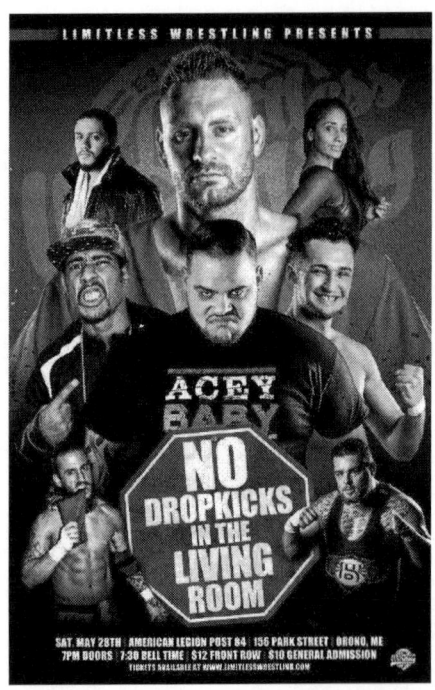

NO DROPKICKS IN THE LIVING ROOM
May 28, 2016 American Legion Post 84 Orono, Maine

- Pre-show matches
- DangerKid pinned Aiden Aggro
- Alexander Lee pinned Danny Miles

- Main Card
- Ace Romero defeated JT Dunn
- EYFBO: Angel Ortiz & Mike Draztik defeated Private Party: Marq Quen & Isiah Kassidy
- Sonya Strong pinned "The Bad Boy" Joey Janela
- Da Hoodz: Davey Cash & Chris Pyro defeated The Influence: Mike Montero & Jason Devine
- Tommaso Ciampa pinned Xavier Bell

- Jeff Cobb defeated Keith Lee
- "All Good" Anthony Greene pinned Warbeard Hanson
- Alex Mason defeated Scott Wild
- Crusade for Change: House of Glory Elite Champion: "The Rogue" Anthony Gangone and M1nute Men: Devin Blaze & Tommy Trainwreck defeated "Dirt Dawg" Jeremy Leary, "Top Shelf" Troy Nelson & Brad Hollister
- Donovan Dijak pinned AR Fox

This show featured the debut of Brad Hollister, Danny Miles, Jeff Cobb, Joey Janela, JT Dunn, Keith Lee, Tommaso Ciampa, and Warbeard Hanson. Alex Mason snapped his four-match losing streak with his victory over Scott Wild, it would also mark Mason's last appearance to date.

HOOK, LINE, & SINKER
July 23, 2016 American Legion Post 84 Orono, Maine

- Pre-Show Matches
- Aiden Aggro defeated Scott Wild
- Triple Threat: House of Glory Elite Champion: "The Rogue" Anthony Gangone defeated Ric King and Mike Graca

- Main Card
- The East Coast Bastard Crew: "Dirt Dawg" Jeremy Leary, Logan Black, & Rude Boy Riley defeated "Top Shelf" Troy Nelson & Devastation Corporation: Flex Rumblecrunch & Max Smashmaster
- "The Octopus" Jonathan Gresham defeated Xavier Bell

- Fans Bring The Weapons Match: DangerKid pinned Alexander Lee
- Luke Robinson pinned "Mr. Remarkable" Adam Booker
- Darius Carter defeated Johnny Torres
- Warbeard Hanson defeated "Raw Dog" John Silver
- Triple Threat: EYFBO: Angel Ortiz & Mike Draztik defeated The Super Savages: Caveman & Mantequilla and Brick n' Bad: Brick Mastone & "Top Talent" Christian Casanova
- Triple Threat: "All Good" Anthony Greene defeated "Fire Brand" Brian Fury and JT Dunn
- Ace Romero pinned Donovan Dijak

This show featured the debut of Darius Carter, Flex Rumblecrunch, Jonathan Gresham, Logan Black, Luke Robinson, Mike Graca, Ric King, and Rude Boy Riley. Matt Riddle was originally supposed to be on the show but he was involved in a car crash and Luke Robinson replaced him on the card. Adam Booker was there to do a spot and ended up wrestling Robinson. Dunn was originally supposed to face Riddle and was added to Green vs. Fury making it a triple threat.

PAST YOUR BEDTIME
September 24, 2016 American Legion Post 84 Orono, Maine

- "All Good" Anthony Greene pinned Xavier Bell
- Veda Scott pinned Davienne
- Mike Bennett defeated Mike Graca
- "Top Shelf" Troy Nelson pinned Scott Wild with Maximum Mecca
- Lince Dorado defeated Flip Gordon
- Flex Rumblecrunch defeated "Kingpin" Brian Milonas
- Scramble Match: Tyler Nitro with Mike Gamble defeated Conner Murphy, Scotty Slade, Johnny Torres, & Sully Banger

- Brick n' Bad: Brick Mastone & "Top Talent" Christian Casanova defeated Maine State Posse: DangerKid & Aiden Aggro
- Anything Goes Match: AR Fox pinned Ace Romero

This show featured the debut of Brian Milonas, Conner Murphy, Davienne, Lince Dorado, Mike Bennett, Scotty Slade, Sully Banger, Tyler Nitro, & Veda Scott. This is Mike Gamble's debut as a manager. This show marks the final indie appearance of Lince Dorado before signing with the WWE. Also, on this show Aiden Aggro and DangerKid first teamed in the promotion together as The Maine State Posse and it also marked the first loss of Ace Romero ending a six-match win streak.

Originally Chris Ridgeway from Liverpool, England had set up a tour and was going to face Mike Bennett, but his travel fell through. Also, Chuck Taylor and "Hot Sauce" Tracy Williams were booked and had travel issues the morning of the show. Randy feels this is one of the best shows he has presented.

Notes from Roy's Reviews on The Wrestling Insomniac blog: Mike Bennett defeated Mike Graca. I wasn't sure how this one would play out. I kind of expected Bennett to be a face just because that's usually how it works with a big name on an indie show but I'm glad he played heel because he is one of the best heels in wrestling right now. Graca held his own well with Bennett. This was a good match. It just was a little too slow for my liking in the middle. The heel ending was perfect.

AR Fox defeated Ace Romero in an Anything Goes Match. Excellent, just excellent. They killed each other just like they knew they would. Gotta see this one. One of the top 3 matches in Limitless Wrestling history. Lots of sick spots.

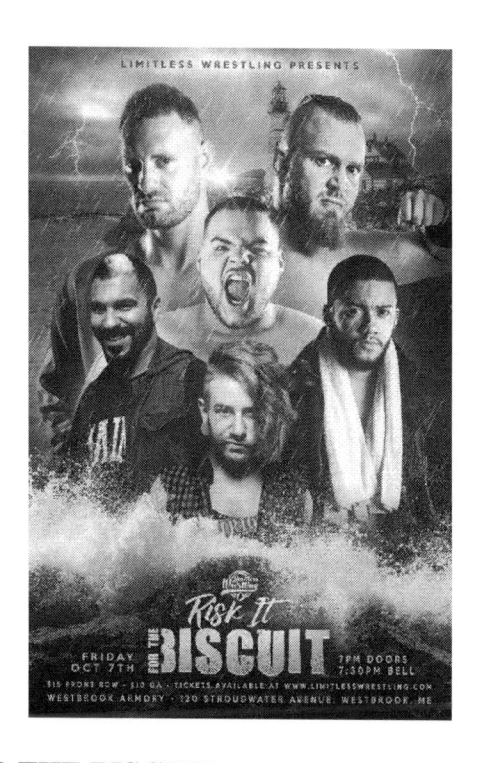

RISK IT FOR THE BISCUIT
October 7, 2016 Westbrook Armory Westbrook, Maine

- "All Good" Anthony Greene pinned Tyler Nitro
- Triple Threat: Scotty Slade defeated Flex Rumblecrunch and Mikey Webb
- Xavier Bell pinned Danny Miles
- JT Dun & Mike Graca defeated The Maine State Posse: DangerKid & Aiden Aggro
- Scramble Match: "Flash" Nick McKenna defeated "Big" Geno Bauer, "Mr. Remarkable" Adam Book, and Owen Brody
- Ace Romero defeated "The Rogue" Anthony Gangone
- "Heart Attack" Tommy Mack pinned Sully Banger

- The Tenacious Two: Johnny Torres & Scott Wild defeated Sass & Fury: "Dirt Dawg" Jeremy Leary & "Hot Scoop" Skylar
- "Fire Brand" Brian Fury defeated Donovan Dijak

This is the first event to be held at the Westbrook Armory. This show featured the debut of Geno Bauer, Mikey Webb, Nick McKenna, the in-ring debut of Skylar, and Tommy Mack. This show was advertised 10 days before it happened as the original Let's Wrestle was supposed to have a show at Thatcher's this night however the fire marshal closed the venue down. The same day the venue was closed, but earlier in the morning Chaotic Wrestling cancelled the show they scheduled for the 7th, so Randy was able to book Fury vs. Dijak and other workers. He then found the armory and was able to draw 150 people on ten days notice. He also rebranded the show as a Limitless Wrestling show. Let's Wrestle would sit on the shelf for almost two years before returning to Orono in July 2018.

Notes from Roy's Reviews on The Wrestling Insomniac blog: JT Dunn and Mike Graca defeated The Maine State Posse: Danger Kid & Aidan Aggro. Good tag match. MSP really stepped it up in this one and showed they can hang with some of the best in New England. I was surprised how well Dunn and Graca worked together since I've never heard of them teaming before. MSP has taken over the role as top tag team in Limitless Wrestling. Ace Romero defeated Anthony Gangone. This was the best performance I've seen from Gangone. He beat up Ace for most of the match and busted open Ace's nose. Lots of good solid action in this one.

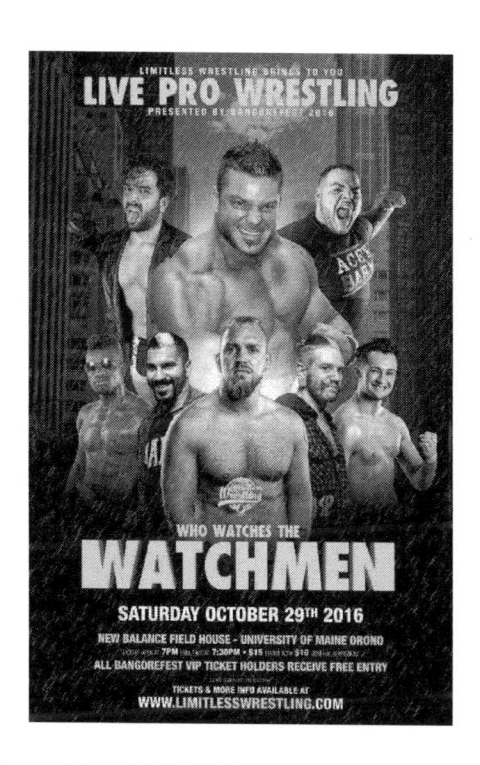

WHO WATCHES THE WATCHMEN?
October 29, 2016 New Balance Field House University of Maine Orono, Maine

- "All Good" Anthony Greene pinned Slyck Wagner Brown
- House of Glory Champion: Anthony Gangone pinned Xavier Bell
- Tornado Match: The Tenacious Two: Scott Wild & Jonny Torres with Maximum Mecca defeated Maine State Posse: Aidan Aggro & DangerKid
- Over the Top Rope & Under the Table Challenge: "Top Shelf" Troy Nelson pinned "Dirt Dawg" Jeremy Leary with "Hot Scoop" Skylar
- Champ Mathews wrestled Mark Moment to a no contest
- "All Good" Anthony Greene pinned Champ Mathews

- Ace Romero pinned "Remarkable" Adam Booker
- Scramble Match: Cam Zagami defeated Tyler Nitro, Skylar, Mike Graca & Mike Montero
- Todo Loco & Danny Miles defeated The M1nute Men: Tommy Trainwreck & Devin Blaze
- "Fire Brand" "Fire Brand" Brian Fury submitted Brian Cage with a Boston crab

This show was held in conjunction with the BanGORE Horror Fest; however, the matches took place after the convention was over. The show featured the debut of Brian Cage, Cam Zagami, Champ Mathews, Mark Moment, and Todo Loco. Champ Mathews vs. Mark Moment went to a No-Contest when Moment was unable to finish the match, to date it is the only No-Contest in Limitless Wrestling. Champ Mathews then wrestled an impromptu match with Anthony Greene who pinned Mathews with a Canadian Destroyer. The Super Savages were originally advertised to face the M1nute Men but were replaced by Todo Loco & Danny Miles.

Notes from my blog The Wrestling Insomniac: House of Glory Champion: Anthony Gangone vs. Xavier Bell Started off as a methodical mat based match with both men exchanging holds. Action picked up along the way and Bell got a three count to win the title. After the fact the ref saw that Gangone's foot was under the bottom rope and restarted the match, which led to a low blow and a win for Gangone.

Over the Top Rope and Under the Table Challenge "Top Shelf" Troy Nelson vs. "Dirt Dawg" Jeremy Leary. Essentially in this match if you are thrown over the top rope and when both feet touch the floor, you must take a shot. So, after several times of them each having to take a shot Nelson threw the referee out of the ring, then Anthony Greene, then Xavier Bell, and a couple other guys, and finally the underage Skylar who all had to take shots. Suddenly Leary grabbed the mic and demanded the music to be hit, which led to a "Don't Stop Believing" Journey sing-along, the entire song. It was pretty amazing! My favorite part through, once they were done Nelson rolled up Leary for a three count.

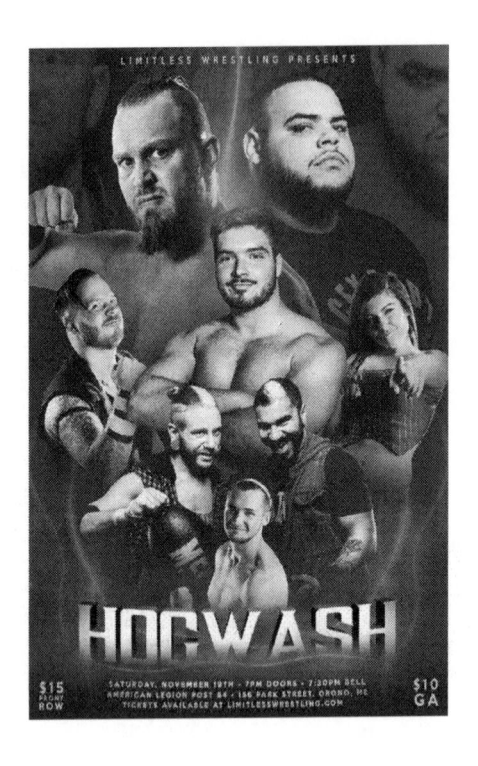

HOGWASH
November 19, 2016 American Legion Post 84 Orono, Maine

- "All Good" Anthony Greene defeated "All Ego" Ethan Page
- Cam Zagami & Tyler Nitro with Mike Gamble defeated Da Hoodz: Davey Cash & Kris Pyro
- Big Daddy Beluga pinned Davienne
- Xavier Bell pinned "Mr. Remarkable" Adam Booker
- Maine State Posse: DangerKid & Aiden Aggro defeated Sass & Fury: "Dirt Dawg" Jeremy Leary & "Hot Scoop" Skylar
- Scramble Match: Mike Graca defeated Rex Lawless, Space Monkey, & Francis Kip Stevens
- Shane Sabre pinned Kobe Durst

- "Top Shelf" Troy Nelson defeated "Smart" Mark Sterling
- Ace Romero defeated "Fire Brand" Brian Fury

This show featured the debut of Ethan Page, Francis Kip Stevens, Kobe Durst, Mark Sterling, Rex Lawless, Shane Sabre, and Space Monkey. Only Page, Sterling, and Lawless have returned to Limitless Wrestling. This was also the final in-ring match of Brian Fury in Limitless Wrestling who had announced his retirement from in-ring competition. This was the first win for the Maine State Posse as a tag team in Limitless.

Notes from Roy's Reviews on The Wrestling Insomniac blog: Big Daddy Beluga defeated Davienne. Before the match Brick Mastone came out and told Davienne that someone else wanted to wrestle her way more than him. He told her to sit in a chair and wait. Out comes Mastone dressed as a male stripper and he proceeded to give her a lap dance.

The match was fun and super entertaining. It was nice to see Mastone and not have people chant baby Rusev.   Ace Romero defeated Brian Fury. Good main event. Fury did some great arm work on Romero. These guys fought hard and gave the crowd a good last match for Fury. Surprisingly Romero got the win. After the match there was an excellent show of respect shown for Fury. Greene came in and challenged Ace to a match, but Fury interrupted and said he would rather see them team.

Sass & Fury: Jeremy Leary & Skylar

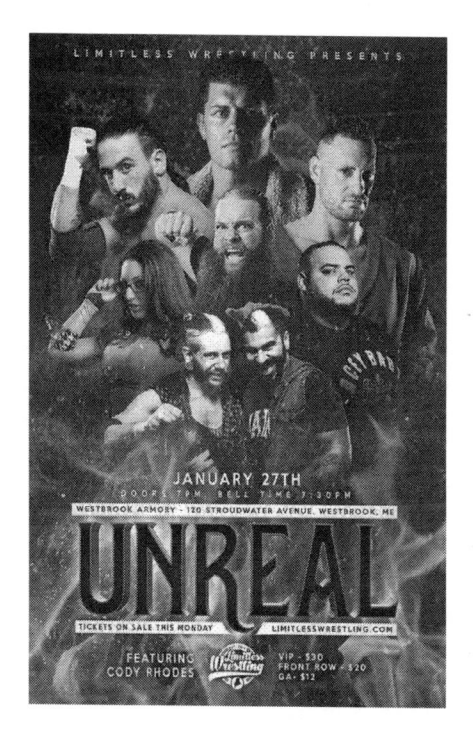

UNREAL
January 24, 2017 Westbrook Armory Westbrook, Maine

- Jon Silver pinned Travis "Flip" Gordon
- Maine State Posse: Aidan Aggro & DangerKid defeated Cam Zagami & Tyler Nitro w/ Mike Gamble
- "Top Shelf" Troy Nelson pinned Mike Gamble; this was an open challenge from Zagami on behalf of Gamble.
- "Celtic" Connor Murphy pinned "The Rogue" Anthony Gangone
- Veda Scott pinned Tessa Blanchard
- "All Good" Anthony Greene & Ace Romero defeated American Destroyers: Donovan Dijak & Mikey Webb when Greene pinned Dijak

- "Kingpin" Brian Milonas defeated Warbeard Hanson, Big Daddy Beluga, & Max Smashmaster
- David Star pinned Xavier Bell
- Skylar pinned Jeremy Leary
- "Mind Eraser" Mike Graca pinned "Remarkable" Adam Booker
- JT Dunn pinned "American Nightmare" Cody Rhodes

This was one of the biggest shows in Limitless Wrestling history. The show featured the debut of Cody Rhodes, David Starr, Mike Gamble in-ring, and Tessa Blanchard. Skylar and Jeremy Leary were supposed to wrestle the M1nute Men in a tag match, however Devin Blaze was injured in a car crash and unable to compete, so the real-life couple wrestled each other. This match was supposed to have a WXW Shotgun Championship match however Starr forgot the title at his house.

Notes from my blog The Wrestling Insomniac: Cody Rhodes was so friendly and took the time to speak to everyone. He saw my son stuck his hand to shake Canaan's and asked him how he was doing. I asked him about wrestling at the Tokyo Dome for Wrestle

Kingdom 11 and he said it was ten of the best minutes of his life. Now I've met a lot of "big name" wrestlers and for most of them that would have been the end of the conversation because the question was answered, and he had a line ahead of him. Instead he kept on talking about the show telling me a story about his entrance for the match. The general consensus I got from everyone that night was how nice and humble Cody is. Anthony Greene & Ace Romero defeated American Destroyers: Donovan Dijak & Mikey Webb. This was the match of the night hands down! First off you have Greene & Romero's entrance to Take Me Home Tonight with live guitar accompaniment that had a large part of the audience singing along. The match itself was fantastic! I don't know if I have the words, but the four of them started slow and then picked up the pace to a tremendous level. I feel like they went 30 minutes until Greene got the pin on Dijak after a 450 splash. Mike Graca pinned Adam Booker. This was an open challenge match that Graca answered. Badass entrance for Grace with a sally port door opening and an ambulance backed partially into the building with Graca coming out of the back. Great match a couple scary moments with Booker suplexing Graca from the floor onto the edge of the ring and Graca tombstone pile driving Booker.

"UNREAL" JANUARY 27TH, 2017 IN WESTBROOK, MAINE

DO WHAT YOU LOVE, FUCK THE REST-FEST
February 25, 2017 American Legion Post 84 Orono, Maine

- Danny Miles defeated Mike Graca
- Mr. Grim defeated Manny Martinez
- Sass & Fury: "Dirt Dawg" Jeremy Leary & "Hot Scoop" Skylar defeated Scott Wild & James Limits
- Xavier Bell defeated Alexander Lee
- Triple Threat: Foxx Vinyer defeated Sebastian Cage and Franco Varga
- Tyler Nitro with Mike Gamble defeated Anthony Bennett
- JT Dunn pinned Sami Callihan
- Take Me Home Tonight: Ace Romero and Anthony Greene defeated Maine State Posse: Aidan Aggro & DangerKid

This show featured the debut of Anthony Bennett, Foxx Vinyer, Franco Varga, James Limits, Manny Martinez, Mr. Grim, Sami Callihan, and Sebastian Cage. This is the return of Alexander Lee to in-ring competition after being out from an injury. Randy disliked Jimmy Limits so much at the time of this show that he intentionally listed him as James Limits, he does not feel this way now. This is another show that as a whole Randy was not happy with.

Notes from Roy's Reviews on The Wrestling Insomniac blog:
Jeremy Leary & Skylar defeated Scott Wild & James Limits. Good tag match here. Wild works really well with Leary and Skylar. Limits did well himself and I would like to see him come back. Wild hit a vicious flying knee on Skylar that almost sent her flying out of the ring. After the match both Leary and Skylar attacked referee Chris Berry. JT Dunn defeated Sami Callihan. This was excellent! They beat the hell out of each other all over the place, including a piledriver through a table. Seemed a little short but it was great despite that. Check this match out. Ace Romero & Anthony Greene defeated The Maine State Posse: Danger Kid & Aidan Aggro. All four guys worked really hard to put on a good match and they did just that. Lots of brutal chops to both Aggro and Kid. There were even a few moves I had never seen before, like the backdrop into a sit out powerbomb by Ace and Greene on Aggro. Ace got the win after a sick piledriver from Greene on Kid. After the match they teased dissension between Greene and Ace.

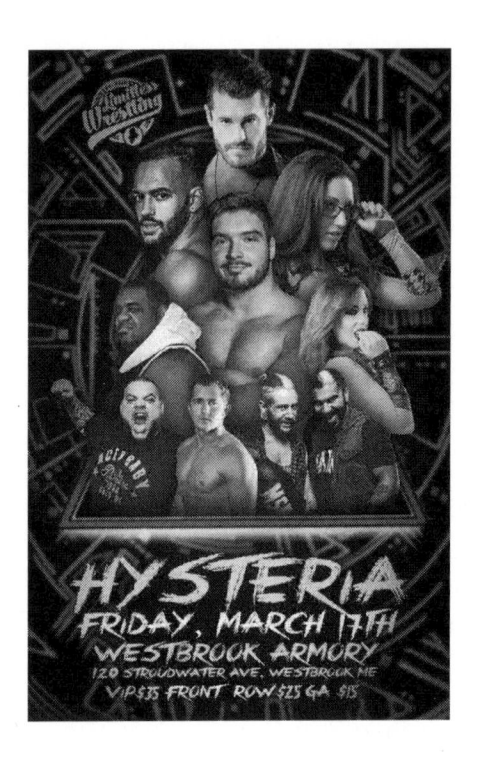

HYSTERIA
March 17, 2017 Westbrook Armory Westbrook, Maine

- Team Limitless Wrestling: Maine State Posse: DangerKid & Aiden Aggro and Sass & Fury: "Dirt Dawg" Jeremy Leary & "Hot Scoop" Skylar defeated Team Freelance Wrestling: Champion: GPA, Matt Knicks, Craig Mitchell, & Rob Matter when Skylar pinned Matter
- "All Ego" Ethan Page defeated Tyler Nitro with Mike Gamble
- Hornswoggle defeated "Rude Boy" Riley in an open challenge
- XWA Champion: Anthony Henry submitted Jay Freddie
- "Top Shelf" Troy Nelson pinned Kikutaro with Sidney Bakabella

- Ace Romero pinned Keith Lee
- "Dirty Daddy" Chris Dickinson pinned Renee Dupree
- Scramble Match: Maxwell Jacob Feinstein defeated Mr. Grim, Xavier Bell, Mike Graca, Dick Justice, and "Celtic" Connor Murphy when Feinstein pinned Bell following a jumping tombstone by Grim
- Veda Scott pinned Taeler Hendrix
- Oleg the Usurper pinned Rex Lawless
- Matt Sydal pinned Ricochet with the shooting star press

This show featured the debut of Anthony Henry, Craig Mitchell, Dick Justice, GPA, Jay Freddie, Kikutaro, Matt Knicks, Matt Sydal, MJF, Oleg the Usurper, Rene Dupree, Ricochet, Rob Matter, Swoggle, and Taeler Hendrix. MJF debuted as Maxwell Jacob Feinstein and by the time he returned at Nothing Gold Can Stay had changed his name to Maxwell Jacob Freidman, before settling on MJF. Taeler Hendrix was injured during this match on a baseball slide fracturing her ankle. Rob Matter was a replacement for Stevie Fierce.

This show features the infamous lost Limitless Wrestling match. Rude Boy Riley had an open challenge and it was accepted by the unadvertised Swoggle, the pop that erupted from the Limitless fans was deafening! What surprised me the most was that this was St. Patrick's Day and that the man who played a Leprechaun in the WWE for a decade was not booked anywhere on the first St. Patrick's Day since his release from the company. Sadly, this match has never been released on home video or on YouTube by Limitless Wrestling as shortly after this event Riley was arrested, and later convicted, for possession of child pornography.

Notes from my blog The Wrestling Insomniac: Ace Romero pinned Keith Lee in a pretty awesome big man match. They did a series of shoulder blocks in and out of the ring that was pretty damn awesome. Everything was high impact and big bumps that had the fans chanting "don't break the ring". Also, the chops they laid in were vicious. Matt Sydal pinned Ricochet with a shooting star press. DAMN, just damn. I mean words simply do not suffice. These two men are just amazing in the ring putting on a flawless acrobatic display that they make look easy. I mean so impressive! They had the crowd popping time after time, myself included. I'm a bigger fan of Ricochet, but ultimately by the end I just didn't care who won. After the match Ricochet cut an impassioned promo about how he looks up to Sydal as a hero back when they first faced each other in 2005 and still does. He got so emotional I thought he was going to cry.

CAN WE KICK IT?
April 28, 2017 Portland Club Portland, Maine

- Lio Rush pinned John Silver
- Triple Threat: Maine State Posse: DangerKid & Aiden Aggro defeated Sass & Fury: "Dirt Dawg" Jeremy Leary & "Hot Scoop" Skylar and Massage Force: VSK & Dorian Graves
- "The Bad Boy" Joey Janela defeated Mr. Grim
- Brandon Watts defeated Tyler Nitro
- Donovan Dijak pinned Mikey Webb
- "All Ego" Ethan Page defeated "The Product" David Starr
- Jay Freddie defeated "Dirty Daddy" Chris Dickinson
- "Top Shelf" Troy Nelson defeated Dick Justice with Sidney Bakabella

- Scramble Match: Xavier Bell defeated Alexander Lee, Josh Briggs, Owen Brody, Kai Katana, Jimmy Lloyd, Manny Martinez, and Dan Barry
- Ace Romero defeated Michael Elgin

This was the Limitless debut at the Portland Club. This show featured the debut of Brandon Watts, Dan Barry, Dorian Graves, Jimmy Lloyd, Josh Briggs, Kai Katana, Lio Rush, Michael Elgin, and VSK. Donovan Dijak vs. Mikey Webb was originally booked to happen this same night for Chaotic Wrestling, however moved the match to this show with their blessing.

Notes from Roy's Reviews on The Wrestling Insomniac blog: Lio Rush defeated Jon Silver. Awesome match and an excellent opener. These guys destroyed each other trading brutal kicks. It seemed a little short, but they filled the time they had with a ton of action. Donovan Dijak defeated Mikey Webb. Awesome match. The best Mikey Webb singles match I have ever seen. Lots of hard-hitting power moves and some ringside brawling as well. Jay Freddie defeated Chris Dickinson. Awesome match. These guys beat the hell out of each other. Jay Freddie is one of the most underrated guys on the Indies right now. This match was really even with both guys answering the others' moves. The finish was kind of dumpy only because the referee messed up the count which really pissed off Dickinson. Ace Romero defeated Michael Elgin. Great main event. These guys beat the hell out of each other with tons of hard strikes. Romero took everything Elgin had and then some. In the end Ace got the win after a Boss Man Slam variation.

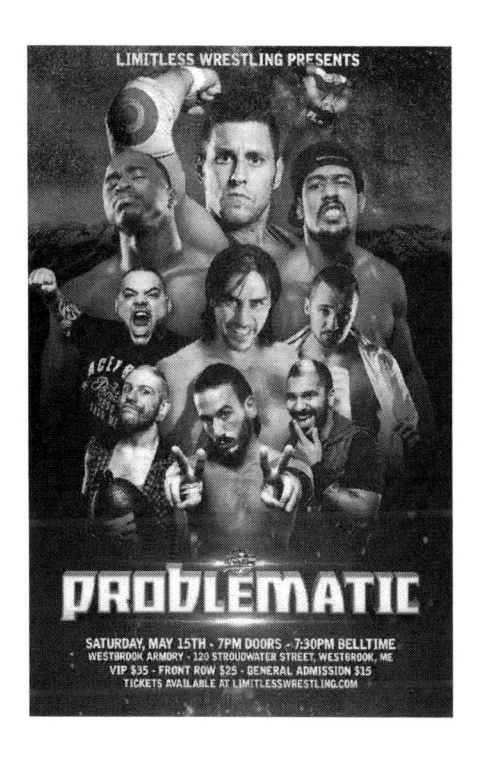

PROBLEMATIC
May 13, 2017 Westbrook Armory Westbrook, Maine

- Brian Cage pinned Flip Gordon
- Sass & Fury: "Dirt Dawg" Jeremy Leary & "Hot Scoop" Skylar defeated Cam Zagami & Tyler Nitro with Mike Gamble when Zagami & Gamble turned on Nitro leaving him on his own
- JT Dunn pinned "The Octopus" Jonathan Gresham
- "Top Shelf" Troy Nelson pinned Colt Cabana with Sidney Bakabella
- "All Good" Anthony Greene pinned Paul London
- The Maine State Posse: DangerKid & Aiden Aggro defeated The Batiri: Kodama & Obariyon

- Le Tabarnak de Team: Mathieu St. Jacques & Thomas Dubois and Buxx Belmar defeated Xavier Bell, "Kingpin" Brian Milonas, & Mike Graca
- Mr. Grim defeated Alex Chamberlain with Jon Alba
- Fans Bring the Weapons: Ace Romero pinned AR Fox, bloody match with lots of light tubes

This show featured the debut of Alex Chamberlain, The Batiri: Kodama & Obariyon, Buxx Belmar, Colt Cabana, Paul London, and Tabarnak de Team: Mathieu St. Jacques & Thomas Dubois. This was originally supposed to be ACH vs. Flip Gordon, Brian Cage was the replacement for ACH, who was booked for a tour with New Japan. London tweaked his knee during this match from a shooting star press.

Notes from my blog The Wrestling Insomniac: Our VIP tickets entitled us a picture and autograph from Paul London, and I must say he is one of the nicest guys I have met. So down to Earth and very friendly and talkative with all the fans. I had heard a lot of positive things about his fan interactions but to see it in person and through-out the show it shows just how genuine he truly is. That being said, anyone I talked to that night, Xavier Bell, Anthony Greene, Johnathan Gresham, Colt Cabana, The Batiri, were awesome. Even Sidney Bakabella.

London serenaded the crowd singing us his entrance music, "Never Too Young To Die" the title song from the hit movie of the same name starring John Stamos and Gene Simmons. I have seen this movie and was familiar with this song.

I must say it was quite the experience. I've been to other Fans Bring the Weapons Matches before and I've seen fans bring light tubes and barbed wire and what not, and they never use those items. I was not expecting to see what we got, which essentially was a death match, and I loved it! These two beat the tar out of each other, it was fantastic! At the start all the plunder was placed on the ring apron including this large light tube contraption. Fox attempted to jumpstart the match with a boot to the face, but Romero was ready for him. After a few minutes of back and forth action they went to the floor. Fox hit Ace in the head with a guitar hero guitar that had no give to it at all, it looked devastating!

Ace then broke a box fan over Fox's head. They returned to the ring and the first of the light tubes were used on both men. Fox's shoulder was torn open and Ace had some lacerations on his head. It really broke down from there with use of the chair and other weapons before more light tubes came into play. Ace had a crown royal bag and we all thought thumbtacks were coming out, but it was gummy bears. He then dumped out a box of Legos, followed by a box full of bottle caps. The canvas was just covered with broken glass, toys, metal, and fruit snacks for an amazing visual. The light tube contraption was brought in the ring and placed on a table near the corner. Eventually Ace put Fox through it was a death valley driver that shredded both of them. It was quite an explosive visual. Ace scored the pin ending the carnage. Post-match Fox told Ace that this wasn't over between them, and in July he challenged Ace and his Take Me Home Tonight partner Anthony Greene to a tag team match against him and his partner Rey Fenix! Once again Limitless produced an outstanding night of wrestling! This night ran the gamut of match styles from comedy, mat based technical style, and closed out with a death match.

Ace through a table

AR Fox flying off the top rope

Ace standing tall on the second rope

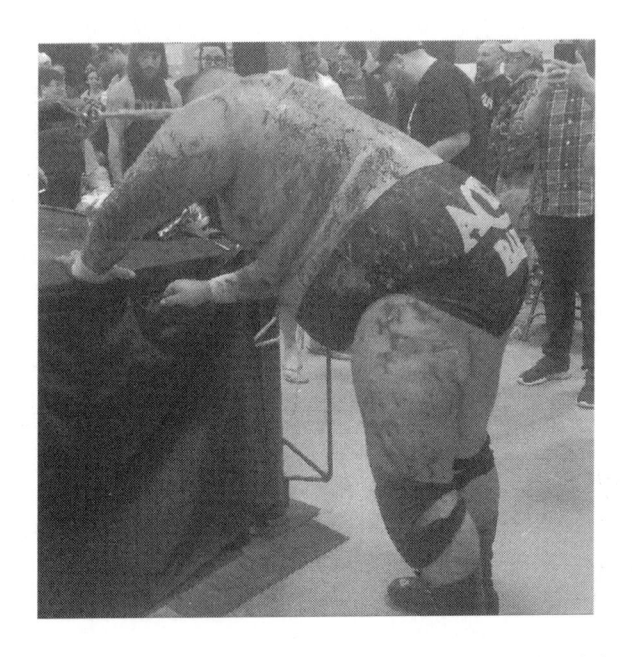

Ace Romero & AR Fox showing the battle wounds of the match

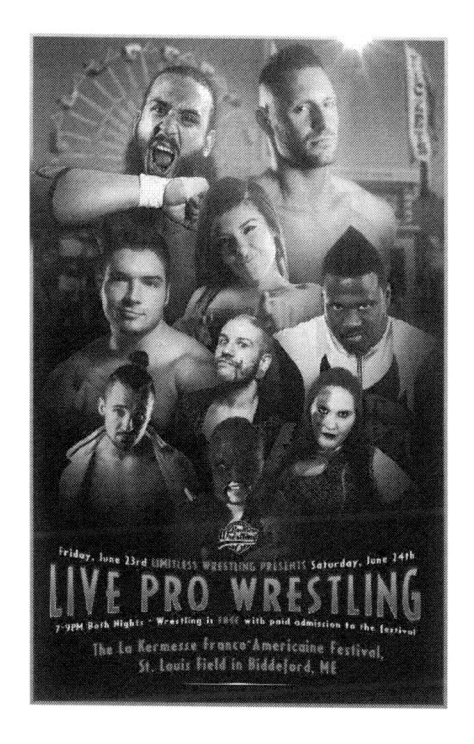

LA KERMESSE FESTIVAL NIGHT 1
June 23, 2017 St. Louis Field Biddeford, Maine

- Buxx Belmar defeated Mike Graca
- Ace Romero pinned "All Ego" Ethan Page
- Jeff Cannonball defeated Alexander Lee
- JT Dunn defeated Josh Briggs
- Terra Calaway defeated Kaitlin Diemond
- Xavier Bell defeated Todd Harris
- Triple Threat: Maine State Posse: DangerKid & Aiden Aggro defeated Le Tabarnak de Team: Mathieu St. Jacques & Thomas Dubois and Sass & Fury: "Dirt Dawg" Jeremy Leary & "Hot Scoop" Skylar
- "All Good" Anthony Greene defeated Donovan Dijak

This was the Limitless Debut in Biddeford and at La Kermesse Festival. This show featured the debut of Jeff Cannonball, Kaitlin Diemond, Terra Calaway, and Todd Harris. This card was stacked because Evolve was running the next night.

LA KERMESSE FESTIVAL NIGHT 2
June 24, 2017 St. Louis Field Biddeford, Maine

- Bear Bronson won a battle royal
- Fatal Four Way: Mr. Grim defeated Tyler Nitro, "Dirt Dawg" Jeremy Leary and James Limits
- Jeff Cannonball & Terra Calaway defeated Xavier Bell & "Hot Scoop" Skylar
- Mike Graca defeated Mike Moretti
- Jessica Troy defeated Kaitlin Diemond
- Travis Huckabee pinned The Whisper
- The Breakfast Club: CPA & Francis Kip Stevens defeated Crummels & Defarge
- Create-A-Pro Champion: "Smart" Mark Sterling pinned Bear Bronson

This show featured the debut of Bear Bronson, CPA, Crummels, Defarge, Jessica Troy, Mick Moretti, The Whisper, and Travis Huckabee. This is the first show to not feature Ace Romero ending his streak of appearing at the first 16 Limitless Shows. This was the first battle royal in Limitless Wrestling.

NOTHING GOLD CAN STAY
July 21, 2017 Westbrook Armory Westbrook, Maine

- Maxwell Jacob Friedman submitted Sami Callihan
- Six Way Scramble: Jon Silver defeated "New Age Enforcer" James Drake, "Mind Eraser" Mike Graca, Mr. Grim, Bear Bronson, & Xavier Bell
- Texas Bullrope Match: "Top Shelf" Troy Nelson defeated Wee BL with Sidney Bakabella
- XWA: Xtreme Wrestling Alliance Heavyweight Champion: Anthony Henry submitted Flip Gordon
- Donovan Dijak pinned Josh Briggs
- Le Tabarnak de Team: Mathieu St. Jacques & Thomas Dubois and Buxx Belmar defeated Maine State Posse: DangerKid, Aidan Aggro, & Alexander Lee

- JT Dunn pinned Super Crazy
- Luke Robinson pinned Cam Zagami with Mike Gamble
- AR Fonix: AR Fox & Rey Fenix defeated Take Me Home Tonight: Ace Romero & "All Good" Anthony Greene when Fox pinned Romero

This show featured the debut of JD Drake, Rey Fenix, Super Crazy, and WeeBL. This was the last Limitless match of Donovan Dijak who had signed with the WWE. This was the last appearance to date of the Quebec based Tabarnak de Team, who I hope can get work visas and return to the States as they are one of the best tag teams in the world. This night featured one of my all-time favorite matches in Limitless Wrestling as TDT & Buxx Belmar defeated the Maine State Posse in a six-man war. Anthony Greene suffered his first loss in Limitless Wrestling ending his 14-match winning streak. It should be noted that it came in a tag team match and his partner Ace Romero took the fall, so even though he lost Greene has not been pinned or submitted.

Notes from my blog The Wrestling Insomniac: Le Tabarnak de Team: Mathieu St. Jacques & Thomas Dubois and Buxx Belmar defeated Maine State Posse: Aidan Aggro, Danger Kid, & Alexander Lee. This match was awesome! I enjoyed Le Tabarnak de Team during their last appearance in May, this performance tonight cemented me as a fan of theirs. Maine State Posse got their normal big reaction as these guys are tremendous fan favorites.

60

However, something happened part way through the match, almost like Rocky overcoming the partisan Russian fans against Ivan Drago, Tabarnak de Team started getting cheers as the match drew to an end. One spot in particular, which was unbelievable, saw one member of TDT piledrive DangerKid onto Alexander Lee who was then hit with two top rope moves from the other members of the team and Lee kicked out. I was surprised at how much the fans booed when he did. I get it, it seemed like that should have been the finish of the match if he kicked out of that what will it take to keep him down? The answer was when Thomas Dubois got the pin on Lee after an SOS Moonsault from the top rope!

QUESTION THE ANSWERS
September 22, 2017 Westbrook Armory Westbrook, Maine

- JT Dunn pinned "Bad Boy" Joey Janela
- Thick Boys: Jay Freddie & Jon Silver defeated LAX: EYFBO: Angel Ortiz & Mike Draztik
- "Top Shelf" Troy Nelson pinned Swoggle with Sidney Bakabella
- Six Way Scramble: Josh Briggs defeated "Smart" Mark Sterling, Jimmy Lloyd, Jeff Cannonball, Mr. Grim, & Dick Justice pinning Sterling
- Jake Hager submitted AR Fox with the ankle lock
- Teddy Hart pinned Maxwell Jacob Friedman

- Joey Ryan & Massage Force: VSK & Dorian Graves defeated The Maine State Posse: Alexander Lee, DangerKid, & Aiden Aggro
- Loser Leaves Town: Cam Zagami with Mike Gamble defeated Tyler Nitro by referee stoppage
- Skylar submitted Willow Nightingale
- "All Good" Anthony Greene pinned Ace Romero with special referee Brian Fury.

This show featured the debut of Jake Hager, Joey Ryan, Teddy Hart, and Willow Nightingale.

This is the first show to not feature Xavier Bell ending his streak of appearing at the first 18 Limitless Shows. Although other wrestlers have appeared at more events, he is the only wrestler to appear at the first eighteen shows. Half of the entrants to this scramble match were, legit, voted on by the fans. Xavier Bell & Christian Casanova were two of the wrestlers that did not receive enough votes to gain entry into the match.

Notes from my blog The Wrestling Insomniac: "All Good" Anthony Greene pinned Ace Romero with special referee Brian Fury. Fantastic match with the action going all over the building at one point. Greene did a dive that pushed them both into the third row. Both wrestlers had tension with their trainer and referee Brian Fury including Romero accidentally back elbowing him. Later Fury tried to superkick Greene but hit Romero. Greene was the bad guy in this match and played it well. He hailed from Funtown USA which if you're from Maine you know is in Saco, which is Romero's hometown. I was surprised how fast the people turned on Greene. He even had new music to mark the occasion with a special introduction on the track. Post-match Fury and Greene squared off and Dunn entered, he went to hit Greene with Death by Elbow but accidentally hit Fury. Not to sound sappy for a moment but I really feel like this show was a giant accomplishment and I truly feel like all of us who support Limitless Wrestling are a part of something special.

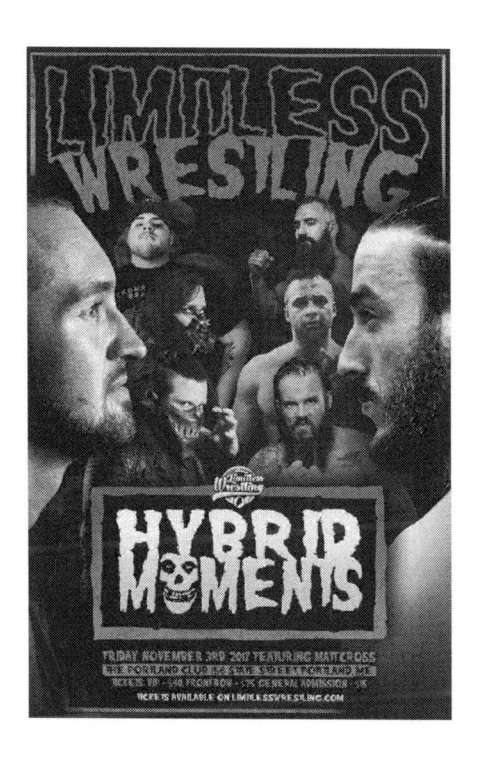

HYBRID MOMENTS
November 03, 2017 Portland Club Portland, Maine

- Ace Romero pinned Sami Callihan
- Jordynne Grace pinned Jessicka Havok
- Josh Briggs pinned Darby Allin
- The Thick Boys: Jon Silver & Jay Freddie defeated The Maine State Posse: Alexander Lee & DangerKid
- Matt Cross pinned Petey Williams
- Maxwell Jacob Friedman submitted Jonathan Gresham
- "Dirty Daddy" Chris Dickinson pinned Cam Zagami
- Christian Casanova with Stokely Hathaway pinned "All Ego" Ethan Page

- Scramble Match: Terra Calaway defeated Skylar, Willow Nightingale, Davienne, Kennedi Copeland, & Ashley Vox pinning Copeland
- "All Good" Anthony Greene & JT Dunn wrestled to a double count-out

This show featured the debut of Ashley Vox, Brett Domino & DL Hurst ringside, Darby Allin, Jessicka Havok, Jordynne Grace, Kennedi Copeland, Matt Cross, Stokely Hathaway, and Petey Williams.
The main event between Anthony Greene and JT Dunn ended in the first and to date only count-out finish in Limitless Wrestling. This show also featured the first ever all ladies scramble match. Christian Casanova made his return for the first time in twelve shows. Ashley Vox was a last-minute replacement and she has only missed two shows since becoming a tremendous fan favorite. Teddy Hart was also scheduled to face Josh Briggs but had to pull off the show for a court appearance in Texas. Originally this show was slated to take place at the Westbrook Armory, however just two weeks prior to the event Limitless was forced to change venues because of a rescheduled military event now taking place there.

Notes from my blog The Wrestling Insomniac: Havok was advertised for the Six Way Scramble but Grace who had no advertised opponent came out and challenged Havok one on one. No complaints at all from me because these two girls put on a hell of a show and really went at each other. This was my first time seeing them both live and they did not disappoint! Stiff wrestling both in the ring and on the floor with back and forth action. Again, they were really laying it into each other but in the end, Grace pushed Havok up on the second rope and threw her down with a powerbomb for the pin. Cam Zagami came out for this American Grit open challenge, music started, and everyone looked towards the entryway when Dickinson hit the ring from behind in his street clothes to a monstrous ovation! He leveled Zagami then hit a Pazuzu bomb kicking Zagami to the floor after while soaking in the thunderous "Dirty Daddy" chant. He then grabbed the mic to cut a promo and said "I fucking forgot that this was an actual match" so he Pazuzu bombed Zagami for the three count.

THE WORLD IS OURS
January 19, 2018 Westbrook Armory Westbrook, Maine

- Kalvin Strange & Xavier Bell defeated Mark Sterling & Jaxon Stone when Strange submitted Stone
- Darby Allin pinned Jeff Cobb
- Triple Threat Match: Martin Stone defeated Fred Yehi & David Starr
- Allie Kat, Kris Statlander, & Ashley Vox defeated The Maine State Posse: DangerKid, Alexander Lee, & Aidan Aggro when Allie Kat pinned Kid after the pussy piledriver
- Whiskey Dick: "Top Shelf" Troy Nelson & Dick Justice defeated Brett Domino & DL Hurst
- Maxwell Jacob Friedman submitted Matt Cross
- Tessa Blanchard pinned Deonna Purrazzo

- "Dirty Daddy" Chris Dickinson pinned Eddie Kingston
- "All Ego" Ethan Page and The Thick Boys: Jon Silver & Jay Freddie defeated The Dream Team: Mr. Grim, Christian Casanova, & Austin Theory with Stokely Hathaway
- Massage NV: Dorian Graves & VSK defeated The Work Horsemen: "New Age Enforcer" James Drake & Anthony Henry
- Fatal Four Way: "All Good" Anthony Greene defeated JT Dunn, Ace Romero, & Josh Briggs pinning Dunn
- Post-Match: Teddy Hart came out and challenged Dunn, Romero, & Briggs to a six-man tag at the next show.

This show featured the debut of Allie Kat, Austin Theory, Brett Domino & DL Hurst in-ring, Deonna Purrazzo, Eddie Kingston, Fred Yehi, Jaxon Stone, Kalvin Strange, Kris Statlander, Martin Stone, and Tessa Blanchard. This is the only appearances to date of Eddie Kingston and Jaxon Stone, it also marks the final appearances to date of Jeff Cobb, Tessa Blanchard, and Xavier Bell. It's interesting to note that Kris Statlander would make her debut teaming with Ashley Vox, who could go on to have one of the wildest feuds in Limitless history. During the Page & Thick Boys vs. The Dream Team the bottom rope broke off and the final two matches were contested without it.

Notes from my blog The Wrestling Insomniac: Cobb is a big powerhouse and Allin is so fast flying around the ring and yet their styles meshed tremendously. Allin got the surprise, dare I say upset win with a unique pinning combination. He stepped through like he was going to go for a sharpshooter but then fell forward tying up Cobb's legs and using his own body weight against him. The three count came out of nowhere for a big pop and shocking finish. Fatal Four Way: Anthony Greene defeated Ace Romero, JT Dunn, & Josh Briggs. The match that was billed to discover the Ace of Limitless Wrestling. This match was exactly what you would expect from these four. It quickly spilled to the floor with all four working their way to the back of the venue where Dunn jumped off the top of the lockers onto the other three. The four then battled back towards the ring past the merchandise tables where among all the chaos Jeff Cobb calmly sat eating his dinner unfazed by everything going on around him. It was hilarious. Greene eventually made his way back to the ring throwing eight steel chairs in a pile in the center. His intention was to splash a prone JT Dunn from the top rope, however Dunn superplexed them both onto the debris it was pretty sick!

The finish came when everyone hit their finishers and Greene rolled up Dunn for the three count with a handful of trunks to win the match officially becoming the Ace of Limitless Wrestling. However, this was overshadowed by what came next. Teddy Hart made his surprise return to the pop of the night. He cut a promo on Briggs, Romero, & Dunn challenging them to a six-man tag team match on March 30th with his partners AR Fox and Sami Callihan!

I applaud the final two matches where the wrestlers didn't seem to let the fact there was no bottom rope stop them from doing their best in the ring. The only thing missing from the show was the staple six-way scramble match.

ONLY FOOLS ARE SATISFIED
March 30, 2018 Westbrook Armory Westbrook, Maine

- Maddison Miles & Ace Austin defeated DL Hurst & Brett Domino with "All Good" Anthony Greene
- Brian Cage defeated "Dirty Daddy" Chris Dickinson
- The Thick Boys: John Silver & Jay Freddie defeated The Workhorsemen: "New Age Enforcer" James Drake & Anthony Henry
- Scramble: Ashley Vox defeated Kris Statlander, Penelope Ford, & Allie Kat
- Jimmy Jacobs pinned DangerKid
- Maxwell Jacob Friedman with Stokely Hathaway defeated Darby Allin with a headlock takeover
- "All Good" Anthony Greene defeated Martin Stone

- Scramble Match: Wheeler YUTA defeated Aiden Aggro, Alexander Lee, Craig Mitchell, Kevin Bennett and Kevin Blackwood
- Whisky Dick: Dick Justice & "Top Shelf" Troy Nelson defeated Bear Country: Bear Bronson & Bear Beefcake with Jon Alba
- "Top Talent" Christian Casanova with Stokely Hathaway defeated Brody King
- Ace Romero, JT Dunn, & Josh Briggs defeated Shane Strickland, AR Fox, and Teddy Hart

This show featured the debuts of Ace Austin, Bear Beefcake, Brandon Kirk, Brody King, Jimmy Jacobs, Kevin Bennett, Kevin Blackwood, Maddison Miles, Penelope Ford, Shane Strickland, and Wheeler YUTA. To date this marks the only appearances of Maddison Miles, Jimmy Jacobs, and Kevin Bennett.

The original main event featured Sami Callihan teaming with AR Fox & Teddy Hart, however he was booked for an overseas tour this weekend as well. Joey Janela was scheduled to wrestle DangerKid in an anything goes match; however, he had an opportunity to wrestle in Ireland and was given Randy's blessing to pull off the card. Multiple flights were delayed with some wrestlers not landing until after the show started causing the match lineups to be shifted around. Other names advertised that cancelled included David Starr and Chase Owens. Jeff Cannonball & Brandon Kirk attacked the Thick Boys after the match, setting up a match at Feed the Need.

FEED THE NEED
May 11, 2018 Portland Club Portland, Maine

- Green Ant, Thief Ant, & DanjerHawk defeated The Whisper, Hermit Crab & Cajun Crawdad
- Brody King pinned Eli Everfly
- Ace Romero defeated AR Fox
- The Dream Team: Christian Casanova & Austin Theory with Stokely Hathaway defeated The Rascalz: Myron Reed & Trey Miguel and The Workhorsemen: "New Age Enforcer" James Drake & Anthony Henry
- Ashley Vox defeated Rachael Ellering
- Portland Street Fight: "All Good" Anthony Greene defeated JT Dunn
- Darby Allin defeated Zachary Wentz

- "Hot Scoop" Skylar defeated Kimber Lee
- Scramble Match: Ace Austin defeated AJ Gray, Kevin Ku, Jake Parnell, Bolt Brady, & Tony Deppen
- Free To Think: "Rogue" Brandon Kirk & Jeff Cannonball defeated The Thick Boys: John Silver & Jay Freddie
- Josh Briggs defeated Teddy Hart

This show featured the debut of AJ Gray, Bolt Brady, Brandon Kirk in-ring, Bryce Remsburg, Cajun Crawdad, Danjerhawk, Eli Everfly, Green Ant, Hermit Crab, Kevin Ku, Kimber Lee, Myron Reed, Rachel Ellering, Thief Ant, Tony Deppen, Trey Miguel, Warhorse, and Zachary Wentz. Warhorse wrestled under the name Jake Parnell.

AR Fox was unadvertised for the match as he answered the Ace Romero open challenge. In an unadvertised match Gangrel was going to wrestle Stokely Hathaway however the arrangement fell through. Jon Alba moderated a confrontation between Joey Eastman and The Maine State Posse causing tension in the group and setting up a triple threat match between the Posse in the first round of the Vacationland Cup. The Josh Briggs vs. Teddy Hart match was originally scheduled to take place back in November 2017.

Notes from Roy's Reviews on The Wrestling Insomniac blog: Anthony Greene defeated JT Dunn in a Street Fight. Sick match. Very brutal. Anthony Greene got slammed on tacks, took a tombstone on a chair and fell through a table from the top rope but somehow still won. Dunn set up what looked like a chair table and went to slam Greene off the top through it, but Brett Domino came out and helped Greene slam Dunn through it instead. After the match Ace Romero came out and told Anthony Greene that in July, they will fight each other in a Steel Cage Match. Skylar defeated Kimber Lee. Very good match here. The best Skylar match I've ever seen. She has improved a ton in her time away from Limitless Wrestling. They beat the hell out of each other for a good 10-15 minutes until Skylar got a surprise roll up for the win. Josh Briggs defeated Teddy Hart. Absolutely sick match. How these guys were able to walk afterwards is beyond me. They hit at least a dozen sick, backbreaker type moves. In the end Briggs got the win after a chokeslam backstabber.

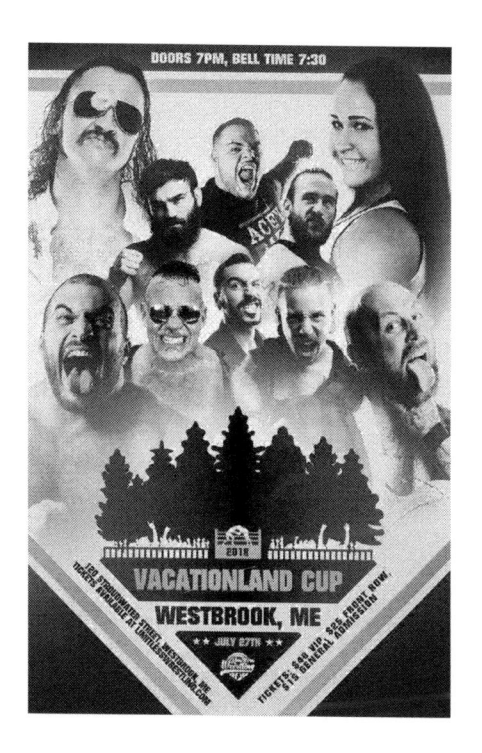

VACATIONLAND CUP
July 27, 2018 Westbrook Armory Westbrook, Maine

- Round 1: Josh Briggs defeated AR Fox
- Round 1: DangerKid defeated Aiden Aggro & Alexander Lee
- Round 1: "Top Talent" Christian Casanova with Stokely Hathaway defeated Ashley Vox
- Round 1: JT Dunn pinned David Starr
- "Dirty Daddy" Chris Dickinson defeated Pierre Carl Ouellet
- Allie Kat pinned Jordynne Grace
- Scramble Match: Kevin Blackwood defeated Austin Theory with Stokely Hathaway, Harlow O'Hara, Eli

Everfly, Jay Freddie with Puff, and Nico Silva with Jon Alba
- Free To Think: "Rogue" Brandon Kirk & Jeff Cannonball defeated Whiskey Dick: Dick Justice & "Top Shelf" Troy Nelson
- Vacationland Cup Finals: JT Dunn defeated DangerKid, Josh Briggs, & "Top Talent" Christian Casanova with Stokely Hathaway
- Steel Cage Match: Ace Romero defeated "All Good" Anthony Greene with Brett Domino & DL Hurst

This show featured the debut of Harlow O'Hara, Nico Silva, Pierre Carl Ouellet, and Puf - ringside. There were several issues and mishaps that happened in and around this show. The morning of the show Randy Carver awoke to several messages from PCO whose flight had been cancelled.

His replacement flight had then been rerouted several times not getting into Boston until 330pm. With bad traffic that day he didn't get to the venue until after 630pm when doors had opened. The ring arrived late at the venue, not getting there until about 5:15pm, all the wrestlers and crew alike pitched together to the ring and chairs set up 630pm when the VIP doors opened.

The cage was not set up correctly and right at the beginning of the match one side of the cage collapsed falling towards the fans. The cage was caught by Kevin Quinn and DL Hurst, Ace Romero took a hard shot from it as well. The fans of Limitless Wrestling held the sides of the cage up so the match could continue.
This was Anthony Greene's first pinfall loss in Limitless Wrestling. With Nico Silva losing the scramble match Jon Alba was banned from Limitless. This was Troy Nelson's first loss after an 11-match winning streak.

2018 HOLLIS PIRATEFEST
August 11, 2018 Hollis Fire Department Hollis, Maine

- Max Caster defeated Manny Martinez
- Kris Statlander pinned Delmi Exo
- Puf pinned Brett Domino
- Alexander Lee defeated "Masshole" Mike McCarthy
- Brandino Davis pinned "Classic" Kalvin Strange
- Davienne defeated Mike Law
- Beefcake Charlie defeated Alvarez
- The Maine State Posse: DangerKid & Aiden Aggro defeated Kevin Blackwood & Daniel Garcia

This was Limitless Wrestling's debut in Hollis. This show featured the debut of Alvin Alvarez, Brandino Davis, Daniel

Garcia, Delmi Exo, Max Caster, Mike Law, Mike McCarthy, and Puf - in-ring.

With the win over McCarthy, Alexander Lee snapped a two-year, ten match losing streak, the longest losing streak in Limitless history. The Maine State Posse also picked up a win ending their four-match losing streak as a team. This was originally scheduled to take place outside however rain forced the ring to be set up inside the Hollis Fire Department.

> **Litchfield Fair**
> May 25, 2018
>
> Hey wrestling fans we have some exciting news for you!!! For the first time ever, the Litchfield Fair will have a wrestling event during the fair.
>
> On Saturday afternoon (September 8th) Maine's very own Limitless Wrestling will be putting on a show. So get ready for some elbow drops, pile drivers and suplexes from some of the best men and women.
>
> More info to come...
>
> Limitless Wrestling
> "The Pine Tree State Pro Wrestling Party"
> Website - www.LimitlessWrestling.com
> Facebook - www.facebook.com/LimitlessWrestling
> Twitter - @LWMaine
> Instagram - @LimitlessWrestling

2018 LITCHFIELD FAIR
September 8, 2018 The Fairgrounds Litchfield, Maine

- Alexander Lee with DangerKid defeated Rob Marsh with Chad Epik
- Brandino Davis pinned Dan Terry
- Richard Holliday defeated "Classic" Kalvin Strange
- Ashley Vox defeated Davienne
- Todo Loco pinned Brett Domino
- DangerKid defeated Nico Silva

This was Limitless Wrestling's debut in Litchfield. This show featured the debut of Dan Terry, Richard Holliday, and Rob Marsh.
I grew up in Litchfield and would go to the fair every year. In fact, back then we could bring a note to school and the bus would drop us off at the fairgrounds after school on Friday. I would ask the

fair every year to have a wrestling show as part of the festivities and they never did, until this show. And, of course, I wasn't just out of town, I was out of the country on vacation with my wife touring Oak Island, Nova Scotia. It is my hope that wrestling will be back to the Litchfield Fair again.

PRETENDERS BEWARE
September 21, 2018 Westbrook Armory Westbrook, Maine

- "Dirty Daddy" Chris Dickinson pinned "The Machine" Brian Cage with a Pazuzu bomb
- Christian Casanova with Stokely Hathaway pinned Kevin Blackwood with a handful of tights
- Maine State Posse: Alexander Lee, DangerKid, & Aiden Aggro defeated Free To Think: Jeff Cannonball, Brandon Kirk, and Casey Katal with Joey Eastman when Kid pinned Cannonball as a result Joey Eastman is now banned from Limitless Wrestling
- Colt Cabana pinned "Retrosexual" Anthony Greene with the Platinum Hunnies

- Wrestling Revolver Open Invite Scramble Champion: Ace Austin defeated Sami Callihan, Jessicka Havok, Daniel Garcia, Mick Morretti, & Matt Cross pinning Calliham
- Josh Briggs pinned Brody King
- Kris Statlander & Davienne defeated Ashley Vox & Willow Nightingale when Statlander pinned Vox
- Austin Theory with Stokely Hathaway pinned DJ Z with Ataxia
- Wet Hot American Street Fight: Thick Boys: John Silver & Jay Freddie defeated "Top Shelf" Troy Nelson & Dick Justice pinning Nelson
- Ace Romero pinned JT Dunn with a lariat
- Post-Match: MJF invaded and Dunn turned on Romero attacking him from behind

This show features the debut of Ava Everett & Angel Sinclair - ringside, DJZ and Kasey Catal. Anthony Greene lost his second straight match by pinfall. Mike McCarthy was scheduled to be the third member of Free to Think but broke his arm two weeks before the show. Kasey Catal, Brandon Kirk's girlfriend, stepped in replacing McCarthy. Alexander Lee and the MSP carried Eastman and his bags, throwing him out of the building after they defeated Free to Think, as Eastman was now banned from Limitless, unless a member of the Maine State Posse had him reinstated.

After defeating Brody King, Josh Briggs issued an open challenge that was answered by Brett Domino, who was given an M5 for his trouble. Chris Dickinson then answered the challenge Pazuzu bombing Domino and setting the match for the next show, Briggs vs. Dickinson.

The major angle was the return of MJF after being gone for six months and he entered the Armory in style riding on the hood of a car through the sally port. JT Dunn attacked Ace from behind joining forces with MJF.

Notes from my blog The Wrestling Insomniac: Fantastic opening match, I think Cage is even bigger than the last time I saw him, he really is a machine. These guys beat the crap out of each other and tossed each other around the ring like it was nothing. Dickinson hit the Pazuzu bomb for the three count. Maine State Posse: Alexander Lee, Aiden Aggro, & Danger Kid defeated Free To Think: Jeff Cannonball, Brandon Kirk, & Kasey Catal with Joey Eastman. If the Posse lose, they must split up in Limitless and if they win then Joey Eastman is banned from Limitless. This match was wild and all over the floor with train wreck after train wreck and we all loved it! Alexander Lee did a trust fall off top rope wiping everyone out, Danger Kid suplex Kasey Catal off the top rope to the floor onto the other four, we got a six-person overhead suplex on the floor. Finish came when MSP hit their finish on Jeff Cannonball pinning him. Colt Cabana pinned "Retro-Sexual" Anthony Greene with the Platinum Hunnies.

This was awesome! It's my first-time seeing AG's new entrance with the Hunnies and I love it. My son didn't even recognize him; he looks that different. He and Colt had a really fun match with great comedy bits, with Colt's flirtatious moves with the Hunnies backfiring on him for a bit before he regained the upper hand and got the win with his superman pin. This was my favorite Colt Cabana match I have seen in person to date. Some great moments in the scramble match with Callihan demanded a kiss from Havok and she punched him in the mouth. Jessicka Havok asking Matt Cross if he was Son of Havok (his gimmick in Lucha Underground) which led to a mother/son reunion mid ring, never mind the fact that Cross is a half dozen years older than Havok. Garcia hit Havok from behind to which Cross yelled, "don't hit my mom!"

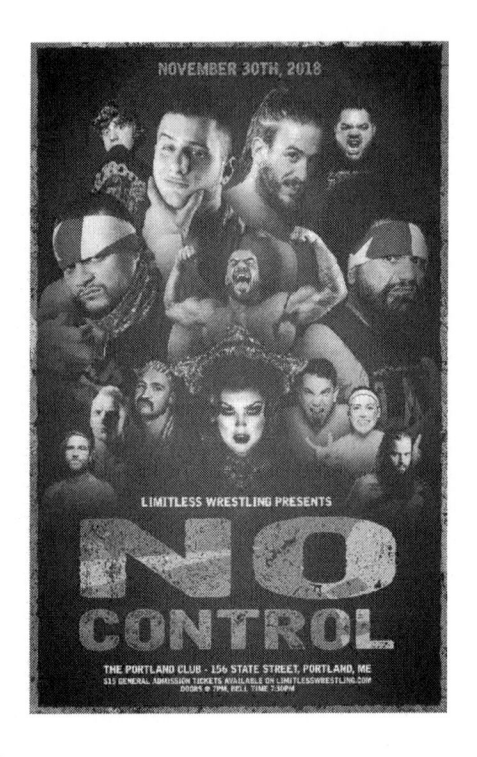

NO CONTROL
November 30, 2018 Portland Club Portland, Maine

- Ace Romero pinned Darby Alin with a lariat
- Kevin Blackwood & Harlow O'Hara defeated DoomFly: Eli Everfly & Delilah Doom
- Ashley Vox submitted "Retro" Anthony Greene with the Platinum Hunnies
- Shooting Gallery: Daniel Garcia & Brandon Thurston defeated Thick Boys: John Silver & Jay Freddie
- "Dirty Daddy" Chris Dickinson submitted Josh Briggs
- DJ Z pinned Christian Casanova with Stokely Hathaway
- Scramble Match: Puf defeated Brandon Kirk, KTB, Bear Bronson, Brett Domino & Troy Nelson
- Kris Statlander pinned Penelope Ford

- Maine State Posse: DangerKid, Aiden Aggro, & Alexander Lee defeated Travis Huckabee, Green Ant, & Thief Ant
- LAX: Ortiz & Santana defeated The Kings: JT Dunn & Brody King with MJF

This show features the debut of Brandon Thurston, Delilah Doom and KTB. This was Anthony Greene's first submission loss in Limitless and his third consecutive loss.

Two debuts were cancelled due to injury when "Filthy" Tom Lawlor broke his wrist and Marko Stunt broke his leg. A broken elbow kept MJF out of the main event. KTB replaced Marko Stunt and DJ Z replaced Lawlor.

After the main event Ace Romero hit the ring to face off with JT Dunn and MJF, Anthony Greene came out siding with Romero super kicked JT Dunn reuniting Take Me Home Tonight.

It was revealed the day after the show that Brody King signed an exclusive deal with Ring of Honor, and this would be his last Limitless show.

Notes from my blog The Wrestling Insomniac: Ashley Vox submitted Anthony Greene, Hands down match of the night!

Sincerely go out of your way to see this match you will not be disappointed. Greene dominated most of the match using his size to his advantage. Vox kept battling back and locking on her finisher wearing Greene down. The Hunnies interfered several times throughout the match until Vox accidentally took them out with a dive after Greene side stepped her. Vox locked on the reel catch for the submission. I loved this match! Crowd was into this big time; they were on their feet and the "tap" chant was deafening!

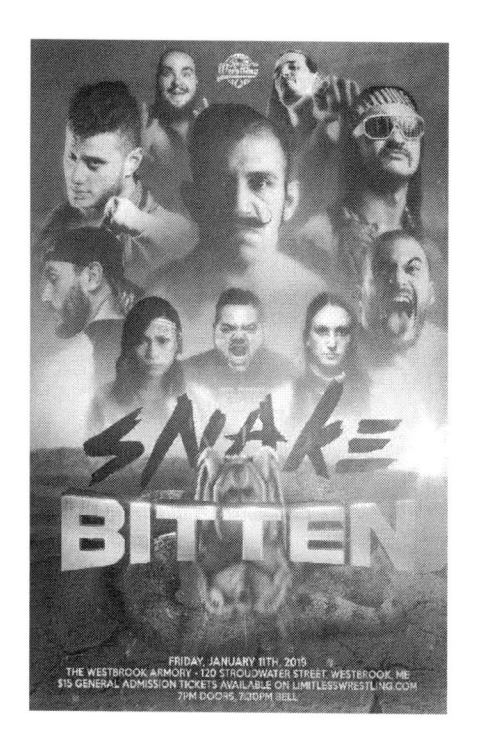

SNAKEBITTEN
January 11, 2019 Westbrook Armory Westbrook, Maine

- Andrew Everett defeated Josh Briggs
- The Dream Team: "Top Talent" Christian Casanova & Austin Theory with Stokely Hathaway defeated Pepper Parks & Harlow O'Hara.
- "Dirty Daddy" Chris Dickinson defeated Simon Grimm
- The Maine State Posse: DangerKid, Aiden Aggro, & Alexander Lee defeated Thick Boys: John Silver, Jay Freddie, & Puf
- Unsanctioned Match: Ashley Vox defeated Kris Statlander
- Amazing Red & "The Rogue" Anthony Gangone defeated Private Party: Marq Quen & Isiah Kassidy

- Scramble Match: "Rogue" Brandon Kirk defeated Ophidian, The Whisper, Willow Nightingale, Jordan Oliver, and Ace Austin
- Mr. Grim pinned Brett Domino
- The Kings: JT Dunn & MJF defeated Take Me Home Tonight: Ace Romero & "Retrosexual" Anthony Greene with The Platinum Hunnies

This show features the debut of Amazing Red, Andrew Everett, Jordan Oliver, Ophidian, Pepper Parks, and Simon Grimm. Private Party made their return to Limitless after nearly three years last appearing at No Dropkicks in the Living Room. Andrew Everett blew out his knee during the match. Pepper Parks replaced Kevin Blackwood as Harlow O'Hara's partner due to the injuries Blackwood suffered in a car crash.

Randy Carver in the ring after the main event about to announce that at the next show the main event will be a fatal four way to declare the first Limitless Wrestling Champion.

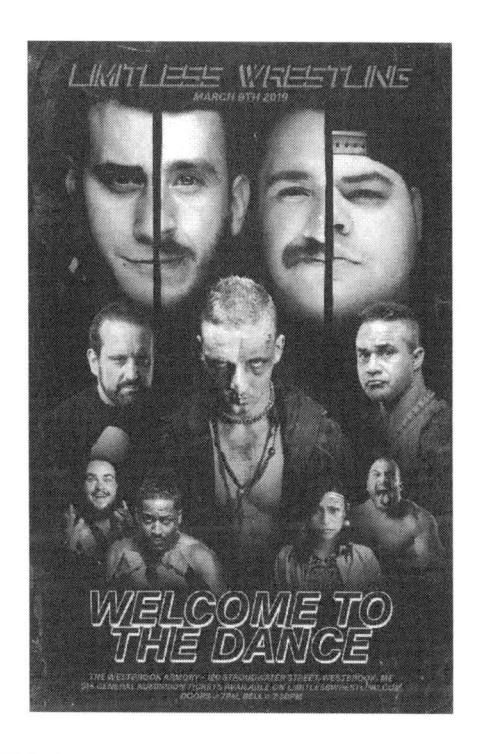

WELCOME TO THE DANCE
March 9, 2019 Westbrook Armory Westbrook, Maine

- DL Hurst pinned "Smart" Mark Sterling
- Teddy Hart pinned Darby Allin
- MSP: Alexander Lee, DangerKid, & Aiden Aggro defeated the Shook Crew: Bobby Orlando, Bryce Donovan, & Max Caster when Aggro pinned Orlando
- Kris Statlander pinned Christian Casanova
- Platinum Hunnies: Angel & Ava Everette pinned Brett Domino
- ECW Rules Match: "Dirty Daddy" Chris Dickinson pinned Tommy Dreamer

- Scramble Match: Brad Hollister defeated Josh Brigs, "Buzzkill" Pat Buck, Antoine Nicholas, Jake Something, and Donovan Danhausen pinning Antoine Nicholas
- Ashley Vox submitted Brandon Kirk
- Thick Boys: Puf & Jay Freddie defeated The Butcher & The Blade: Andy Williams & Pepper Parks when Parks was pinned
- Limitless Wrestling Championship: MJF defeated "Retro" Anthony Greene, JT Dunn, & Ace Romero pinning Anthony Greene to win the championship

This show features the debut of The Butcher Andy Williams, Antoine Nicolas, Ava Everett & Angel Sinclair in-ring, Bobby Orlando, Bryce Donovan, Danhausen, Jake Something, Pat Buck, and Tommy Dreamer. Brad Hollister returned after nearly three years last appearing at No Dropkicks in the Living Room. "Hurricane" Shane Helms was advertised to be at the show and was the VIP headliner, however the WWE pulled him from the event. That changed the card as originally Kris Statlander was going to wrestle Mark Sterling and DL Hurst wasn't booked to appear on the card. Stokely Hathaway was also set to appear on the show but was signed by the WWE.

Notes from my blog The Wrestling Insomniac: To say that this was a packed house is an understatement, I've never seen so many people crammed in this building. They even removed the gimmick tables from the back and side of the venue for the standing room, and it was a raucous crowd! I'm so happy to have a promotion in Maine that others from around the country look at and wish they had close to them like I used. Teddy Hart pinned Darby Allin. This was tremendous and lived up to the hype I built up in my mind. Both of these guys are so good, and both displayed their unique offense. Allin took a beating this match but battled back several times, but in the end, Teddy got the pin after one of his signatures moves, a splash mountain into a sitout powerbomb but Darby did a full flip before landing.

I have been a fan of Tommy Dreamer for over 20 years back to the days of ECW that I watched live thanks to my buddy Jay's satellite dish. Seeing Dreamer come out to Man in the Box, I got all emotional, I just can't help it wrestling does that to me sometimes. The main event was a damn great match! These four guys showed why they deserved to be in the main event fighting for this title. At the beginning of the match it was primarily The Kings staying together, until Dunn hit Death by Elbow and MJF threw Dunn to the floor to steal the pin. The match went to the floor and around the ring. They went through the crowd to the lockers, this time Greene and Dunn climbed on top, with Greene falling off and then Dunn jumping on everyone. Back in the ring the finish came when Dunn hit everyone with Death by Elbow, the last being MJF which caused MJF to fall back on top of Greene for the three count as Ace pulled Dunn out of the ring.

There was a huge pop when MJF won the championship, I think part excitement and part disbelief. I myself was rooting for Anthony Greene to pick up the win. In my opinion he has been the true ace of Limitless Wrestling over the years.

HOOKED ON A FRIEDMAN
May 10, 2019 Westbrook Armory Westbrook, Maine

- Vacationland Cup Fatal Four Way Qualifying Match: Ace Romero defeated Jon Silver, Mance Warner, & Chris Dickinson pinning Silver
- Brad Hollister pinned Christian Casanova
- Kris Statlander pinned "Buzzkill" Pat Buck
- Vacationland Cup Fatal Four Way Qualifying Match:
- JT Dunn defeated "The Rogue" Brandon Kirk, Adam Brooks, & "All Ego" Ethan Page pinning Kirk
- Skylar with Jeremy Leary pinned Victoria after hitting her with "brass" knux
- DL Hurst & Brett Domino pinned Thick Boys: Puf & Jay Freddie when Hurst pinned Freddie

- Allie Kat pinned Shazza Mackenzie
- New Hart Foundation: Teddy Hart & Davey Boy Smith Jr. defeated Maine State Posse: Aidan Aggro & DangerKid when Smith pinned Kid
- Limitless Champion: Maxwell Jacob Friedman with JT Dunn pinned Ashley Vox

This show features the debut of Adam Brooks, Davey Boy Smith Jr., Mance Warner, Shazza McKenzie, and Victoria. This was Domino's first and only win to date after seven losses. Kevin Blackwood made his return after injuries sustained from a car crash in January distracting Christian Casanova, costing him the match to Brad Hollister. Both Statlander and Buck requested to wrestle this match as in their home state the New York State Athletic Commission will not allow intergender matches.

This was MJF's second Limitless Wrestling World Title defense but his first on a Limitless event.
Vehicle crashes on the interstate delayed the arrival of fans and wrestlers causing the doors to open late. For instance, Teddy Hart was driving from Philadelphia and didn't arrive until 8:45pm. This

resulted in the card being shuffled as the New Hart Foundation vs. MSP was supposed to be the match before intermission.

Notes from my blog The Wrestling Insomniac: Reporter Rob Caldwell from the local NBC affiliate WCSH 6 was on hand doing a story on Limitless. New Hart Foundation: Davey Boy Smith Jr & Teddy Hart defeated Maine State Posse: Aidan Aggro & Danger Kid This was tremendous! Smith and Hart dominated the match with their high impact offense but Aggro and Danger Kid hung with them the whole time. We saw Davey Boy deliver the shoulder powerslam both running from the corner and off the second rope. Smith pressed DangerKid and Teddy jumped off the top rope grabbing on the way down for a DDT, it was nuts! Kid even took the Doomsday Canadian Destroyer with Smith pinning Kid for the win. Fans were hot through the whole match. Post-match both Smith and Hart cut promos thanking the fans, putting over Limitless Wrestling and wrestling as a whole in general. Limitless Wrestling World Champion: Maxwell Jacob Friedman with JT Dunn pinned Ashley Vox. MJF opened with a scathing promo about putting down Vox and women in general generating a lot of hate and discontent from the crowd. Mikey LaFreniere mentioned he's surprised that no one has attacked him yet, I'd have to agree with Mikey as MJF gets that old-school white-hot heat. Dunn came out with MJF but a few minutes into the match was ejected from ringside. Ashley would take a tremendous beating repeatedly in this match but each time she would battle back with some high impact offense much to the delight of the crowd. I was excited to see MJF bust out both a bear hug and torture rack style back breaker in the match. Late in the match while on the floor MJF pressed Ashley over his head and just threw her into the crowd on both sides of the ring. Probably would have been nice if they would have tried to catch her. This was a fantastic visual! Back in the ring the ref was knocked down and MJF got the title belt, Vox said that she would kiss his boot as he demanded at the beginning of the match, but she hit him in the junk instead. Then hit him with the belt and locked on her finish, MJF tapped out but the ref didn't see it. Eventually the ref came around again and Vox locked her reel catch submission back on, MJF then violently bit down hard on her finger covering her hand and his mouth with blood. It was vicious!

He then drove her into the mat with Cross Rhodes for the pin. Post-match the fans threw trash into the ring which MJF encouraged. I've never been to a show where trash was thrown at a wrestler like trash was thrown at MJF on this show, this is how much MJF gets the people to hate him. He cut a promo saying we were trash and that JT Dunn was going to win the Vacationland Cup and forfeit his title match. Dunn hit MJF with Death by Elbow and cut a promo saying he was going to take the title from MJF.

LA KERMESSE FESTIVAL NIGHT 1
June 22, 2019 St. Louis Field Biddeford, Maine

- Best of 7 Falls: "Retrosexual" Anthony Greene with The Platinum Hunnies defeated "Smart" Mark Sterling
- DL Hurst pinned Nico Silva
- The Sea Stars: Ashley Vox & Delmi Exo defeated The Platinum Hunnies: Ava Everett & Angel Sinclair
- "The Prize" Alex Price defeated Channing Thomas
- Davienne defeated CJ Cruz
- Mac Daniels pinned Doug Wyzer
- Eric Johnson defeated Mac Daniels
- Maine State Posse: DangerKid & Aiden Aggro defeated Sass & Fury: "Dirt Dawg" Jeremy Leary & "Hot Scoop" Skylar

This show features the debut of Alec Price, Channing Thomas, CJ Cruz, Doug Wyzer, Eric Johnson, and Mac Daniels. This was

Jeremy Leary's in-ring return at Limitless after two years. Right before the show started a passing storm soaked the ring, it was drying fast, but it was still wet when the card started. This led to the standard one fall match between AG and Sterling to be a best of 7 falls.

LA KERMESSE FESTIVAL NIGHT 2
June 23, 2019 St. Louis Field Biddeford, Maine

- CJ Cruz won a battle royal
- The Top Dogs: Davienne & "Hot Scoop" Skylar with "Dirt Dawg" Jeremy Leary defeated The Platinum Hunnies: Ava Everett & Angel Sinclair
- DL Hurst pinned Max Caster
- Triple Threat: Alexander Lee defeated Bryce Donovan and "Dirt Dawg" Jeremy Leary
- M.A.D.: Tomahawk & Perry Von Vicious defeated Off The Hop Rope: "Top Shelf" Troy Nelson & CPA
- "The Prize" Alec Price defeated Kid Curry
- Sierra defeated Bobby Orlando with Bobby Jr
- The Stigma: Eric Johnson & Brandino Davis defeated The Dirty Drifters: Jacob Drifter & Doug Wyzer
- Street Fight: ¡Let's Wrestle! Champion: Kalvin Strange defeated CJ Cruz

This show features the debut of Jacob Drifter, Kid Curry, Perry Von Vicious, Tomahawk aka Rip Byson, and Sierra. This was only the second battle royal in Limitless. Tyler Nitro made his return to Limitless after two years.

2019 VACATIONLAND CUP
July 12, 2019 Portland Club Portland, Maine

- Round 1: Kevin Blackwood defeated "Top Talent" Christian Casanova
- Round 1: Ace Romero pinned DL Hurst
- The Maine State Posse: DangerKid & Aiden Aggro defeated The Workhorsemen: "New Age Enforcer" James Drake & Anthony Henry
- Round 1: JT Dunn pinned Eli Everfly
- Round 1: "Retro" Anthony Greene with The Platinum Hunnies defeated Shawn Spears & Tommy Dreamer
- Daniel Garcia defeated Pepper Parks

- Scramble Match: Ashley Vox defeated Swoggle, Lil Blay, "Dirt Dawg" Jeremy Leary, Covey Christ, and Channing Thomas
- "Hot Scoop" Skylar defeated Kris Statlander
- Puf pinned "Smart" Mark Sterling
- Vacationland Cup Finals: "Retro" Anthony Greene with The Platinum Hunnies defeated Ace Romero, Kevin Blackwood, & JT Dunn to become the number one contender

This show features the debut of Covey Christ, Lil Blay and Shawn Spears. On January 6, 2019 Kevin Blackwood and Daniel Garcia, along with others were involved in a serious vehicle crash. Tonight, marked not only both wrestlers returning to Limitless Wrestling, but this was Kevin Blackwood's first match in the ring after the crash.

This was Swoggle's first appearance in two years. Brad Hollister suffered a knee injury taking him out of the tournament with DL Hurst replacing him. Shawn Spears was pulled from the card and replaced by Tommy Dreamer, then Spears was able to work the show after all and the match was made a three-way dance. Alexander Lee turned on the Maine State Posse joining the returning Brandon Kirk and Joey Eastman.

Leon Ruff was slated to be in the Scramble match, but his flight was delayed beyond his ability to make it to the show, he was replaced by Channing Thomas.

KNOW YOUR ENEMY
September 6, 2019 Portland Expo Portland, Maine

- Ace Romero pinned Dan Maff
- Christian Casanova pinned Leyla Hirsch
- The New Hart Foundation: Teddy Hart & Davey Boy Smith Jr. defeated The Work Horsemen: James Drake & Anthony Henry when Smith pinned Henry
- Kevin Blackwood pinned JT Dunn
- Street Fight: Maine Street Posse: Aiden Aggro & DangerKid defeated Alexander Lee & "Rogue" Brandon Kirk with Joey Eastman when Lee was pinned
- The Butcher & The Blade defeated "Dirty Daddy" Chris Dickinson & "Filthy" Tom Lawlor when Butcher pinned Lawlor

- Scramble Match: DL Hurst defeated Jody Threat, Jon Silver, Puf, & Harlow O'Hara when Hurst pinned Threat
- Hair vs. Career: Kris Statlander & Ashley Vox defeated Jeremy Leary & Skylar when Kris Stat pinned Leary. Bradford shaved Leary's head post-match
- Retro Anthony Greene pinned Limitless Wrestling World Champion: MJF to win the championship

This is the Portland Expo debut for Limitless. This show features the debut of Dan Maff, Jody Threat, Leyla Hirsch, and Tom Lawlor. Alexander Lee suffered his first loss after a seven-match winning streak. MJF's title reign ended at 181 days, this would also be his final Limitless Wrestling match to date. AR Fox was scheduled to face Christian Casanova and simply didn't get on the plane for the show, he was replaced by Leyla Hirsch who was slated for the scramble match. A couple weeks prior to this show Fox was supposed to face Casanova for NorthEast Wrestling and Fox didn't get on the plane for that show either. Evil UNO dropped off the show the week of with a hip injury, Puf was his replacement. Brandon Kirk suffered a deep laceration on his head from the lobster trap.

Notes from my blog The Wrestling Insomniac: I was very excited to have front row for this show because this is one of the most historic buildings for wrestling in Maine. Built in 1914 it is the second oldest arena in continuous operation in the United States. On March 5, 1929 World Heavyweight Champion Gus Sonnenberg defeated Ned McGuire in two straight falls. On April 2, 1945 Leo Numa defeated Manuel Cortez by disqualification when referee Babe Ruth called for the bell. The first time I can find that the WWWF ran at the Expo was July 19, 1966 with King Curtis Iaukea defeating Johnny Valentine in the main event. In his book Bob Backlund talks about wrestling then WWF Champion "Superstar" Billy Graham to a bloody double count-out on December 6, 1977 at the Expo. For over 11 years the WWWF/WWF ran monthly shows at the venue. In 1978 the WWF would move to the newly opened and larger Cumberland County Civic Center, now Cross Insurance Arena. My dad went to the matches here regularly and saw the legends like Graham, Backlund, Putksi, Andre the Giant and others. I myself have only attended one wrestling show at the Expo, which was the last wrestling show the venue hosted. March 16, 2003 Maine Event Wrestling featuring Robbie Ellis, X-Pac, Brian Christopher, Raven, Mike Quackenbush vs. Reckless Youth in a 2 out of 3 falls masterpiece and The Fabulous Moolah and The Great Mae Young in tag team action against Don Montoya & Towel Boy Adams, I sat in the bleachers on that night.

Ace Romero pinned Dan Maff. This was a hell of a fight and what a great way to open the show. It got the crowd to their feet for the entire contest and these guys beat the hell out of each other. Maff got Romero in a torture rack position and gave him a burning hammer right on the top of Ace's head! It was sick, in a good way! Ace got the pin after a monster clothesline. Hair vs. Career: Kris Statlander & Ashley Vox defeated Jeremy Leary & Skylar In this match it was Stat's career and Leary's hair on the line. If you would have told me that Leary was going to lose this match and have his head shaved, I would have lost that bet. The match was great with Leary being a giant asshole the whole contest. After Statlander pinned him with her finisher the crowd erupted! They started cutting his hair in the ring and then at ringside Bradford finished the job. It was an awesome moment.

Vox & Statlander start the cut

Bradford finishes the job

"Retro" Anthony Greene defeated Limitless Wrestling World Champion: MJF. This was a highly anticipated match and the perfect finish to the Limitless Wrestling four-year anniversary event. About two minutes into the match MJF hit Greene with a deliberate low blow for which the referee called for the bell. Randy Carver, Limitless owner, restarted the match making it no DQ. The match quickly went to the floor and around ringside. This match was not as crazy as the street fight, but they did their fair share of damage to each other. Finish came right in the center of the ring after a step up tomikaze by Greene on MJF. Biggest pop of the night when referee Eric Greenleaf hit the three count. Every person in the building was on their feet! We all wanted this bad for AG!

Danger Kid flies onto Alexander Lee in the Expo Street Fight

The Butcher and the Blade

FRESH BLOOD
October 25, 2019 AMVets Yarmouth, Maine

- ¡Let's Wrestle! Showcase: CJ Cruz pinned "The Prize" Alec Price

- Leyla Hirsch pinned Jon Silver
- Maine State Posse: Aiden Aggro & DangerKid defeated Violence is Forever: Kevin Ku & Dominic Garrini when Kid pinned Ku
- Kris Statlander pinned Caleb Konley
- Fatal Four Way Elimination: Gangrel defeated DL Hurst, Danhausen, & Alexander Lee with Joey Eastman; Lee pinned Hurst, Lee pinned Danhausen, and Gangrel pinned Lee

- Anything Goes: Dan Maff pinned Matthew Justice
- Scramble Match: Ashley Vox defeated Masha Slamovich, Allie Kat, Jody Threat, & Skylar with Jeremy Leary when Vox submitted Slamovich
- "Red Death" Daniel Garcia submitted Fred Yehi
- JT Dunn, Christian Casanova, & Joshua Bishop defeated Kevin Blackwood, and The Butch & The Blade when Dunn pinned Blackwood
- Limitless Wrestling World Champion: Anthony Greene pinned Josh Briggs

This was the debut of Limitless at the AMVets in Yarmouth. This show features the debut of Caleb Konley, Dominic Garrini, Gangrel, Joshua Bishop, Masha Slamovich, and Matthew Justice.

Notes from my blog The Wrestling Insomniac: CJ Cruz pinned "The Prize" Alec Price. They brought everything that they had tonight and absolutely killed it! Honestly this match set a very high standard for the rest of the card to have to follow. Cruz pinned Price after a wicked missile dropkick. Women's Scramble

Match: Ashley Vox defeated Masha Slamovich, Jody Threat, Allie Kat, & Skylar with Jeremy Leary. This was the first match back after intermission and it got the crowd back up. Got to see Slamovich with a sweet wheelbarrow suplex on Vox and Saito suplex on Kat. Threat was Irish whipped by Kat on her skateboard into Slamovich spearing her into the chairs. Vox got the win when she submitted Slamovich.

Post-match Kris Stat came out to celebrate with Vox, who got up on Stat's shoulders. Stat then cut a promo stating that they were a team and proposed they take on MSP. Then she said they should challenge the winner of Greene vs. Briggs in a triple threat match. But ultimately, she decided "How about I finish what I started and fucking murder you" dropping Vox on her face. After a pull apart brawl Statlander challenged Vox to a Last Creature Standing Match.

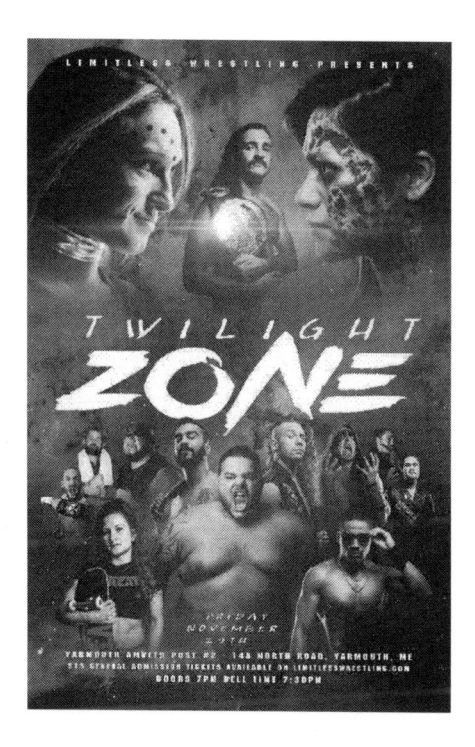

TWILIGHT ZONE
November 29, 2019 AMVets Yarmouth, Maine

- Independent Wrestling Champion: Warhorse pinned Jon Silver
- Christian Casanova pinned Myron Reed
- "Blue Collar Badass" James Drake pinned "The Prize" Alec Price
- Masha Slamovich pinned Jody Threat
- Take Me Home Tonight: Limitless Wrestling World Champion: "Retro" Anthony Greene & Ace Romero defeated MSP: Aiden Aggro & DangerKid when Ace pinned Kid
- CJ Cruz defeated Kevin Ku, One Called Manders, Oswald Project, & Pinkie Sanchez pinning Ku

- JT Dunn pinned Jake Something
- Last Creature Standing: Ashley Vox defeated Kris Statlander

This event was streamed live on IWTV. This show features the debut of 1 Called Manders, Oswald Project, and Pinkie Sanchez. This was also Warhorse's first appearance as Warhorse with the IWTV Championship. Dan Maff was slated to appear against JD Drake; however, he suffered an unfortunate death in the family and cancelled, he was replaced by Alec Price. The internet crashed halfway through MSP vs. Take Me Home Tonight cutting the live streaming feed for about five minutes.

Notes from my blog The Wrestling Insomniac: James Drake vs "The Prize" Alec Price. This was supposed to be Drake vs. Dan Maff, but he couldn't attend because of a death in the family. The surprise opponent was Alec Price. Boy oh boy did the Prize shine bright tonight! I have to give Randy a lot of credit for putting Prize in the match, it was the right choice. This was a fantastic match, lots of hard-hitting action, very fast paced at times, and the big man James Drake nailed a moonsault for the pin. If last month's pre-show got his foot in the door, tonight's performance should guarantee Price a permanent roster spot. Take Me Home Tonight: Limitless Wrestling World Champion: "Retro" Anthony Greene & Ace Romero vs. Maine State Posse: Danger Kid & Aiden Aggro. This was as awesome as I expected it to be! Action was inside and outside the ring, lots of back and forth action. No one team had the upper hand for any extended period of time, but I legit thought MSP was going to get the win. Ace pinned DangerKid with a package piledriver. Post-match Ace got on the mic, put over MSP and then challenged AG to a title match in January. Casanova came to the ring; said he deserved a title shot. AG accepted both of their challenges for a triple threat match on January 24th. JT Dunn vs. Jake Something. This match was awesome! They were different in the fact that they stayed in the ring with a stiff and snug match. Jake Something was over huge and the people hated JT Dunn. I really dug this match a lot and I really hope we get more of Jake Something in Limitless. Dunn got the pin with death by elbow.

Last Creature Standing: Kris Statlander vs. Ashley Vox. This did not disappoint. We got brutality, we got broken furniture, we got the ring boards exposed, and both ladies busted open. Ashley Vox won, that's all I'm going to say, go watch it, you will not regret it.

After the crash

Kevin Quinn reaching the 10 count

120

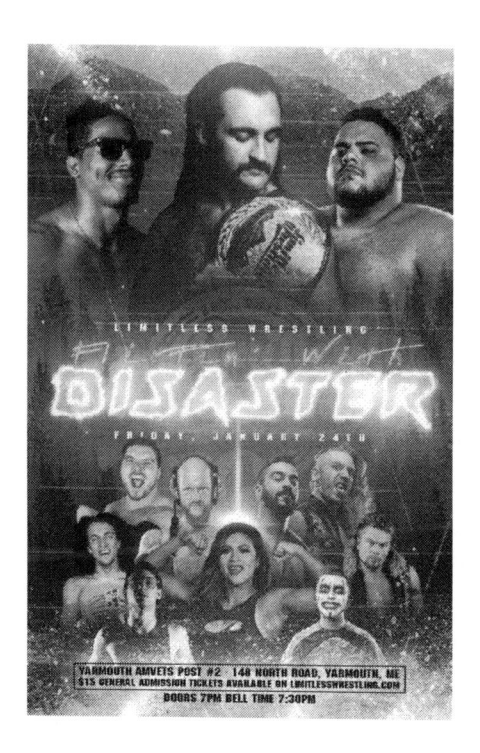

FLIRTIN' WITH DISASTER
January 24, 2020 AMVets Yarmouth, Maine

- 'Blue Collar Badass" James Drake pinned Brian Pillman Jr.
- "The Prize" Alec Price pinned Danhausen
- "Red Death" Daniel Garcia submitted Oswald Project
- Kris Statlander pinned "Red Death" Daniel Garcia
- Ashley Vox pinned Tasha Steelz
- MSP: Aiden Aggro & DangerKid defeated Impact Wrestling Tag Team Champions: The North: "All Ego" Ethan Page & Josh Alexander in a non-title match when Aggro pinned Alexander
- Josh Briggs defeated Jody Threat, Kevin Blackwood, and Alexander Lee with Joey Eastman when Briggs pinned Blackwood

- Puf pinned Jon Silver
- CJ Cruz defeated JT Dunne by reverse decision
- Limitless Wrestling World Champion: "Retro" Anthony Greene defeated Christian Casanova & Ace Romero pinned Romero

This show features the debut of Brian Pillman Jr., Josh Alexander, and Tasha Steelz.

Notes from my blog The Wrestling Insomniac: The AMVets hall was a packed sold out standing room only with over 40 people turned away at the door. From the moment the name of this show was announced it reminded me of the Molly Hatchet song of the same name. Every time I saw a new post or notification of the show the song popped into my head. If Randy didn't open the show with this blaring over the speakers it would be a crime. Well he didn't start with a recording of the song, it started with Ryan Curry rocking it out on the guitar and Rich Palladino belted an awesome rendition of the track! What a way to start the show! "Red Death" Daniel Garcia vs. Oswald Project. Garcia getting that big-time heat from the moment he entered the ring. At first, he seemed to be the reluctant heel but by the end of the match he was embracing the hate. I'm still not overly impressed with Oswald; we saw a lot more of what he could do in this match than the last but that still wasn't a lot. Project spent the majority of the match getting ass handed to him while he begged off not wanting the fight, then when he decided to fight, he busted out some interesting offense. In the end Garcia locked in the sharpshooter and leaned back far enough that he even hooked Project around the head getting the submission win with a nasty move. Post-match Garcia got on the mic and said that this is what happens when someone who gets in the ring isn't prepared for the fight. That he wanted real competition and issued an open challenge that led to.... "Red Death" Daniel Garcia vs. Kris Statlander.

Kris Statlander with the unadvertised surprise appearance. I thought for sure after November's Last Creature Standing match and with her signing with AEW we had seen the last of our favorite alien. This was an excellent match! Statlander is one of the best wrestlers of any gender in wrestling today. I don't care who she is wrestling, Statlander gets a good match out of them. Not that she needed to work that hard with Garcia who is excellent as well. Near the end Stat was going for big bang theory when Garcia reversed it into a roll up and the two rolled back and forth exchanging a couple dozen two counts. In the end though Kris Stat picked up the win. Post-match Garcia attacked Statlander until Ashley Vox made the save.

Maine State Posse: Danger Kid & Aiden Aggro vs. The North: "Walking Weapon" Josh Alexander & "All Ego" Ethan Page. This was announced as a non-title match as The North are the Impact Wrestling World Tag Team Champions. Mikey and I attempted to start a Monster Mafia chant but were not successful. I like that name much better than The North. This was Alexander's first time in Maine whereas Page has been here a bunch. As one would expect that was a tremendous match! Posse continues to get better and with teams like The North coming in to work with them they will continue to get better. Page and Alexander brought their A game tonight, but it wasn't enough as Aggro stole a cradle pin from Alexander giving MSP the upset victory. JT Dunn vs. CJ Cruz. This was a great match! The two meshed together very well with Dunn continuing to tell Cruz that he wasn't worthy and Cruz proving him wrong. Cruz went for the BDE: Best Dropkick Ever, but Dunn side stepped him and hit DBE: Death by Elbow scoring the three count. After being declared the victor Dunn continued the punishment on Cruz. Dunn knew even though he got the pinfall he didn't prove what he set out to do which was show that Cruz couldn't hang with him. When referee Kevin Quinn attempted to pull Dunn off Cruz, Dunn shoved Quinn to the mat. Quinn then reversed the decision awarding the contest to CJ Cruz. Dunn continued the beat down on Cruz and Rich Palladino tried to get Dunn to stop the assault when Dunn shoved Rich to the ground. Well that move pissed off the entire Limitless crowd as they jumped to their feet letting Dunn know that, that was not cool. Sincerely you could feel the hostile tension towards Dunn for his actions, and Dunn could too as he wisely left the ring returning to the back.

PRACTICE WHAT YOU PREACH
February 22, 2020 AMVets Yarmouth, Maine

- Christian Casanova pinned Myron Reed
- MSP Invitational: "Smart" Mark Sterling & VSK defeated Kevin Blackwood, Demorest & Oswald Project, and Maine State Posse: Aiden Aggro & DangerKid when Sterling pinned Blackwood
- Trevor Murdoch pinned Atticus Cogar
- "Red Death" Daniel Garcia pinned Ashley Vox
- Kris Statlander pinned Jody Threat
- Independent Wrestling Champion: Warhorse pinned Rip Byson
- JT Dunn & Hammerstone defeated Josh Briggs & CJ Cruz when Dunn pinned Cruz

- Jake Something pinned "The Prize" Alex Price
- Limitless Wrestling Champion: "Retro" Anthony Greene pinned "Dirty Daddy" Chris Dickinson
- Post-Match: Kris Statlander challenged Greene

This show features the debut of Alex Hammerstone, Demorest, and Trevor Murdoch.

Notes from my blog The Wrestling Insomniac: Daniel Garcia vs. Ashley Vox. Great match! The crowd loves Ashley and hates Garcia. Garcia really beat the crap out of Vox throughout the match, hard slams on the floor, tying her in knots in the ring. Ashley fought back through and sunk in her reel catch submission finisher, but Garcia rolled through somehow and rolled her up for the pin. Limitless Wrestling World Champion: Retro AG vs. "Dirty Daddy" Chris Dickinson. The Dirty Daddy jump started this match when he nailed AG with a missile dropkick during his entrance. It looked like Dickinson was going to win the Championship, but AG reversed a lateral press into one of his own for a quick three count. Post-match Dickinson hits AG with the Pazuzu Bomb and Kris Stat cut a promo on AG about challenging him next month.

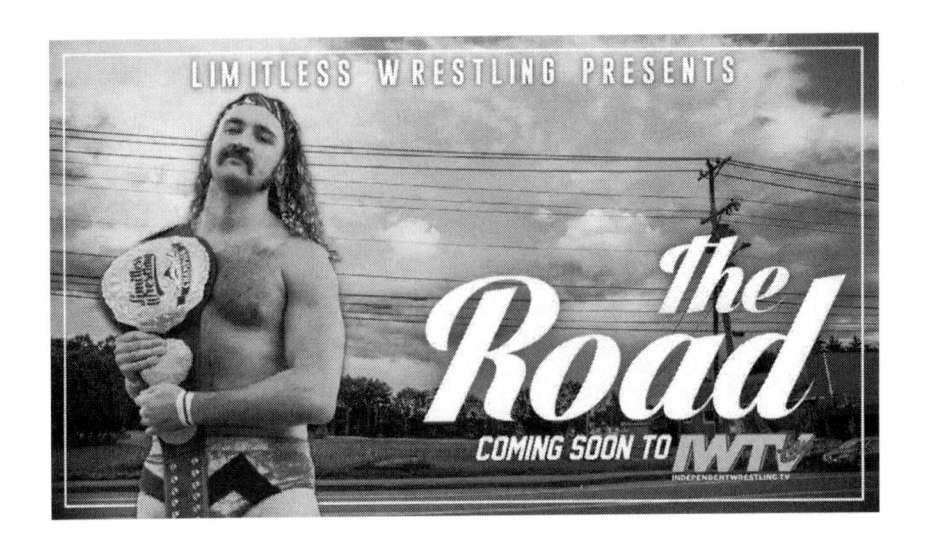

The Road: Season 1

The weekend of July 11 & 12, 2020 the talent from Limitless Wrestling, ¡Let's Wrestle!, and new competitors looking to earn future opportunities gathered at the American Legion Hall in Orono, Maine for a round of closed set tapings. This new series called *The Road* debuted on IWTV on Wednesday July 29, 2020 at 7pm and ran for eleven episodes concluding on October 7, 2020.

Episode 1 *Aired July 29, 2020*
Commentary by Randy Carver, featuring promos by DangerKid, Armani Kayos, Waves & Curls, Kirby Wackerman, Eric Johnson, Alec Price,

- DangerKid defeated Armani Kayos
- The Sea Stars: Ashley Vox & Delmi Exo defeated Waves & Curls: Jaylen Bradyn & Traevon Jordan when Delmi pinned Jordan
- Eric Johnson pinned Kirby Wackerman
- Ace Romero defeated "The Prize" Alec Price

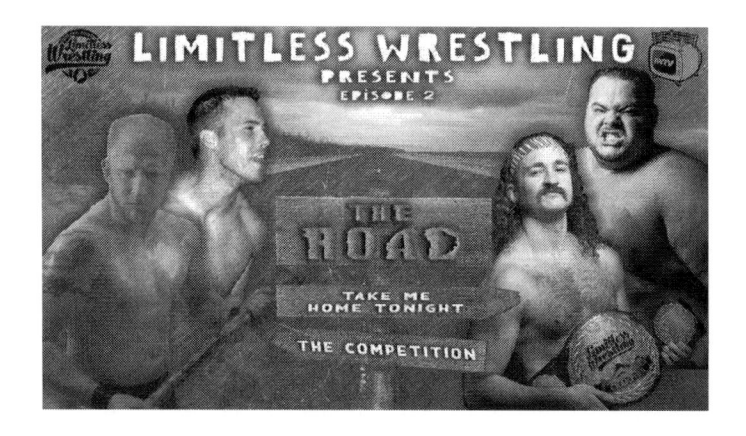

Episode 2 *Aired August 5, 2020*
Commentary by Randy Carver, featuring promos by Dylan Nix, Alexander Lee, Frank Jaeger, Delmi Exo, and Rip Byson

- The Kids: Basic Becca, CJ Cruz, & Ricky Archer defeated The High Society of Love: Paris Van Dale, Armani Kayos, & Love Doug when Becca pinned Doug after a 3D
- Best of 5 Series Match 1: "Frisky" Frank Jaeger pinned Alexander Lee with a quick roll up
- Take Me Home Tonight: World Champion: Anthony Greene & Ace Romero defeated The Competition: Champ Mathews & Paul Hudson when AG pinned Murphy after a back-body bomb
- "Iron" Rip Byson pinned Delmi Exo with an Oklahoma Stampede

Episode 3 *Aired August 12, 2020*
Commentary by Randy Carver, featuring promos by Nick Stapp, Alexander Lee, Ave Everett & Davienne, and Eric Johnson

- Kennedi Copeland submitted "Baby Girl" Nick Stapp with Fujiwara armbar

- Best of 5 Series Match 2: "Frisky" Frank Jaeger defeated Alexander Lee by disqualification, the first disqualification in Limitless Wrestling
- 2 on 1 Handicapped Match: Eric Johnson defeated Dylan Nix & Konnor Hex pinning Nix with the Johnson Special
- "Iron" Rip Byson pinned DangerKid with a lariat

Episode 4 *Aired August 19, 2020*
Commentary by; Randy Carver, featuring promos by The Sea Stars, The Girls Room, Alec Price, Basic Becca, Jacob Drifter, a video package on Rip Byson vs Ace Romero, and a video package on the Alexander Lee vs. Frank Jaeger match that lead to Lee vs. Kid

- The Girls Room: Ava Everett & Davienne defeated The Sea Stars: Delmi Exo & Ashley Vox
- Ace Romero pinned Dozer
- "The Prize" Alec Price defeated Basic Becca
- Alexander Lee defeated DangerKid

Episode 5 *Aired August 26, 2020*
Commentary by; Randy Carver, featuring promos by Dave Dyer, Eric Johnson, Anthony Greene post-match, Ava Everett post-match

- Ace Romero pinned "Iron" Rip Byson with a Lariat
- 2 on 1 Match: Eric Johnson defeated The Dirty Drifters: Jacob Drifter & Doug Wyzer when Johnson pinned them both after the Johnson Special
- Best of 5 Series Match 3: Alexander Lee pinned "Frisky" Frank Jaeger
- Non-Title: Limitless Wrestling World Champion: "Retro" Anthony Greene pinned "Avataker" Ava Everett

Episode 6 *Aired September 2, 2020*

Commentary by; Randy Carver, featuring promos by Doug Wyzer, Rip Byson, Ava Everette, Higher Society, video with Traevon Jordan, Basic Becca & Love Doug, backstage pull apart between Rip Byson & Eric Johnson post-match promo by Ricky Archer and Ace Romero

- Dave Dyer defeated Doug Wyzer
- Limitless Wrestling World Champion: Anthony Greene & Ava Everette defeated The Higher Society: Armani Kayos & Paris Van Dale
- Best of Five Series Match 4: Alexander Lee defeated Frank Jaeger
- Ace Romero defeated Ricky Archer

Episode 7 *Aired September 9, 2020*

Commentary by; Randy Carver, featuring promos by Rip Byson, Alexander Lee, video with Basic Becca, Traevon Jordan, & Love Doug, and Alec Price

- Waves & Curls: Jaylen Bradyn & Traevon Jordan defeated The Higher Society: Armani Kayos & Paris Van Dale
- Nick Stapp defeated Kirby Wackerman

- BA Tatum pinned Jacob Drifter
- Eric Johnson defeated Rip Byson

Episode 8 *Aired September 16, 2020*
Commentary by; Randy Carver, featuring promos by Eric Johnson, Traevon Jordan & Love Doug, highlight video of the best of five series, and post-match promo by Alexander Lee

- Traevon Jordan pinned Love Doug
- ¡Let's Wrestle! Tag Team Champions: The Stigma: Eric Johnson & Valentino Davis defeated The Competition: Champ Mathews & Connor Murphy
- Best of Five Series Match 5: Dojo Street Fight: Alexander Lee defeated Frank Jaeger
- "The Prize" Alec Price pinned Ace Romero

Episode 9 *Aired September 23, 2020*
Commentary by; Randy Carver, featuring promos by Love Doug & Basic Becca video, Dylan Nix, post-match promo by Davienne

- Body Slam Challenge: Traevon Jordan defeated Love Doug
- Roll UP: Jaylen Bradyn defeats Love Doug
- Traevon Jordan defeated Love Doug
- Kennedi Copeland defeated Dave Dyer
- Dylan Nix pinned Nick Stapp
- Davienne defeated Rip Byson

Episode 10 *Aired September 30, 2020*
Commentary by; Randy Carver, featuring promos by DangerKid confronting and challenging Dylan Nix, Ashley Vox, Jacob Drifter, Love Doug & Basic Becca video

- Armani Kayos defeated CJ Cruz

- Davienne pinned Paris Van Dale
- Jacob Drifter defeated Ace Romero
- Basic Becca defeated Love Doug

Episode 11 *Aired October 7, 2020*
Commentary by; Randy Carver, featuring promos by Anthony Greene, BA Tatum, Ashley Vox, Dylan Nix, post-match promo by Anthony Greene praising Ashley Vox, video package closes the show with Anthony Greene setting down the championship stating that his road has come to an end.

- Delmi Exo pinned Nick Stapp
- Brandido Davis pinned BA Tatum
- DangerKid pinned Dylan Nix
- World Champion: "Retro" Anthony Greene pinned "Reel Catch" Ashley Vox

These show features the debut of Armani Kayos, Basic Becca, Dave Dyer, Dozer, Dylan Nix, Frank Jaeger, Jaylen Bradyn, Kirby Wackerman, Konnor Hex, Love Doug, Paris Van Dale, Ricky Archer, and Traevon Jordan

The Breakdown:
34 wrestlers competed in 47 matches with 13 wrestlers making their Limitless debut, Ace Romero had the most matches at seven while Eric Johnson was undefeated in all five of his matches, while four other wrestlers went undefeated as well, eight were unable to pick up a win.

2020 VACATIONAL CUP Qualifying Match
December 12, 2020 AMVets Yarmouth, Maine

- Four Way Match: CJ Cruz defeated Mac Daniels with Jon Alba, Ricky Archer, & Tyree Taylor

2020 VACATIONLAND CUP
December 19, 2020 AMVets Yarmouth, Maine

- First Round: "Red Death" Daniel Garcia defeated Lee Moriartiy
- First Round: "Top Talent" Christian Casanova defeated CJ Cruz
- First Round: JD Drake defeated Kevin Blackwood
- First Round: "The Price" Alec Price defeated Ace Romero

- The Beverage Barons: Puf & Megabyte Ronnie defeated The Prestige: Brett Ryan Gosselin & Channing Thomas
- Maine State Posse: Aiden Aggro & DangerKid defeated The Sea Stars: Ashley Vox & Delmi Exo
- "Iron" Rip Byson pinned Big Beef Gnarls Garvin
- Vacationland Cup Finals: Fatal Four Way Elimination Match: "Top Talent" Christian Casanova outlasted "Red Death" Daniel Garcia, "The Prize" Alec Price, and JD Drake to capture the vacant Limitless Wrestling World Championship. Prize pinned Drake, Garcia eliminated Price via referee stoppage, and Casanova pinned Garcia

This is the first full Limitless show in ten months. This show features the debut of Big Beef Gnarls Garvin, Lee Moriarty, and Megabyte Ronnie. It was not announced, the original first round match for Alec Price was Leyla Hirsh, however she made an appearance on AEW. Ace Romero was slated to face Rip Byson in the first round. Myron Reed was slated to face Kevin Blackwood in the first round but missed his flight resulting in the four-way qualifying match. Another first round match Christian Casanova vs. JD Drake was also shuffled around.

What Would Have Happened

When 2020 started the plan for Limitless Wrestling was to run monthly shows with four tent pole shows over the year. Those four shows were to be the *Vacationland Cup* singles tournament with the winner advancing to *Welcome to The Dance* which would become the annual September anniversary show. *Fresh Blood* would be a card featuring a lot of new talent debuting in Limitless. Finally, *WrestleProm*, an open invitation tag team tournament with the same set up as the *Vacationland Cup* with four opening round matches with the winners advancing to a four-way elimination tag team final. The show would also feature scramble matches called Ballroom Blitz.

When the Covid-19 Pandemic caused a lockdown in the state of Maine Limitless had announced *Cause for Alarm* which had been scheduled for March 21, 2020, but the show was cancelled on March 15th. The announced show featured;

- **Limitless Wrestling World Champion:** "Retro" Anthony Green vs. Kris Statlander
- Maine State Posse: DangerKid & Aiden Aggro vs. Bear Country: Bear Bronson & Bear Boulder vs Violence is Forever: Kevin Ku & Dominic Garrini
- Fatal Four Way: "Reel Catch" Ashley Vox vs Kevin Blackwood vs "Man Scout" Jake Manning vs Covey Christ
- "The Prize" Alec Price vs. Matt Cross
- CJ Cruz vs. Josh Briggs
- Hardcore Match: Alexander Lee with Joey Eastman vs. Brandon Kirk
- Number 1 Contenders Match: Christian Casanova vs. Daniel Garcia
- Unannounced: Ace Romero vs. "Smart" Mark Sterling

This show would have led into the first *WrestleProm* on April 18, 2020. The fans would have been encouraged to dress up like they were going to a prom with sashes awarded to the best dressed couple. The teams slated to appear were:

- **Limitless Wrestling World Champion:** "Retro" Anthony Green & Ava Everette
- Maine State Posse: DangerKid & Aiden Aggro
- The Bird and The Bee: Willow Nightingale & Solo Darling
- The Shook Crew: Max Caster & Bobby Orlando
- "Reel Catch" Ashley Vox & "Legit" Leyla Hirsch
- Christian Casanova & Tasha Steelz
- Whatever It Takes: "Smart" Mark Sterling & VSK
- Kris Statlander & Nick Gage

Randy does plan to implement the monthly schedule and the tent pole shows once Limitless can run again, however with contract status of some of these competitors it is unlikely we will ever see these complete cards come to fruition.

Alternate Show Art

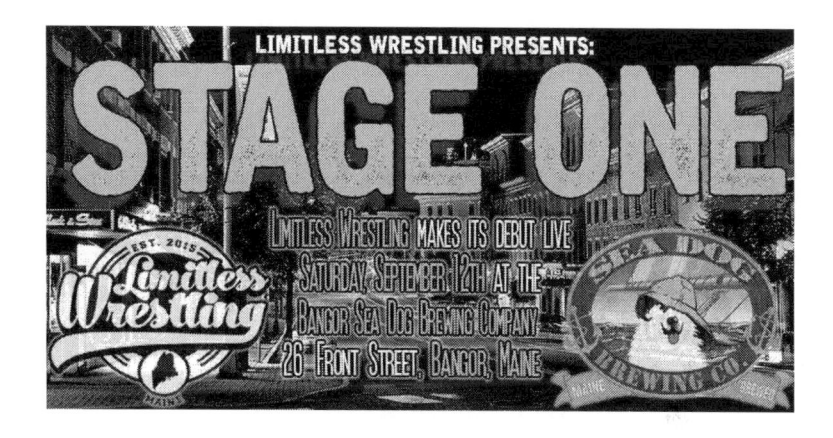

Stage One

Who Watches The Watchmen?

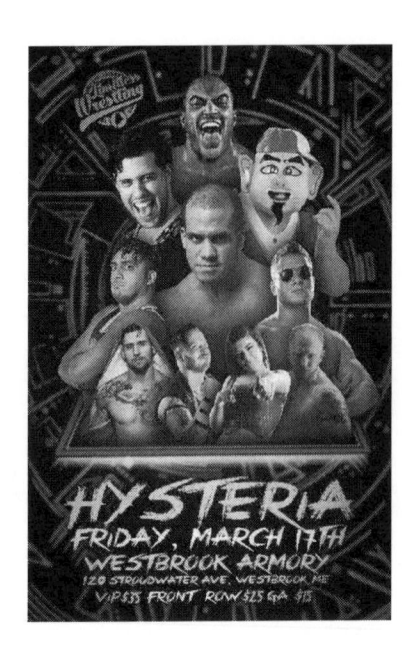

Hysteria

Nothing Gold Can Stay

Question The Answers September 22, 2017 Westbrook, Maine

Only Fools Are Satisfied March 30, 2018 Westbrook, Maine

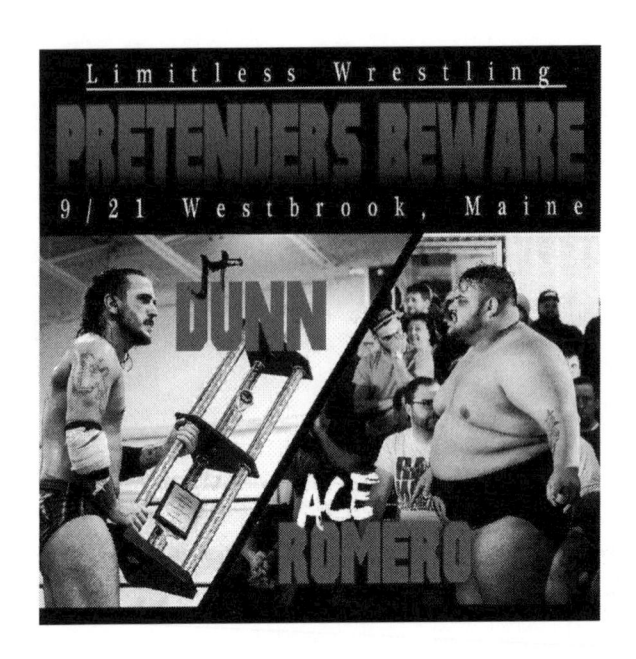

Pretenders Beware September 21, 2018 Westbrook, Maine

The Road Season 1

The Road Season 1

The 2020 Vacationland Cup December 19, 2020

143

The 2020 Vacationland Cup December 19, 2020

Bitter Rivals

Anthony Greene vs. JT Dunn

Anthony Greene and JT Dunn have competed in more matches against each other in Limitless Wrestling than any other two competitors, seven matches. AG got the better of JT Dunn winning four matches, losing one and one match ended in a double count-out. The seventh match they were involved in was a fatal four way where neither man came out on top.

July 23, 2016 *Hook, Line, & Sinker* American Legion Post 84 Orono
Triple Threat: Anthony Greene defeated JT Dunn & Brian Fury

November 03, 2017 *Hybrid Moments* Portland Club
Anthony Greene & JT Dunn wrestled to a double count-out

January 19, 2018 *The World Is Ours* Westbrook Armory
Fatal Four Way: Anthony Greene defeated Ace Romero, Josh Briggs, & JT Dunn

May 11, 2018 *Feed The Need* Portland Club
Portland Street Fight: Anthony Greene defeated JT Dunn

January 11, 2019 *Snakebitten* Westbrook Armory
The Kings: JT Dunn & MJF defeated Take Me Home Tonight: Ace Romero & Anthony Greene

March 09, 2019 *Welcome to the Dance* Westbrook Armory
Fatal Four Way: MJF defeated JT Dunn, Anthony Greene, & Ace Romero to become the first Limitless Wrestling World Champion

July 12, 2019 *2019 Vacationland Cup* Portland Club
Finals: Fatal Four Way Elimination Match: Anthony Greene outlasted Ace Romero, JT Dunn, & Kevin Blackwood to win the Vacationland Cup

Ace Romero vs. JT Dunn

Ace Romero and JT Dunn have competed in six matches against each other in Limitless Wrestling. In the six encounters Ace won two, Dunn one, and the other three involved other wrestlers and neither came walked out with the win.

May 28, 2016 *No Dropkicks in the Living Room* American Legion Post 84 Orono
Ace Romero pinned JT Dunn

January 19, 2018 *The World Is Ours* Westbrook Armory
Fatal Four Way: Anthony Greene defeated Ace Romero, Josh Briggs, & JT Dunn

September 21, 2018 *Pretenders Beware* Westbrook Armory
Ace Romero pinned JT Dunn

January 11, 2019 *Snakebitten* Westbrook Armory
The Kings: JT Dunn & MJF defeated Take Me Home Tonight: Ace Romero & Anthony Greene

March 09, 2019 *Welcome to the Dance* Westbrook Armory
Fatal Four Way: MJF defeated JT Dunn, Anthony Greene, & Ace Romero to become the first Limitless Wrestling World Champion

July 12, 2019 *2019 Vacationland Cup* Portland Club
Finals: Fatal Four Way Elimination Match: Anthony Greene outlasted Ace Romero, JT Dunn, & Kevin Blackwood to win the Vacationland Cup

Anthony Greene vs. Ace Romero

Between teaming with each other and fighting against each other AG & Ace have been involved in 13 matches, however in 6 of them were the opponents. AG got the best of Ace securing four victories, Ace only once however it was the only Steel Cage match to date in Limitless. One other match neither man walked out with the win.

September 22, 2017 *Question The Answers* Westbrook Armory
Anthony Greene defeated Ace Romero with Special Referee Brian Fury

January 19, 2018 *The World Is Ours* Westbrook Armory
Fatal Four Way: Anthony Greene defeated Ace Romero, Josh Briggs, & JT Dunn

July 27, 2018 *Vacationland Cup* Westbrook Armory
Steel Cage: Ace Romero pinned Anthony Greene

March 09, 2019 *Welcome to the Dance* Westbrook Armory
Fatal Four Way: MJF defeated JT Dunn, Anthony Greene, & Ace Romero to become the first Limitless Wrestling World Champion

July 12, 2019 *2019 Vacationland Cup* Portland Club
Finals: Fatal Four Way Elimination Match: Anthony Greene outlasted Ace Romero, JT Dunn, & Kevin Blackwood to win the Vacationland Cup

January 24, 2020 ***Flirtin' With Disaster*** AMVets Hall Yarmouth
Triple Threat: Limitless Wrestling World Champion: Anthony Greene defeated Ace Romero & Christian Casanova

Ace Romero vs. AR Fox

In one of the most memorable feuds in the first couple years of Limitless Wrestling was Ace Romero vs. AR Fox. Of their six encounters Ace won four of them with AR Fox taking only two victories, however both of these wins gave Ace Romero and later Anthony Greene their first losses in Limitless Wrestling. This feud also featured the bloodiest match in Limitless to date the Fans Bring The Weapons Match at *Problematic*.

January 30, 2016 ***Under Fire*** American Legion Post 84 Orono
Ace Romero pinned AR Fox

September 24, 2016 ***Past Your Bedtime*** American Legion Post 84 Orono
Anything Goes: AR Fox pinned Ace Romero

May 13, 2017 ***Problematic*** Westbrook Armory
Fans Bring The Weapons Match: Ace Romero pinned AR Fox

July 21, 2017 ***Nothing Gold Can Stay*** Westbrook Armory
AR Fox & Rey Fenix defeated Ace Romero & Anthony Greene when Fox pinned Romero

March 30, 2018 ***Only Fools Are Satisfied*** Westbrook Armory
Ace Romero, Josh Briggs, & JT Dunn defeated AR Fox, Shane Strickland, & Teddy Hart

May 11, 2018 ***Feed The Need*** Portland Club
Ace Romero defeated AR Fox

DangerKid vs. Alexander Lee

The story of DangerKid and Alexander Lee is one of the most unusual stories in Limitless. They started out rough when Kid, working as a cameraman allegedly got in Lee's way costing him a match. The two teamed up, but that one match ended badly leading towards their first match against each other. Eventually they reconciled for a couple years until Lee turned on DangerKid and Aiden Aggro and now they are fighting in a battle that is destined to last. In their six matches Kid has defeated Lee four times with Lee defeating Kid twice.

March 19, 2016 *Don't Fear The Sleeper* American Legion Post 84 Orono
Alexander Lee & Aiden Aggro defeated DangerKid & Wrecking Ball Legursky

July 23, 2016 *Hook, Line, & Sinker* American Legion Post 84 Orono
Fans Bring The Weapons: DangerKid defeated Alexander Lee

July 27, 2018 *Vacationland Cup* Westbrook Armory
First Round Triple Threat: DangerKid defeated Alexander Lee & Aiden Aggro

September 06, 2019 *Know Your Enemy* Portland Expo
The Maine State Posse: DangerKid & Aiden Aggro defeated Alexander Lee & Brandon Kirk with Joey Eastman

The Road Season 1 Episode 4 *Aired August 19, 2020*
Alexander Lee defeated DangerKid

Ashley Vox vs. Kris Statlander

The feud that is Kris Statlander vs. Ashley Vox goes beyond the four matches they have competed in against each other. Both have run in at the end of each other's matches to "steal their thunder". Statlander destroyed Vox's sister Delmi Exo at the Hollis Pirate Festival as a message to Vox. Strangely though after their Unsanctioned Match at Snakebitten Statlander seemed to bury the hatchet with Vox even teaming with her defeating Skylar and Jeremy Leary at Know Your Enemy with Statlander putting her career on the line against Leary's hair. At Fresh Blood Statlander came out in what seemed like a celebration with Vox that ended with her turning on Vox and challenging her to their Last Creature Standing match. In their four matches Ashley Vox has won three times and Statlander only once. However, their Unsanctioned and Last Creature Standing matches are two of the wildest and most violent matches in Limitless history.

March 30, 2018 *Only Fools Are Satisfied* Westbrook Armory
Fatal Four Way: Ashley Vox defeated Kris Statlander, Allie Kat, & Penelope Ford

September 21, 2018 *Pretenders Beware* Westbrook Armory
Kris Statlander & Davienne defeated Ashley Vox & Willow Nightingale

January 11, 2019 *Snakebitten* Westbrook Armory
Unsanctioned Match: Ashley Vox defeated Kris Statlander

November 29, 2019 *Twilight Zone* AMVets Hall Yarmouth
Last Creature Standing: Ashley Vox defeated Kris Statlander

WRESTLER PROFILES

For this section of the book I contacted many of the wrestlers directly to gather the most accurate information. For those I was unable to contact I sourced interviews and the internet for the data. If information is missing it is because I was not able to contact the wrestler and could not find information on the internet.

1 Called Manders *"Corn Belt Cowboy"*
6'1" 229 lbs Great State of Iowa

Record: 0 – 1
Shows wrestled on:
November 29, 2019 ***Twilight Zone*** AMVets Hall Yarmouth

1 Called Manders has made just one appearance to date with Limitless in a five-way scramble that included Oswald Project, Pinkie Sanchez, Kevin Ku, and was won by CJ Cruz. A product of the Black & Brave Wrestling Academy, he debuted in April 2017.

Ace Austin *"The Ace of Spades"*
5'8" 174 lbs Atlantic City, New Jersey

Record: 3 – 1
Shows wrestled on:
March 30, 2018 ***Only Fools Are Satisfied*** Westbrook Armory
May 11, 2018 ***Feed The Need*** Portland Club
September 21, 2018 ***Pretenders Beware*** Westbrook Armory
January 11, 2019 ***Snakebitten*** Westbrook Armory

Trained at the CZW Dojo he debuted in April 2015. He is currently signed to Impact wrestling where he is a former X-Division Champion holding the title for 171 days. His biggest win in Limitless came at Pretenders beware where he successfully defended the Pro Wrestling Revolver Scramble Championship against Daniel Garcia, Jessicka Havok, Matt Cross, Mick Moretti, & Sami Calliham

Ace Romero *"Acey Baby"*
6'0" 376lbs Saco, Maine

Record: 30 – 11
Shows wrestled on:
September 12, 2015 **Stage One** City Side Restaurant, Brewer
November 15, 2015 **Killin' & Thrillin** American Legion Post 84 Orono
January 30, 2016 **Under Fire** American Legion Post 84 Orono
March 19, 2016 **Don't Fear The Sleeper** American Legion Post 84 Orono
May 28, 2016 **No Dropkicks in the Living Room** American Legion Post 84 Orono
July 23, 2016 **Hook, Line, & Sinker** American Legion Post 84 Orono
September 24, 2016 **Past Your Bedtime** American Legion Post 84 Orono
October 07, 2016 **Risk It For The Biscuit** Westbrook Armory

October 29, 2016 *Who Watches the Watchmen?* The Field House at University of Maine Orono
November 19, 2016 *Hogwash* American Legion Post 84 Orono
January 27, 2017 *Unreal* Westbrook Armory
February 25, 2017 *Do What You Love, Fuck The Rest-Fest* American Legion Post 84 Orono
March 17, 2017 *Hysteria* Westbrook Armory
April 28, 2017 *Can We Kick It?* Portland Club
May 13, 2017 *Problematic* Westbrook Armory
June 23, 2017 *La Kermesse Festival Night 1* St. Louis Field Biddeford
July 21, 2017 *Nothing Gold Can Stay* Westbrook Armory
September 22, 2017 *Question The Answers* Westbrook Armory
November 03, 2017 *Hybrid Moments* Portland Club
January 19, 2018 *The World Is Ours* Westbrook Armory
March 30, 2018 *Only Fools Are Satisfied* Westbrook Armory
May 11, 2018 *Feed The Need* Portland Club
July 27, 2018 *Vacationland Cup* Westbrook Armory
September 21, 2018 *Pretenders Beware* Westbrook Armory
November 30, 2018 *No Control* Portland Club
January 11, 2019 *Snakebitten* Westbrook Armory
March 09, 2019 *Welcome to the Dance* Westbrook Armory
May 10, 2019 *Hooked on a Friedman* Westbrook Armory
July 12, 2019 *2019 Vacationland Cup* Portland Club
September 06, 2019 *Know Your Enemy* Portland Expo
November 29, 2019 *Twilight Zone* AMVets Hall Yarmouth
January 24, 2020 *Flirtin' With Disaster* AMVets Hall Yarmouth
The Road Season 1 *Episodes 1, 2, 4, 5, 6, 8, 10, & 11* American Legion Post 84, Orono
December 19, 2020 *2020 Vacationland Cup* AMVets Hall Yarmouth

Romero got his start training in 2008 at the New England Pro Wrestling Academy, then the Chaotic Training Center. He had written an essay in school about wanting to become a pro wrestler and with the support of his teacher she drove him to his first class where at a tryout he earned three months of free training. He trained at the school for about two years and felt he wasn't progressing. He moved to Florida with the thought of training at the WWE developmental Florida Championship Wrestling. He arrived at FCW and feeling a bit overwhelmed and intimidated he never got out of the car. He then searched out other schools and started training at Team 3D Academy where he trained another two years on and off before he finally had his first match in Florida for Iron Fist Pro Wrestling. He wrestled under the name Batuka which he describes as a jungle savage type character, with his first official match being a battle royal. He also wrestled a series of matches in June 2012 for Florida Underground Wrestling.

He returned to New England and started training in Providence, Rhode Island with Biff Busick. Romero states he owes a lot to Biff for encouraging him to change his gear into wearing trucks and giving him confidence in himself. After Biff signed with the WWE, Romero started training with Mike Bennett and Matt Taven. He also credits JT Dunn with helping him with indie style wrestling psychology.

Ace with partner Roadblock, and others in 2014

He made his Maine debut for Brewer based IWE: Independent Wrestling Entertainment and worked there consistently while training with Busick. He quickly formed the tag team The Leatherheads with partner Roadblock and the duo would win the

IWE Tag Team Championships on two occasions. He also held the IWE Heavyweight and Twin Cities Championships during his time in the promotion.

In 2014, he started branching outside New England wrestling for promotions in New York and New Jersey. In September 2016, while in California for personal reasons he contacted Empire Wrestling Federation, promotion that has been in operation since 1996, and was booked on their September 9th show in Covina picking up a win over Jacob Tarasso. In 2017, he held the New Jersey based Pro Wrestling Magic Heavyweight Championship for 35 days. Also, in 2017, he and Anthony Greene as Take Me Home Tonight won the XWA: Xtreme Wrestling Alliance Tag Team Championships.

In 2018, he moved to Ohio to train with Sami Callihan and wrestling for AAW, IWA Mid-South, Pro Wrestling Revolver, and Rockstar Pro where he, along with MJF and Clayton Jackson, held the Rockstar Pro Wrestling Trios Championship for 40 days. While living in the Midwest he would return to Maine to wrestle for Limitless. In 2018, he signed with MLW spending a year with the promotion appearing in a series of matches including defeating Simon Gotch in the Simon Gotch Prize Fight Challenge. He wrestled at the AEW *Double or Nothing* PPV in the 21 Man Casino Battle Royal on May 25th in Las Vegas at the

MGM Grand. In October 2019 he signed with Impact Wrestling where he currently teams with Larry D as XXXL.
In Limitless Wrestling he main evented the first ever show, *Stage One* defeating Alex Mason. He would also main event Limitless second show *Killin' & Thrillin'* defeating Scott Wild. Romero has competed in more matches than anyone else in a Limitless ring, he has also appeared in the most main events headlining 19 shows. He's been involved in some of the most famous and controversial matches in Limitless Wrestling history including three of the top 10 moments in Limitless history; his fans bring the weapons match with AR Fox at *Problematic*, when the cage collapsed against Anthony Greene at the *2018 Vacationland Cup*, and the fatal four way at *Welcome to the Dance* to crown the first Limitless Wrestling World Champion.
His entrance music "Your Love" by The Outfield was inspired by Matt Tremont's use of Journey's "Separate Ways". He wanted a song that the fans could sing along with and get behind that also pumped him up during his entrance.

Adam Booker *"Mr. Remarkable"*
6 '4" 242 lbs Saco, Maine

Record: 0 – 5
Shows wrestled on:
July 23, 2016 **Hook, Line, & Sinker** American Legion Post 84 Orono
October 07, 2016 **Risk It For The Biscuit** Westbrook Armory
October 29, 2016 **Who Watches the Watchmen?** The Field House at University of Maine Orono
November 19, 2016 **Hogwash** American Legion Post 84 Orono
January 27, 2017 **Unreal** Westbrook Armory

The former "Trendsetter" debuted September 16, 1999 teaming with the "Boogie Woogie Man" Jimmy Valiant against two of Valiant's students. He returned to Maine becoming a mainstay in the Eastern Wrestling Alliance winning their Heavyweight, New England, & Hardcore championships.

Adam Brooks *"GLOAT: Greatest Ledge Of All Time"*
5' 11" 176 lbs Melbourne, Victoria, Australia

Record: 0 – 1
Shows wrestled on:
May 10, 2019 ***Hooked on a Friedman*** Westbrook Armory

Trained by Buddy Murphy, Brooks wrestled in Independents around the world before being signed by Ring of Honor in February of 2020.

Adam Falcon
5' 11" 235 lbs Farmingdale, New York

Record: 0 – 2
Shows wrestled on:
September 12, 2015 ***Stage One*** City Side Restaurant, Brewer
January 30, 2016 ***Under Fire*** American Legion Post 84 Orono

Trained by the Amazing Red, he debuted in House of Glory Wrestling in 2014 and is a former Grand Slam Wrestling Tag Team Champion with partner Joe Quick.

AJ Gray "Rich Homie Juice"
Lexington, Tennessee

Record: 0 – 1
Shows wrestled on:
May 11, 2018 ***Feed The Need*** Portland Club

Debuting in 2016, AJ has found his best career success since joining Game Changer Wrestling in 2019. On December 8, 2019 he ended Nick Gage's historic 722 day run as GCW Heavyweight Champion.

Alec Price *"The Prize"*
6' 175 lbs East Boston, Massachusetts

Record: 6 – 5
Shows wrestled on:
June 22, 2019 *La Kermesse Festival Night 1* St. Louis Field Biddeford
June 23, 2019 *La Kermesse Festival Night 2* St. Louis Field Biddeford
October 25, 2019 *Fresh Blood* AMVets Hall Yarmouth
November 29, 2019 *Twilight Zone* AMVets Hall Yarmouth
January 24, 2020 *Flirtin' With Disaster* AMVets Hall Yarmouth
February 22, 2020 *Practice What You Preach* AMVets Hall Yarmouth
The Road Season 1 *Episodes 1, 4, & 8* American Legion Post 84, Orono
December 19, 2020 *2020 Vacationland Cup* AMVets Hall Yarmouth

Trained by Beau Douglas at the Bell Time Club, Price debuted in. In ¡Let's Wrestle! he had an amazing feud with CJ Cruz culminating in an Iron Man match. An explosive dark match at *Fresh Blood* between the Prize City OG and Cruz punched their ticket to the main roster. On Episode 8 of *The Road* Price scored an impressive victory over Ace Romero. At the *2020 Vacationland Cup* Price once again defeated Romero in the opening round before being eliminated in the finals for the vacant Limitless Wrestling World Championship.

Alex Chamberlain
6' 0" 240lbs Bangor, Maine

Record: 0 – 1
Shows wrestled on:
May 13, 2017 **Problematic** Westbrook Armory

Trained by "Brutal" Bob Evans, Chamberlain debuted in 2003 where he and Alexander Lee, then going by Scotty Vegas, were the original Maine State Posse. He relocated to Florida where he has continued his successful run on the indie scene while dabbling in acting. He competes in the Fantasy Super Cosplay Wrestling promotion as Skeletor from the He-Man series.

Alex Mason *"The Carnivore"*
Queens, New York

Record: 1 – 4
Shows wrestled on:
September 12, 2015 **Stage One** City Side Restaurant, Brewer
November 15, 2015 **Killin' & Thrillin** American Legion Post 84 Orono
January 30, 2016 **Under Fire** American Legion Post 84 Orono
March 19, 2016 **Don't Fear The Sleeper** American Legion Post 84 Orono

May 28, 2016 *No Dropkicks in the Living Room* American Legion Post 84 Orono

A product of the House of Glory wrestling school, Mason debuted in 2013. In Maine, Mason wrestled for IWE: Independent Wrestling Entertainment before appearing on Limitless' debut show. Was part of the tag team Booty & The Beast with Sonny Kiss.

Alexander Hammerstone
6' 3" 251lbs Glendale, Arizona

Record: 1 – 0
Shows wrestled on:
February 22, 2020 *Practice What You Preach* AMVets Hall Yarmouth

Debuted in 2013 in Arizona, Hammerstone quickly became a powerhouse on the west coast indie scene capturing several championships. 2019 would see Hammerstone sign with both Major League Wrestling, where he is the first and current MLW National Openweight Champion, winning the title on June 1, 2019. He also debuted in Japan for Pro Wrestling NOAH representing MLW in the 2019 N1-Victory tournament.

Alex Reynolds
6' 04" 196lbs Long Island, New York

Record: 0 – 1
Shows wrestled on:
March 19, 2016 *Don't Fear The Sleeper* American Legion Post 84 Orono

Reynolds debuted in 2006 after training with Mikey Whipwreck. In 2011 he formed the tag team The Beaver Boys with John Silver, since then they have captured numerous tag team championships including: NYWC, PWS, & PWG. Currently the duo is signed with AEW and are members of the Dark Order.

Alexander Lee *"Bald Beautiful Bastard of Bangor"*
5' 10" 220lbs Bangor, Maine

Record: 14 – 17
Shows wrestled on:
September 12, 2015 ***Stage One*** City Side Restaurant, Brewer
November 15, 2015 ***Killin' & Thrillin*** American Legion Post 84 Orono
January 30, 2016 ***Under Fire*** American Legion Post 84 Orono
March 19, 2016 ***Don't Fear The Sleeper*** American Legion Post 84 Orono
May 28, 2016 ***No Dropkicks in the Living Room*** American Legion Post 84 Orono
July 23, 2016 ***Hook, Line, & Sinker*** American Legion Post 84 Orono
February 25, 2017 ***Do What You Love, Fuck The Rest-Fest*** American Legion Post 84 Orono
March 17, 2017 ***Hysteria*** Westbrook Armory
April 28, 2017 ***Can We Kick It?*** Portland Club

May 13, 2017 ***Problematic*** Westbrook Armory
June 23, 2017 ***La Kermesse Festival Night 1*** St. Louis Field Biddeford
July 21, 2017 ***Nothing Gold Can Stay*** Westbrook Armory
September 22, 2017 ***Question The Answers*** Westbrook Armory
November 03, 2017 ***Hybrid Moments*** Portland Club
January 19, 2018 ***The World Is Ours*** Westbrook Armory
March 30, 2018 ***Only Fools Are Satisfied*** Westbrook Armory
July 27, 2018 ***Vacationland Cup*** Westbrook Armory
August 11, 2018 ***2018 Hollis Pirate Festival*** Hollis Fire Department
September 08, 2018 ***2018 Litchfield Fair***
September 21, 2018 ***Pretenders Beware*** Westbrook Armory
November 30, 2018 ***No Control*** Portland Club
January 11, 2019 ***Snakebitten*** Westbrook Armory
March 09, 2019 ***Welcome to the Dance*** Westbrook Armory
June 23, 2019 ***La Kermesse Festival Night 2*** St. Louis Field Biddeford
September 06, 2019 ***Know Your Enemy*** Portland Expo
October 25, 2019 ***Fresh Blood*** AMVets Hall Yarmouth
January 24, 2020 ***Flirtin' With Disaster*** AMVets Hall Yarmouth
The Road Season 1 *Episodes 2, 3, 4, 5, 6, & 8* American Legion Post 84, Orono

Alexander Lee began his wrestling career in 2003 training with Legion Cage at Rampage Pro Wrestling. Lee also credits "Brutal" Bob Evans & Chris Hamrick with helping to mold him into the wrestler he would become. His first match was April 23, 2003 under the name Scotty "By God" Vegas, a name he would use for a dozen years. A veteran and leader of the Maine independent scene Lee has wrestled for almost every promotion that has sprung up in Maine. In 2004 Lee teaming with Alex Chamberlain were the original Maine State Posse wrestling around the New England region until 2009 when Chamberlain relocated to Florida. During this run the Original MSP held the NCW Tag Team Championships for 364 days.

Scotty "By God" Vegas May 11, 2012 Intergalactic Wrestling

Lee has collected numerous championships during his 18 years in the ring including;

IWE: Independent Wrestling Entertainment
6-time Heavyweight Champion
3-time Tag Team champion with Larry Huntley, Viper the Ninja, & Scott Wild
2011 King of New England Rumble winner

SAW: Slam All-Star Wrestling
Tag Team Championships with Big Vigo

NCW: Northeast Championship Wrestling
Heavyweight Champion
2-time New England champion
Tag Team Champion with Alex Chamberlain

PWA: Pro Wrestling America
2-time New England Championship

NAWA: North Atlantic Wrestling Association

North Atlantic Champion
Tag Team Championships with Johnny Primer

Scotty "By God" Vegas vs. Robbie Ellis February 21, 2007

In 2015 with the launch of Limitless Wrestling, a new name was needed to go along with a new attitude and Alexander Lee was born defeating former UFC MMA fighter "Cold Steel" Chuck O'Neil. At this time DangerKid, having already made his professional wrestling debut in another promotion, was working for Limitless Wrestling as a cameraman. At *Killin' & Thrillin'* DangerKid cost Lee the scramble match. As Lee was taking his aggression out on DangerKid, Randy Carver made them a tag team for the next show. Lee and DangerKid did not succeed as a team at *Under Fire*. Lee then brought in a friend of DangerKid in Aiden Aggro as his protégé to show DangerKid what he could do for him if he just listened to Lee. *At Don't Fear the Sleeper*, Lee & Aggro defeated Kid and Wrecking Ball Legurksy in tag team competition. At Hook, Line, & Sinker DangerKid defeated Lee in a Fans Bring the Weapons match with Aggro hitting Lee with a chair solidifying his loyalty to DangerKid.

Eventually the trio put their differences aside and in early 2016, DangerKid and Aiden Aggro teamed up Lee to reform the Maine State Posse. At first Lee was in a managerial role, and then was out of commission with an injury. However, in July 2017 he returned, and the Maine State Posse became a trio with the full support of the fans. They had several outstanding matches with Tabarnak de Team, Free To Think: Jeff Cannonball, Brandon Kirk, & Casey Katal, and others making six-man tag teams a must-see match at Limitless events.

At *Hybrid Moments* Joey Eastman came to the ring offering his services to MSP, which was rejected showing the unity of the trio. However, in early 2018 tensions between the three started coming forward. Kid & Aggro wanted to strike out on their own whereas Lee didn't want to dismantle what he had worked so hard in building the Maine State Posse.

After months of speculation, at the *2019 Vacationland Cup*, Alexander Lee joined Joey Eastman and Brandon Kirk attacking DangerKid & Aggro with his goal to end the Maine State Posse. This led to a Portland Street Fight at *Know Your Enemy* where the Maine State Posse defeated Lee and Kirk. The battle between Kirk and Lee is far from over.

Alexander Lee is also an intricate part of ¡Let's Wrestle! contributing even more to the professional wrestling scene in Maine. During Season 1 of *The Road* he won a best of Five series against "Frisky" Frank Jaeger defeating him in a Dojo Brawl to end the series. He also won a decisive victory over DangerKid on Episode 4.

Allie Kat
5' 03" 128lbs Escaped from the Local Animal Shelter

Record: 3 – 2
Shows wrestled on:
January 19, 2018 **The World Is Ours** Westbrook Armory
March 30, 2018 **Only Fools Are Satisfied** Westbrook Armory
July 27, 2018 **Vacationland Cup** Westbrook Armory
May 10, 2019 **Hooked on a Friedman** Westbrook Armory
October 25, 2019 **Fresh Blood** AMVets Hall Yarmouth

Allie Kat debuted in Texas in 2015 and traveled around the US indie scene building her reputation. She debuted in Limitless Wrestling the same night as Kris Statlander, the two teamed with Ashley Vox defeating the Maine State Posse in a six-person tag when Allie Kat pinned DangerKid with the pussy piledriver. In recent months she has become a mainstay with Game Changer Wrestling.

Alvin Alvarez *"Absolute" "Problem Solver"*
5' 11" 268lbs Coram, New York

Record: 0 – 1

Shows wrestled on:
August 11, 2018 *2018 Hollis Pirate Festival* Hollis Fire Department

Was trained by Alex Reynolds and Tony Nese, Alvin debuted in 2012. Wrestling primarily in the New York & New Jersey area winning championships NYWC, ACE, and VPW

Amazing Red
5' 06" 154lbs New York

Record: 0 – 1
Shows wrestled on:
January 11, 2019 *Snakebitten* Westbrook Armory

Trained by Mikey Whipwreck, Red debuted in 1998 and for the last 22 years has been one of the most influential wrestlers in the Indies. As a wrestler he has innovated many moves that wrestlers use today and has trained some of the best wrestlers from the Northeast region. He is a former multiple time champion holding titles in CZW, Ring of Honor, and most famously a three-time TNA X-Division Champion.

Andrew Everett *"The Apex of Agility"*
5' 09" 214lbs Burlington, North Carolina

Record 1 – 0
Shows wrestled on:
January 11, 2019 *Snakebitten* Westbrook Armory

Debuting in 2007 after being trained by Matt & Jeff Hardy Everett is one of only two people, I have ever seen do a double rotation moonsault. He has wrestled around the world in the United Kingdom, Japan, and Mexico, as well across the United States. He wrestled in Impact from 2015 – 2018 capturing the Tag Team

Championship with DJZ and most recently working for Ring of Honor.

Andy Williams *"The Butcher"*
6' 03" 273lbs Buffalo, New York

Record: 1 – 2
Shows wrestled on:
March 09, 2019 **Welcome to the Dance** Westbrook Armory
September 06, 2019 **Know Your Enemy** Portland Expo
October 25, 2019 **Fresh Blood** AMVets Hall Yarmouth

The Butcher started wrestling late debuting in 2016 and began teaming with Pepper Parks, The Blade, in 2017. The duo in a short time has become a formidable tag team eventually signing with AEW in December of 2019. He is the guitarist for the metalcore band Every Time I Die.

Angel Sinclair *"Queen of Booty Style"*
Pawtucket, Rhode Island
Record: 1 – 2
Shows wrestled on:
March 09, 2019 **Welcome to the Dance** Westbrook Armory
June 22, 2019 **La Kermesse Festival Night 1** St. Louis Field Biddeford
June 23, 2019 **La Kermesse Festival Night 2** St. Louis Field Biddeford

She started her training at the New England Pro Wrestling Academy. In March 2018 at Chaotic Wrestling Cold Fury 17 she made her debut as one of the Platinum Hunnies, with Ava Everett, being part of a grand entrance for Anthony Greene. This was supposed to be a one-time moment; however, it was so popular with the fans they became part of AG's regular entrance. With Ava Everett they duo started out as a tag team, but by mid-2019 had gone their separate ways with one final match as a team in

December 2019. Together they held the Empowered and WSU Tag Team Championships. As a singles she has wrestled in the Northeast US Indies region including winning the APW: Atlantic Pro Wrestling Women's Championship.

Anthony Bennett *"The Hightop Fading Hip-Hop Parading"*
5' 11" 165lbs Paulsboro, New Jersey

Record 0 – 1
Shows wrestled on:
February 25, 2017 ***Do What You Love, Fuck The Rest-Fest***
American Legion Post 84 Orono

Debuted in 2013 after training with the Monster Factory, holding their Heavyweight Championship. He stays primarily in the New York / New Jersey area.

Anthony Gangone *"The Rogue"*
5' 5" 189lbs New York

Record: 3 – 4
Shows wrestled on:
January 30, 2016 ***Under Fire*** American Legion Post 84 Orono
May 28, 2016 ***No Dropkicks in the Living Room*** American Legion Post 84 Orono
July 23, 2016 ***Hook, Line, & Sinker*** American Legion Post 84 Orono
October 07, 2016 ***Risk It For The Biscuit*** Westbrook Armory
October 29, 2016 ***Who Watches the Watchmen?*** The Field House at University of Maine Orono
January 27, 2017 ***Unreal*** Westbrook Armory
January 11, 2019 ***Snakebitten*** Westbrook Armory

Gangone was trained by Amazing Red & Brian XL debuting in 2013. Wrestling primarily in the Northeast region he has captured several titles including holding the House of Glory Heavyweight

Championship for a combined 1048 days. His match vs Sonya Strong in Limitless wrestling has over 33 million views on the Limitless YouTube channel.

Anthony Greene *"All Good" "Retrosexual" "Retro AG"*
6' 02" 191lbs Dangertown USA

Record: 30 – 6 – 1
Shows wrestled on:
September 12, 2015 *Stage One* City Side Restaurant, Brewer
November 15, 2015 *Killin' & Thrillin* American Legion Post 84 Orono
March 19, 2016 *Don't Fear The Sleeper* American Legion Post 84 Orono
May 28, 2016 *No Dropkicks in the Living Room* American Legion Post 84 Orono
July 23, 2016 *Hook, Line, & Sinker* American Legion Post 84 Orono

September 24, 2016 ***Past Your Bedtime*** American Legion Post 84 Orono
October 07, 2016 ***Risk It For The Biscuit*** Westbrook Armory
October 29, 2016 ***Who Watches the Watchmen?*** The Field House at University of Maine Orono
November 19, 2016 ***Hogwash*** American Legion Post 84 Orono
January 27, 2017 ***Unreal*** Westbrook Armory
February 25, 2017 ***Do What You Love, Fuck The Rest-Fest*** American Legion Post 84 Orono
June 23, 2017 ***La Kermesse Festival Night 1*** St. Louis Field Biddeford
July 21, 2017 ***Nothing Gold Can Stay*** Westbrook Armory
September 22, 2017 ***Question The Answers*** Westbrook Armory
November 03, 2017 ***Hybrid Moments*** Portland Club
January 19, 2018 ***The World Is Ours*** Westbrook Armory
March 30, 2018 ***Only Fools Are Satisfied*** Westbrook Armory
May 11, 2018 ***Feed The Need*** Portland Club
July 27, 2018 ***Vacationland Cup*** Westbrook Armory
September 21, 2018 ***Pretenders Beware*** Westbrook Armory
November 30, 2018 ***No Control*** Portland Club
January 11, 2019 ***Snakebitten*** Westbrook Armory
June 22, 2019 ***La Kermesse Festival Night 1*** St. Louis Field Biddeford
July 12, 2019 ***2019 Vacationland Cup*** Portland Club
September 06, 2019 ***Know Your Enemy*** Portland Expo
October 25, 2019 ***Fresh Blood*** AMVets Hall Yarmouth
November 29, 2019 ***Twilight Zone*** AMVets Hall Yarmouth
January 24, 2020 ***Flirtin' With Disaster*** AMVets Hall Yarmouth
February 22, 2020 ***Practice What You Preach*** AMVets Hall Yarmouth
The Road Season 1 *Episodes 2, 5, 6, & 11* American Legion Post 84, Orono

Greene started his wrestling journey in 2009 as a referee under the name Josiah Matthews. He had his first match in May 2012 but didn't start formal training until June 2012. Although many people had a hand in training Greene, he credits the New England Pro Wrestling Academy with helping him the most.

Switching from wearing the stripes to full time wrestler also called for a name change and "All Good" Anthony Greene was born. In the last eight years Greene has wrestled all around the United States with tours in Canada, Mexico, Germany, and the United Kingdom. He's held multiple championships with his first being the PLW: Power League Wrestling tag team championships with Rob Araujo holding them from May 19, 2013 – August 10, 2014. He also held titles in Chaotic Wrestling, Lucky Pro Wrestling, Top Rope Promotions and more including being a former CZW World Champion.

At Chaotic Wrestling Cold Fury 17 in 2018 Retro AG appeared with the Platinum Hunnies: Ava Everett & Angel Sinclair for a grand entrance in his match with Cam Zagami. What was supposed to be a one-time enhancement to his entrance became part of his roadshow and elevated Greene to another level. Greene is one of 4 wrestlers who appeared on *Stage One* and is still active in the promotion through the rating period of this book. Greene came out victorious in his first fourteen matches in Limitless Wrestling, a record that stands with the promotion to this day. Greene's first loss was at *Nothing Gold Can Stay* when he and Ace Romero faced off against AR Fox and Rey Fenix, in that match Romero took the fall. Greene's first pinfall loss was at the *2018 Vacationland Cup* in a Steel Cage Match at the hands of Ace Romero.

This loss would be the first of a five-match losing streak that saw Greene drop matches to Colt Cabana, Ashley Vox, a tag match with Ace against JT Dunn & MJF, and the four-way match featuring Dunn, Ace, & MJF where MJF won the Limitless Wrestling World Championship.

Greene rebounded, winning the *2019 Vacationland Cup* and then going on to defeat MJF to win the Limitless Wrestling World Championship at the Portland Expo. Since then Greene has had numerous successful title defenses and not just in Limitless Wrestling. On October 7, 2020, after 397 days as champion with 8 successful title defenses Greene vacated the championship. That same day it was announced that he had been signed by the WWE and had reported to the performance center. He currently wrestles on NXT and 205 Live as August Grey.

Anthony Henry *"Saint" "The 5 Star King"*
5' 10" 180lbs Augusta, Georgia

Record: 2 – 5
Shows wrestled on:
March 17, 2017 ***Hysteria*** Westbrook Armory
July 21, 2017 ***Nothing Gold Can Stay*** Westbrook Armory
January 19, 2018 ***The World Is Ours*** Westbrook Armory
March 30, 2018 ***Only Fools Are Satisfied*** Westbrook Armory
May 11, 2018 ***Feed The Need*** Portland Club
July 12, 2019 ***2019 Vacationland Cup*** Portland Club
September 06, 2019 ***Know Your Enemy*** Portland Expo

Henry was trained by Sal Rinauro and Todd Sexton and debuted in 2002. For the first several years of his career he wrestled primarily in Georgia and the Carolinas winning championships in NWA regional promotions Anarchy, North Georgia, and Southern States. In 2016 he signed with the World Wrestling Network where he and James Drake captured the Evolve Tag Team Championships. Henry also wrestled for WWN's FIP where he held the Heavyweight Championship for 509 days.

Antoine Nicolas
5' 8" 170lbs Manchester, Connecticut

Record: 0 – 1
Shows wrestled on:
March 09, 2019 ***Welcome to the Dance*** Westbrook Armory

Nicolas started training in 2015 making his in-ring debut in 2016. His appearance at the ¡Let's Wrestle! Rumble 2019 wrote his ticket to this Limitless appearance. He attempted a shooting star press however landed on the ring post and top turnbuckle and came out of it uninjured. At *Welcome to the Dance* he was involved in the Scramble match and took the fall being pinned by

Brad Hollister. Nicolas states his favorite opponent to be Anthony Greene.

AR Fox *"The Whole Foxin' Show"*
6' 0" 185lbs Mableton, Georgia

Record: 4 – 5
Shows wrestled on:
January 30, 2016 ***Under Fire*** American Legion Post 84 Orono
May 28, 2016 ***No Dropkicks in the Living Room*** American Legion Post 84 Orono
September 24, 2016 ***Past Your Bedtime*** American Legion Post 84 Orono
May 13, 2017 ***Problematic*** Westbrook Armory
July 21, 2017 ***Nothing Gold Can Stay*** Westbrook Armory
September 22, 2017 ***Question The Answers*** Westbrook Armory
March 30, 2018 ***Only Fools Are Satisfied*** Westbrook Armory
May 11, 2018 ***Feed The Need*** Portland Club
July 27, 2018 ***Vacationland Cup*** Westbrook Armory

Trained by Mr. Hughes he debuted in 2007 and has traveled around the Indies and around the world wrestling in Dragon Gate, Dragon Gate USA, CZW, FIP Evolve, Lucha Underground and more. He was the first ever Evolve Champion defeating Sami Callihan in the finals of a one-night tournament. He is best known in Limitless Wrestling for his feud with Ace Romero. They have been in the ring with each other six times in singles and tag team competition with Ace coming out on top four times, including the bloody Fans Bring The Weapons Match at Problematic. Fox is responsible for handing both Ace Romero and Anthony Greene their first losses in Limitless Wrestling.

Armani Kayos
5' 9" Skinny Legend from the Upper East Side

Record 1 - 4

Shows wrestled on:
The Road Season 1 *Episodes 1, 2, 6, 7, & 10* American Legion Post 84, Orono

Kayos began training at the New England Pro Wrestling Academy in August 2018 wrestling his first match in October 2019. His favorite moment in all of wrestling started on November 23, 2014 when Nikki Bella won the Divas Championship through September 15, 2015 when she became the longest reigning Divas Champion.

Ashley Vox *"Reel Catch"*
5' 03" 114lbs Providence, Rhode Island

Record: 14 – 8
Shows wrestled on:
November 03, 2017 **Hybrid Moments** Portland Club
January 19, 2018 **The World Is Ours** Westbrook Armory
March 30, 2018 **Only Fools Are Satisfied** Westbrook Armory
May 11, 2018 **Feed The Need** Portland Club
July 27, 2018 **Vacationland Cup** Westbrook Armory
September 08, 2018 **2018 Litchfield Fair**
September 21, 2018 **Pretenders Beware** Westbrook Armory
November 30, 2018 **No Control** Portland Club
January 11, 2019 **Snakebitten** Westbrook Armory
March 09, 2019 **Welcome to the Dance** Westbrook Armory
May 10, 2019 **Hooked on a Friedman** Westbrook Armory
June 22, 2019 **La Kermesse Festival Night 1** St. Louis Field Biddeford
July 12, 2019 **2019 Vacationland Cup** Portland Club
September 06, 2019 **Know Your Enemy** Portland Expo
October 25, 2019 **Fresh Blood** AMVets Hall Yarmouth
November 29, 2019 **Twilight Zone** AMVets Hall Yarmouth
January 24, 2020 **Flirtin' With Disaster** AMVets Hall Yarmouth
February 22, 2020 **Practice What You Preach** AMVets Hall Yarmouth

The Road Season 1 *Episodes 1, 4, & 11* American Legion Post 84, Orono
December 19, 2020 *2020 Vacationland Cup* AMVets Hall Yarmouth

Trained by Doug Summers she debuted in 2014 forming a tag team The Sea Stars with her sister Delmi Exo in 2015. She debuted for CHIKARA in 2016 at the 12th Young Lions Cup, with the Sea Stars arriving two months later. As a duo they have won the tag team championships in Battle Club Pro, Sabotage, and Shimmer. In Limitless Wrestling Ashley is known for her wild and violent feud with Kris Statlander defeating Statlander in an Unsanctioned Match at *Snakebitten* and a Last Creature Standing Match at *Twilight Zone*. She also had two amazing matches you should go out of your watch. First against Anthony Greene at *No Control* and against MJF for the Limitless Wrestling World Championship at *Hooked on a Friedman*.

In 2020, The Sea Stars were featured in the Pro Wrestling Illustrated 500 wrestlers, the PWI Female 100, and the PWI Top 50 Tag Teams. This was the first year that PWI released the tag team ratings making this the first year this could be accomplished. Ashley Vox ranked 471 in the 500 and 66 in the Female 100, Delmi Exo ranked 477 in the 500 and 75 in the Female 100, while the team was ranked 26th in the tag team rankings. They are the only two people to be ranked in all three listings. In 2020 the Sea Stars competed in Impact wrestling and in 2021 AEW.

Atticus Cogar
5' 10" 175lbs Cleveland, Ohio

Record: 0 – 1
Shows wrestled on:
February 22, 2020 *Practice What You Preach* AMVets Hall Yarmouth

Cogar was trained by Ricky Shane Page making his debut in 2015. With Otis Cogar they simultaneously held the MEGA and PCW Tag Team Championships, he also held those promotions top singles titles. As a member of RSP's 44.OH! they have run roughshod over GCW. His Limitless debut was not an easy task as he was pitted against Trevor Murdoch and even though he lost he proved his toughness to the Limitless fans. His favorite moment to date is wrestling at GCW Run Rickey Run February 15, 2020 after RSP defeated Nick Gage to retain the GCW Championship when the fans rained garbage down upon 44.OH!

Austin Theory
6' 01" 220lbs Atlanta, Georgia

Record: 3 – 2
Shows wrestled on:

January 19, 2018 ***The World Is Ours*** Westbrook Armory
May 11, 2018 ***Feed The Need*** Portland Club
July 27, 2018 ***Vacationland Cup*** Westbrook Armory
September 21, 2018 ***Pretenders Beware*** Westbrook Armory
January 11, 2019 ***Snakebitten*** Westbrook Armory

Austin Theory was trained by AR Fox and in only his second match on May 5, 2016 he defeated Fox for the WWA4 Heavyweight Championship. A few months later he signed with the World Wrestling Network winning championships in FIP, Evolve, and becoming a 2-time WWN Champion. He wrestled in Mexico for Crash and CMLL in 2019 signing with WWE later in the year debuting on an NXT house show. In March 2020 he debuted on Raw as one of Seth Rollins Disciples.

Ava Everett *"Avataker"*
5' 8" 130lbs Somewhere Near Death Valley

Record: 3 – 3
Shows wrestled on:
March 09, 2019 ***Welcome to the Dance*** Westbrook Armory
June 22, 2019 ***La Kermesse Festival Night 1*** St. Louis Field Biddeford
June 23, 2019 ***La Kermesse Festival Night 2*** St. Louis Field Biddeford
The Road Season 1 *Episodes 4, 5, & 6* American Legion Post 84, Orono

Ava's passion for professional wrestling began with Nikki Bella and Total Divas. However, it wasn't until after watching a triple threat match at WrestleMania 32 between Charlotte Flair, Becky Lynch, and Sasha Banks that made her want to step in the ring. She started her training in August 2017 at the New England Pro Wrestling Academy. In March 2018 at Chaotic Wrestling Cold Fury 17 she made her debut as one of the Platinum Hunnies being part of a grand entrance for Anthony Greene. This was supposed to be a one-time moment; however, it was so popular

with the fans she became part of AG's regular entrance. She made her in-ring debut in September 2018. Ava with Angel Sinclair started out as a tag team, but by mid-2019 had gone their separate ways with one final match as a team in December 2019. Together they held the Empowered and WSU Tag Team Championships. With only a few short years in the ring Ava Everett has proven that her future is looking bright in the world of professional wrestling.

BA Tatum *"Bad Ass"*
6' 0" 250lbs Brooklyn, New York

Record: 2 – 1
Shows wrestled on:
September 12, 2015 ***Stage One*** City Side Restaurant, Brewer

The Road Season 1 *Episodes 7 & 11* American Legion Post 84, Orono

Tatum was trained by Steve Bradley and Maverick Wild before debuting in 2008. His favorite moment in wrestling is becoming tag team champions with Owen Brody.

Basic Becca
5' 2" 120lbs Columbus, Ohio

Record: 2 - 1
Shows Wrestled on:
The Road Season 1 *Episodes 2, 4, & 10* American Legion Post 84, Orono

Becca started training at the Bell Time Club in April 2019 and eight months later moved to the New England Pro Wrestling Academy where she trains to this day. Her first match was a loss to Ava Everett on January 10, 2020 for Chaotic Wrestling in Lowell, Massachusetts. Her favorite moment so far in wrestling was in this debut match where Ava "superkicked me in the face nearly taking my head off!"

The Batiri: Kodama 5' 07" 166lbs Obariyon 5' 08" 192lbs Bled Island

Record: 0 – 1
Shows wrestled on:
May 13, 2017 *Problematic* Westbrook Armory

Trained by Mike Quackenbush & Claudio Castagnoli the duo debuted in CHIKARA in 2010. The duo had good success in CHIKARA but branched out in 2012. They are two-time AIW Tag Team Champions and have held the STAR Pro tag Team Championships since March 16, 2019.

Bear Boulder
6' 5" 290lbs Bear Mountain

Record: 1 – 1
Shows wrestled on:
March 30, 2018 *Only Fools Are Satisfied* Westbrook Armory
August 11, 2018 *2018 Hollis Pirate Festival* Hollis Fire Department

Also known as Beefcake or Bear Beefcake with a history of matches dating back to September 2012. He wrestled across the Midwest and northeast US Indies. He formed the team Bear Country with Bear Bronson in 2017 winning the Chaotic Wrestling tag team championships in 2018 holding them for 224 days. In 2019 the duo made their Canadian debut Alpha-1 wrestling and later C*4 Wrestling. In 2020 they made their AEW debut on *Dark* signing with the promotion. In 2021, they made their debut on *Dynamite* and appeared on the *Revolution* PPV.

Bear Bronson
6' 2" 260lbs Bear Mountain

Record: 2 – 3
Shows wrestled on:
June 24, 2017 *La Kermesse Festival Night 2* St. Louis Field Biddeford
July 21, 2017 *Nothing Gold Can Stay* Westbrook Armory
March 30, 2018 *Only Fools Are Satisfied* Westbrook Armory
November 30, 2018 *No Control* Portland Club

Debuting in 2015, Bronson was trained by Pat Buck and Brian Myers at Create-A-Pro Wrestling Academy. He is a former CAP Champion and billed as Santa Claus a former WWE 24/7 Champion defeated Akira Tozawa on December 22, 2019 (airing on the 23rd) and losing it moments later to R-Truth. In 2017, he and Bear Beefcake formed the formidable tag team Bear

County. They have wrestled in the US Indies and made their Canadian debut in 2019. They have appeared on several episodes of AEW *Dark* including picking up a win on the January 12, 2021 episode. In 2021, they made their debut on *Dynamite* and appeared on the *Revolution* PPV.

Big Beef Gnarls Garvin
6' 0" 251lbs Shepherdyville, Kentucky

Record: 0 – 1
December 19, 2020 *2020 Vacationland Cup* AMVets Hall Yarmouth

Began training in 2015 with Apollo Garvin and Dave Christ, Garvin made his in-ring debut in January 2016. He has wrestled mostly in the Midwest region with Limitless being his debut in the Northeast region. He held the Zero1 USA Tag Team Championships with Jake Lander for 322 days.

Big Daddy Cruz
5' 9" 330lbs From the Top of Lust Mountain

Record: 0 – 1
Shows wrestled on:
March 19, 2016 *Don't Fear The Sleeper* American Legion Post 84 Orono

Began his training with Amazing Red in 2014, having his first match on June 14th of that year. His favorite moment in wrestling to date is making his debut on AEW Dark teaming with M'Badu in a loss to The Gunn Club: Austin & Billy Gunn

Bobby Orlando *"The Greatest of all Time"*
5' 10" 202lbs Mahopac, New York

Record: 0 – 2

Shows wrestled on:
March 09, 2019 *Welcome to the Dance* Westbrook Armory
June 23, 2019 *La Kermesse Festival Night 2* St. Louis Field Biddeford

A student of Brian Myers and Pat Buck's Create-A-Pro Academy he debuted in 2017. He is one third of The Shook Crew with Bryce Donovan & Max Caster. Orlando is a two-time CAP Tag Team Champion having separate reigns with both Donovan and Caster. The trio is well known for their Diss Tracks about upcoming opponents.

Bolt Brady *"The Human Dynamo" "The Super Charged Superstar"*
6' 0" 209lbs Round Rock, Texas

Record: 0 – 1
Shows wrestled on:
May 11, 2018 *Feed The Need* Portland Club

Trained by Luke Hawx, Mr. Mexico II, & Ray Campos he debuted in 2004 wrestling primarily in the middle states from Texas to Illinois.

Brad Hollister *"Big Bacon"*
5' 10" 222lbs Chicopee, Massachusetts

Record: 2 – 1
Shows wrestled on:
May 28, 2016 *No Dropkicks in the Living Room* American Legion Post 84 Orono
March 09, 2019 *Welcome to the Dance* Westbrook Armory
May 10, 2019 *Hooked on a Friedman* Westbrook Armory

A staple of the New England independent scene he was trained by Antonio Thomas and debuted in 2008. He became a mainstay first in NECW and then in NEW capturing both of their heavyweight championships. He also has held the Pioneer Valley Promotions Heavyweight and Tag Team Championships three times each.

Brandino Davis *"All Pro" "The Big Deal"*
6' 3" 250lbs Lynn, Massachusetts

Record: 5 – 0
Shows wrestled on:
August 11, 2018 *2018 Hollis Pirate Festival* Hollis Fire Department
September 08, 2018 *2018 Litchfield Fair*
June 23, 2019 *La Kermesse Festival Night 2* St. Louis Field Biddeford
The Road Season 1 *Episodes 8 & 11* American Legion Post 84, Orono

Davis debuted in late 2011 after training with Jason Rumble, Beau Douglas, and DC Dillinger. Prior to entering professional wrestling, he was a college standout even attending NFL combines. With Eric Johnson they make up the tag team The Stigma capturing the ¡Let's Wrestle! Tag Team Championships.

Brandon Kirk *"The Rogue"*
6' 1" 200lbs Sayreville, New Jersey

Record: 3 – 5
Shows wrestled on:
May 11, 2018 *Feed The Need* Portland Club
July 27, 2018 *Vacationland Cup* Westbrook Armory
September 21, 2018 *Pretenders Beware* Westbrook Armory
November 30, 2018 *No Control* Portland Club
January 11, 2019 *Snakebitten* Westbrook Armory
March 09, 2019 *Welcome to the Dance* Westbrook Armory
May 10, 2019 *Hooked on a Friedman* Westbrook Armory
September 06, 2019 *Know Your Enemy* Portland Expo

Kirk made his wrestling debut in 2012 training with Corey Havoc. The first few years of his career is wrestled primarily in the New Jersey indie scene debuting with GCW and CZW in 2015. Today he is primarily known as a deathmatch wrestler even though he didn't have his first deathmatch until 2016 when he wrestled Jimmy Lloyd in a No Ropes Barbed Wire match on GCW *Deck the Halls With Ultraviolence*. Kirk and Lloyd have been feuding for four years and it appears to be a dance that will go on forever.

In an interview Kirk said wrestling in a deathmatch is something that he wanted to check off his bucket list, but after that first match, he grew a passion for it. He's defeated Matt Tremont in a CZW Tangled Web match, competed in the 2018 Tournament of Death, defeated Homicide in a street fight, and tore the house down with Masashi Takeda in a death match in January 2020. He is one of the most technically sound deathmatch wrestlers on the scene today.

In Limitless Wrestling he teamed with Alexander Lee against the MSP at *Know Your Enemy* getting severely busted open. Lee blames Kirk for their loss and was very vocal about it. Kirk returned on January 24, 2020 *Flirtin' With Disaster* jamming skewers into Lee's head and chasing away Joey Eastman. They were scheduled for a Hardcore Match at the cancelled *Cause for the Alarm,* a match that will no doubt be rescheduled. He is married to wrestler Kasey Catal.

Brandon Thurston *"The Patron Saint of Professional Wrestling"*
5' 7" 178lbs Buffalo, New York

Record: 1 – 0
Shows wrestled on:
November 30, 2018 **No Control** Portland Club

Thurston debuted in 2004 wrestling primarily in the upstate New York and Pennsylvania area becoming a three-time Empire State Wrestling and one-time Pro Wrestling Rampage heavyweight champion. Since 2019 he has become a regular with Beyond Wrestling.

Brandon Watts *"Shred God"*
5" 8" 174lbs New York City

Record: 1 – 0
Shows wrestled on:
April 28, 2017 **Can We Kick It?** Portland Club

One half of the tag team Milk Chocolate with Randy Summers, Watts debuted in 2013. The duo are three-time NYWC tag team champions and one time Five Borough Wrestling tag champs. He wrestles primarily in the northeast region of the United States.

Brett Domino *"The Domino Effect"*
Worcester, Massachusetts

Record: 1 – 7
Shows wrestled on:

January 19, 2018 *The World Is Ours* Westbrook Armory
March 30, 2018 *Only Fools Are Satisfied* Westbrook Armory
August 11, 2018 *2018 Hollis Pirate Festival* Hollis Fire Department
September 08, 2018 *2018 Litchfield Fair*
November 30, 2018 *No Control* Portland Club
January 11, 2019 *Snakebitten* Westbrook Armory
March 09, 2019 *Welcome to the Dance* Westbrook Armory
May 10, 2019 *Hooked on a Friedman* Westbrook Armory

Domino trained at the New England Pro Wrestling Academy and made his first appearance in Limitless Wrestling at *Hybrid Moments*, November 3, 2017 at the Portland Club with DL Hurst as part of Anthony Greene's entourage. AG would replace Domino and Hurst with the Platinum Hunnies. At *No Control* he would break out on his own coming up short in a scramble match. At *Welcome to the Dance* he would last a two on one match against the Platinum Hunnies. In his final Limitless Match to date he reunited with DL Hurst getting the upset victory over The Thick Boys. Hurst was fast becoming a fan favorite with his catchphrase "I'm Brett Domino motherfucker!"

Brett Ryan Gosselin
5' 5" 175lbs West Greenwich, Rhode Island

Record: 0 – 2
Shows wrestled on:
June 23, 2017 *La Kermesse Festival Night 1* St. Louis Field Biddeford
December 19, 2020 *2020 Vacationland Cup* AMVets Hall Yarmouth

Trained with Matt Taven and Mike Bennett he debuted in 2015 as Todd Harris. A regular with Northeast Championship Wrestling three times for a combined 322 days. Competed in ¡Let's Wrestle! getting a pinfall victory over Davienne. Recently made his return to Limitless Wrestling after a three-year absence on *The Road* Season 2. With partner Channing Thomas they lost to the Beverage Brothers at the *2020 Vacationland Cup*.

Brian Cage *"The Machine"*
6' 0" 278lbs From The 559

Record: 2 – 2
Shows wrestled on:
October 29, 2016 **Who Watches the Watchmen?** The Field House at University of Maine Orono
May 13, 2017 **Problematic** Westbrook Armory
March 30, 2018 **Only Fools Are Satisfied** Westbrook Armory
September 21, 2018 **Pretenders Beware** Westbrook Armory

A protégé of Chris Kanyon, Brian Cage began his wrestling journey in 2004. In 2008 he signed with WWE going to Florida Championship Wrestling where he won the tag team championships with Justin Gabriel. He spent a year with the promotion and was released in September 2009. In the years since he has toured the world wrestling for Indies like PWG but also TNA and later Impact Wrestling, Lucha Underground, Lucha Libre AAA, and is currently signed to All Elite Wrestling. He is a former Impact World and X-Division Champion, Lucha Underground Gift of the Gods Champion and held numerous other championships. In AEW he is managed by Taz and the current FTW World Champion.

Brian Fury *"Firebrand"*
5' 11" 209lbs Rochester, New Hampshire

Record: 3 – 3
Shows wrestled on:
September 12, 2015 **Stage One** City Side Restaurant, Brewer
January 30, 2016 **Under Fire** American Legion Post 84 Orono

July 23, 2016 ***Hook, Line, & Sinker*** American Legion Post 84 Orono
October 07, 2016 ***Risk It For The Biscuit*** Westbrook Armory
October 29, 2016 ***Who Watches the Watchmen?*** The Field House at University of Maine Orono
November 19, 2016 ***Hogwash*** American Legion Post 84 Orono

Trained by Steve Bradley, Fury debuted in the year 2000. He has wrestled primarily in the New England area becoming a mainstay in Chaotic Wrestling where he took over the training center, later renaming it the New England Pro Wrestling Academy. The biggest exposure in his career was competing in the 2016 Ring of Honor Top Prospect Tournament coming up short against Lio Rush in the finals. Fury retired in 2016, came back for a match in 2018 and again in 2019 and was slated to make his Limitless return in March 2020 before the pandemic caused the cancellation of the show.

Brian Milonas *"The Kingpin"*
6' 4" 339lbs Manchester, New Hampshire

Record: 1 – 2
Shows wrestled on:
September 24, 2016 ***Past Your Bedtime*** American Legion Post 84 Orono
January 27, 2017 ***Unreal*** Westbrook Armory
May 13, 2017 ***Problematic*** Westbrook Armory

Trained at Killer Kowalski's wrestling school, Milonas debuted in 2001, best known in the New England area for his long tenure with Chaotic Wrestling where is a three-time heavyweight champion holding the crown for a combined 896 days. On May 25, 2007, Chaotic Wrestling held a benefit show where Milonas wrestled "Big" Rick Fuller with Johnny Fabulous in his corner and John Cena as special guest referee. Vince McMahon made a surprise appearance laying out Cena and raising Milonas' hand. In 2017,

Milonas won the Ring of Honor Top Prospect Tournament. He is currently signed to the promotion teaming with the Beer City Bruiser as the tag team The Bouncers.

Brian Myers *"Prince of Queens"*
6' 1" 216lbs Queens, New York

Record: 0 – 1
Shows wrestled on:
March 19, 2016 ***Don't Fear The Sleeper*** American Legion Post 84 Orono

Trained by Mikey Whipwreck, Myers debuted in 2004 quickly forming a tag team with Matt Cardona capturing the NYWC tag team championships in 2005. The duo would team on and off until today. Their names would change along the way, but they won tag team championships in Deep South Wrestling, Ohio Valley Wrestling, Florida Championship Wrestling, and the WWE. In March 2014, Myers and Pat Buck opened Create A Pro Wrestling Academy and are responsible for training a tremendous group of current wrestlers including Kris Statlander. Myers is currently on his second run in Impact Wrestling.

Brian Pillman Jr. *"The Price That Was Promised"*
6' 1" 205lbs Cincinnati, Ohio

Record: 0 – 1
Shows wrestled on:
January 24, 2020 ***Flirtin' With Disaster*** AMVets Hall Yarmouth

Trained by Lance Storm, this second-generation wrestling has huge shoes to step into and seems to be accomplishing it with ease. Debuting in December 2017 in less than three years he has traveled around the US Indies signing with MLW in late 2018 forming the New Era Hart Foundation with Teddy Hart and Davey Boy Smith Jr capturing the MLW Tag Team Championships. He is a former Warrior Wrestling champion holding the title for 224 days. He is currently signed with AEW where he and Griff Garrison team as the Varsity Blondes.

Brick Maston / Big Daddy Beluga
5' 11" 242lbs Boulder, Colorado

Record: 6 – 1
Shows wrestled on:
September 12, 2015 **Stage One** City Side Restaurant, Brewer
November 15, 2015 **Killin' & Thrillin** American Legion Post 84 Orono
January 30, 2016 **Under Fire** American Legion Post 84 Orono
July 23, 2016 **Hook, Line, & Sinker** American Legion Post 84 Orono
September 24, 2016 **Past Your Bedtime** American Legion Post 84 Orono
November 19, 2016 **Hogwash** American Legion Post 84 Orono
January 27, 2017 **Unreal** Westbrook Armory

Trained at the New England Pro Wrestling Academy he debuted in 2015 as a rough and tumble powerhouse. He had an excellent run in Limitless winning his first six matches before suffering a loss as part of a scramble match. He appears to have left wrestling having his last match in February 2018.

Brody King
6' 5" 285lbs Van Nuys, California

Record: 1 – 3
Shows wrestled on:
March 30, 2018 **Only Fools Are Satisfied** Westbrook Armory
May 11, 2018 **Feed The Need** Portland Club
September 21, 2018 **Pretenders Beware** Westbrook Armory
November 30, 2018 **No Control** Portland Club

King trained at the Santino Bros Wrestling Academy and debuted in July 2015. Traveled the US Indies scene including PWG and a year with MWL. Signed with Ring of Honor in December 2018 joining Villain Enterprises with Marty Scrull and PCO, the trio would win the ROH Six-Man Tag Team Championships, at the same time Scrull & King would hold the Australia based World Series Wrestling Tag Team Championships while King and PCO would win the 2019 Crockett Cup and the NWA World Tag Team Championship holding all three titles simultaneously. PCO & King are also former ROH World Tag Team Champions. King has also wrestled for New Japan Pro Wrestling most recently appearing on the NJPW Strong series.

Bryce Donovan
6' 4" 220lbs Long Beach, New York

Record: 0 – 2
Shows wrestled on:
March 09, 2019 *Welcome to the Dance* Westbrook Armory
June 23, 2019 *La Kermesse Festival Night 2* St. Louis Field Biddeford

Trained at Create A Pro Wrestling Academy he debuted in 2016. A member of the Shook Crew with Bobby Orlando and Max Caster. A former CAP Tag Team Champion with Orlando, the trio is well known for their Diss Tracks about upcoming opponents.

Buxx Belmar *"Dirty"*
5' 11" 194lbs Montreal, Quebec, Canada

Record: 3 – 0
Shows wrestled on:
May 13, 2017 *Problematic* Westbrook Armory
June 23, 2017 *La Kermesse Festival Night 1* St. Louis Field Biddeford
July 21, 2017 *Nothing Gold Can Stay* Westbrook Armory

Trained by Jacque Rougeau Buxx debuted in 2004. He's wrestled his entire career in Canada with a few shots in the States in the New England region. At times he has formed a trio with Le Tabarnak de Team. He is a former two-time C*4 Champion, held the International Wrestling Syndicate World Heavyweight Championship for over a year, and several other championships in Canada. His biggest win in Limitless was an outstanding match teaming with TDT defeating the Maine State Posse.

Cajun Crawdad *"The Brawler from the Bayou"*
6' 2" 196lbs The Bayou

Record: 0 – 1
Shows wrestled on:
May 11, 2018 *Feed The Need* Portland Club

A product of The Wrestle Factory Crawdad debuted in 2015 and is a member of Creatures Of The Deep with Hermit Crab, Merlok, & Oceanea.

Caleb Konley *"The Midnight Son" "The Obsession"*
6' 0" 207lbs Cartersville, Georgia

Record: 0 – 1
Shows wrestled on:
October 25, 2019 ***Fresh Blood*** AMVets Hall Yarmouth

Trained by George South he made his debut in 2005 and in the last fifteen years has held over seventeen championships including the FIP World Championship for 329 days. He has wrestled across the US Indies, Canada, United Kingdom and even in China with the WWN tour. Since 2016, he has wrestled on and off in Impact Wrestling as himself and under the guise of Suicide, a character he has also played on many shows outside of Impact. Since 2015 he has been the leader of the faction Revolt!.

Cam Zagami
5' 8" 187lbs Salem, New Hampshire

Record: 3 – 4
Shows wrestled on:
October 29, 2016 ***Who Watches the Watchmen?*** The Field House at University of Maine Orono
November 19, 2016 ***Hogwash*** American Legion Post 84 Orono
January 27, 2017 ***Unreal*** Westbrook Armory
May 13, 2017 ***Problematic*** Westbrook Armory
July 21, 2017 ***Nothing Gold Can Stay*** Westbrook Armory
September 22, 2017 ***Question The Answers*** Westbrook Armory
November 03, 2017 ***Hybrid Moments*** Portland Club

Zagami debuted in 2012 after training with Brian Fury. He's wrestled mostly in the New England area primarily as a heel. On March 31, 2018, he defeated Omari in the finals of the CHIKARA Young Lions Cup XIV to win the title. In Limitless he had a memorable feud with Tyler Nitro and in the end defeated Nitro in a loser leaves town match. However, his final Limitless match to date did not go as well as "Dirty Daddy" Chris Dickinson destroyed Zagami in 30 seconds after answering Zagami's open challenge.

Champ diving onto his opponents July 12, 2012

Champ Mathews
5' 10" 177lbs Unity, Maine by way of The Island of Misfit Toys

Record: 0 – 3 – 1
Shows wrestled on:
October 29, 2016 ***Who Watches the Watchmen?*** The Field House at University of Maine Orono
The Road Season 1 *Episodes 2 & 8* American Legion Post 84, Orono

Began his training at the Bangor, Maine based Rampage Pro Wrestling with Legion Cage and Hardware making his in-ring debut in early 2001. Later received additional training from Scott Hall, "Lobsterman" Jeff Costa, Dr. Heresy, and "Confederate Currency" Chris Hamrick. In 2005, he scored two victories over Kenny Omega in a tag team match and triple threat match in NWA: New England in Sanford, Maine and with New Wrestling

Horizons in Gray, Maine. On February 21, 2007, he challenged Steve Corino for the AWA World Championship in Fairfield, Maine for AWA North Atlantic. Has held several championships in Maine including being a former IWE Heavyweight Champion, NWA Maine State Champion, and RPW: Cruiserweight Champion. He has promoted several successful events over the years as well under the banner of Live Pro Wrestling. In 2020, he reunited with Conner Murphy to re-form the tag team The Competition. The duo first teamed up in 2002 under the team name 69 Degrees and are former NWH Tag Team Champions.

Channing Thomas *"The Brofessional"*
6' 0" 229lbs Saugus, Massachusetts

Record: 0 – 3
Shows wrestled on:
June 22, 2019 *La Kermesse Festival Night 1* St. Louis Field Biddeford
July 12, 2019 *2019 Vacationland Cup* Portland Club
December 19, 2020 *2020 Vacationland Cup* AMVets Hall Yarmouth

Thomas began his training in 2017 with the Lockup Academy with Ryan Waters and later trained at the Kingdom School with Matt Taven and Vinny Marseglia.

Chris Dickinson *"Dirty Daddy"*
5' 10" 235lbs New York City

Record: 8 – 6
Shows wrestled on:
March 19, 2016 *Don't Fear The Sleeper* American Legion Post 84 Orono
March 17, 2017 *Hysteria* Westbrook Armory
April 28, 2017 *Can We Kick It?* Portland Club
November 03, 2017 *Hybrid Moments* Portland Club

January 19, 2018 *The World Is Ours* Westbrook Armory
March 30, 2018 *Only Fools Are Satisfied* Westbrook Armory
July 27, 2018 *Vacationland Cup* Westbrook Armory
September 21, 2018 *Pretenders Beware* Westbrook Armory
November 30, 2018 *No Control* Portland Club
January 11, 2019 *Snakebitten* Westbrook Armory
March 09, 2019 *Welcome to the Dance* Westbrook Armory
May 10, 2019 *Hooked on a Friedman* Westbrook Armory
September 06, 2019 *Know Your Enemy* Portland Expo
February 22, 2020 *Practice What You Preach* AMVets Hall Yarmouth

The leader of Team Pazuzu Dickinson has a background in Taekwondo and backyard wrestling as Paco Loco, before making his pro debut in 2008 for Jersey All Pro Wrestling. Dickinson's in-ring style I would consider to be the Japanese Strong Style. His feud with Kimber Lee in Beyond in 2015 went viral and elevated both of them on the US Indies. Dickinson and Jaka are two-time former Evolve Tag Team Champions with the second reign lasting 400 days. As champions they defended their titles against Oney Lorcan and Danny Burch during WrestleMania 34 Access. Dickinson held the Interspecies Wrestling Undisputed King of Crazy Championship for 1,624 days, from April 19, 2014 – September 29, 2018. In 2019, he made his debut for AAA in both their Invades New York show and later in Mexico. In 2020 he made his debut in Japan when GCW ran shows in the country. Dickinson is one of the biggest US stars on the Indie scene with a large fan following even when he's not being a fan favorite. Dickinson is one of the few wrestlers on the Indie scene that gets a Road Warrior pop every time he makes his entrance. He has signed with New Japan Pro Wrestling appearing on their US television show Strong Style.

Chris Hero *"The Knockout Artist"*

Record: 0 – 1
Shows wrestled on:
January 30, 2016 **Under Fire** American Legion Post 84 Orono

Hero debuted September 12, 1998 and in the last 22 years has established a reputation as being one of the greatest wrestlers of all time. Hero has trained under some of the all-time greats, Les Thatcher, Dory Funk Jr., William Regal, Dave Taylor, Fit Finlay, Johnny Saint, & The NOAH Dojo to name a few. He and Claudio Castagnoli had an amazing tag team as the Kings of Wrestling. Signed to WWE developmental twice, TNA, CZW, PWG, Ring of Honor, Pro Wrestling NOAH, Progress and too many other numerous promotions around the world. Hero may have had only one match in Limitless Wrestling, but it's one of the greatest matches that I have ever seen live. At *Under Fire* he wrestled Zack Sabre Jr in a 25-minute bout that blew us all away.

Christian Casanova *"Top Talent" "Thrillanova"*
5' 10" 176lbs Boston, Massachusetts

Record: 14 – 10
Shows wrestled on:
September 12, 2015 ***Stage One*** City Side Restaurant, Brewer
November 15, 2015 ***Killin' & Thrillin*** American Legion Post 84 Orono
January 30, 2016 ***Under Fire*** American Legion Post 84 Orono
July 23, 2016 ***Hook, Line, & Sinker*** American Legion Post 84 Orono
September 24, 2016 ***Past Your Bedtime*** American Legion Post 84 Orono
November 03, 2017 ***Hybrid Moments*** Portland Club
January 19, 2018 ***The World Is Ours*** Westbrook Armory
March 30, 2018 ***Only Fools Are Satisfied*** Westbrook Armory
May 11, 2018 ***Feed The Need*** Portland Club
July 27, 2018 ***Vacationland Cup*** Westbrook Armory
September 21, 2018 ***Pretenders Beware*** Westbrook Armory
November 30, 2018 ***No Control*** Portland Club
January 11, 2019 ***Snakebitten*** Westbrook Armory
March 09, 2019 ***Welcome to the Dance*** Westbrook Armory
May 10, 2019 ***Hooked on a Friedman*** Westbrook Armory
July 12, 2019 ***2019 Vacationland Cup*** Portland Club
September 06, 2019 ***Know Your Enemy*** Portland Expo
October 25, 2019 ***Fresh Blood*** AMVets Hall Yarmouth
November 29, 2019 ***Twilight Zone*** AMVets Hall Yarmouth
January 24, 2020 ***Flirtin' With Disaster*** AMVets Hall Yarmouth
February 22, 2020 ***Practice What You Preach*** AMVets Hall Yarmouth
December 19, 2020 ***2020 Vacationland Cup*** AMVets Hall Yarmouth

Casanova trained at the New England Pro Wrestling Academy and had his first match in 2014 against Mikey Webb, Maine fans may remember him as he worked several dates for IWE. He wrestled primarily in the New England area. 2020 looked to be a breakout year for Top Talent until the pandemic shut down Indie wrestling, however it will not stop Casanova from reaching the levels the Limitless fans know he will reach. He also has the distinction of being one of the four wrestlers that wrestled on *Stage One* that is still active with the promotion during the ranking period of this book.

He states his favorite moment in wrestling to date was being in the Main Event at *Flirtin' With Disaster*. Casanova returned to Limitless Wrestling at the *2020 Vacationland Cup* where he captured the Limitless Wrestling World Championship defeating Daniel Garcia, Alex Price, and JD Drake in the finals. Moments after winning the championship he was offered to sign with the WWE. He competed in his final indie wrestling match on March 19, 2021 at *Double Vision* losing the Limitless Wrestling World Championship to "Red Death" Daniel Garcia.

Chuck O'Neil *"Cold Steel"*
6' 2" 185lbs Falmouth, Massachusetts

Record: 0 – 2
Shows wrestled on:
September 12, 2015 **Stage One** City Side Restaurant, Brewer
November 15, 2015 **Killin' & Thrillin** American Legion Post 84 Orono

In 2006, O'Neil made his MMA debut and would eventually find himself on UFC's The Ultimate Fighter Team Lesnar vs. Team Dos Santos on Team Lesnar. He retired from MMA 2016 as the Cage Titans Fighting Championship Welterweight Champion. He joined the world of Professional Wrestling in 2015 training with Ryan Drew at Lock Up Pro Wrestling Academy with his first match in march 2015 against fellow UFC veteran Eric Spicely.

CJ Cruz *"The Little Brick Shithouse"*
5' 6" 200lbs Lowell, Massachusetts

Record: 6 – 5
Shows wrestled on:
June 22, 2019 **La Kermesse Festival Night 1** St. Louis Field Biddeford
June 23, 2019 **La Kermesse Festival Night 2** St. Louis Field Biddeford
October 25, 2019 **Fresh Blood** AMVets Hall Yarmouth
November 29, 2019 **Twilight Zone** AMVets Hall Yarmouth
January 24, 2020 **Flirtin' With Disaster** AMVets Hall Yarmouth
February 22, 2020 **Practice What You Preach** AMVets Hall Yarmouth
The Road Season 1 *Episodes 2 & 10* American Legion Post 84, Orono
December 19, 2020 **2020 Vacationland Cup** AMVets Hall Yarmouth

Began training in 2017 with the New England Pro Wrestling Academy with his first match in 2018. Started out in ¡Let's Wrestle! feuding with "The Prize" Alec Price, having an outstanding Last Man Standing match with each other. Cruz' favorite moment in wrestling is the match with Price at Fresh Blood that led to their full-time roster spot. Cruz has an impressive missile dropkick dubbed The BDE: Best Dropkick Ever.

Cody Rhodes *"American Nightmare"*
6' 2" 220lbs Atlanta, Georgia

Record: 0 – 1
Shows wrestled on:
January 27, 2017 ***Unreal*** Westbrook Armory

Second generation star that debuted in May 2006 for the WWE developmental territory Ohio Valley Wrestling and made his WWE debut July 2007 on Monday Night Raw. In May 2016 he requested and was granted his release from WWE. In the ten years he was with the promotion he became a six-time Tag Team Champion and two-time Intercontinental Champion. He spent the next two and a half years wrestling all over the world in various promotions winning the IWGP United States Championship, ROH World Heavyweight Championship, & the NWA World Heavyweight Championship. In January 2019 he, along with Tony Kahn, Kenny Omega, and The Young Bucks announced the formation of All Elite Wrestling changing the landscape of professional wrestling in the United States since its launch.

Colt Cabana *"Boom Boom"*
6' 1" 242lbs Maxwell St in Chicago, Illinois

Record: 1 – 1
Shows wrestled on:
May 13, 2017 ***Problematic*** Westbrook Armory
September 21, 2018 ***Pretenders Beware*** Westbrook Armory

Training at Steel Dominion Colt debuted in June 1999 and in the last 21 years has traveled the world defining what it means to be a DIY wrestler launching an extremely successful podcast, merchandise line, and following. He has won championships around the world including being a two-time Ring of Honor World Tag Team Champion and a two-time NWA World Heavyweight Champion. He is currently signed to All Elite Wrestling.

Conner Murphy *"Celtic"*
5' 8" 185lbs Newport News, Virginia

Record: 1 – 4
Shows wrestled on:
September 24, 2016 ***Past Your Bedtime*** American Legion Post 84 Orono
January 27, 2017 ***Unreal*** Westbrook Armory
March 17, 2017 ***Hysteria*** Westbrook Armory
The Road Season 1 *Episodes 2 & 8* American Legion Post 84, Orono

The former "Hot Stuff" Paul Hudson started out in wrestling as a referee for Eastern Wrestling Alliance before debuting on April 6, 2002 as an in-ring competitor. He's held numerous championships including being a former New Wrestling Horizons tag team champion with The Honky Tonk Man. He also is a former PWF

Northeast Junior Heavyweight Champion, NWA Maine State and Cruiserweight Champion, NWA New England Cruiserweight Champion, and NCW New England Champion. Through-out his career he had feuded and teamed with Champ Mathews in several outstanding matches. The first teamed in 2002 as 69 Degrees, and currently are running roughshod around Maine as The Competition. In 2005 he and Mathews teamed up in NWA New England in Sanford, Maine defeating Kenny Omega and Danny Duggan. Outside the ring Murphy is a passionate fan of the now named Washington Football Team.

Covey Christ
5' 11" 181lbs Cape Breton Island, Nova Scotia, Canada

Record: 0 – 1
Shows wrestled on:
July 12, 2019 *2019 Vacationland Cup* Portland Club

Trained by Scott D'Amore, Christ debuted in 2016 and has been a mainstay in the Canadian Maritimes. He has been the Ultimate Championship Wrestling Junior Heavyweight Champion since October 28, 2017. He is also a former UCW Maritime Heavyweight Champion. In August 2019, he toured the United Kingdom with All Star Wrestling. On November 7, 2020 he captured the Nova Scotia based Kaizen Pro Wrestling Championship.

Craig Mitchell
5' 7" 220lbs Berwyn, Illinois

Record: 0 – 2
Shows wrestled on:
March 17, 2017 *Hysteria* Westbrook Armory
March 30, 2018 *Only Fools Are Satisfied* Westbrook Armory

Trained by Benjamin Bryce and Steve Boz, Mitchell debuted in 2009 and has wrestled primarily in the Illinois area. He is a former Southland Championship Wrestling Heavyweight Champion and former Freelance Wrestling Tag Team Champion with Kenny Sutra.

Cornelius Crummels
5' 7" 172lbs Chagrin Falls, Ohio

Record: 0 – 1
Shows wrestled on:
June 24, 2017 *La Kermesse Festival Night 2* St. Louis Field Biddeford

Trained at the Wrestle Factory, Crummels debuted in 2016. He and Sonny Defarge have formed a successful tag team winning the Premier Championship Wrestling tag team championships twice and the CHIKARA Campeonatos de Parejas.

Da Hoodz: Davey Cash *"Hi Lite"*
6' 1" 189lbs New Bedford, Massachusetts

Record: 1 – 2
Shows wrestled on:
November 15, 2015 *Killin' & Thrillin* American Legion Post 84 Orono
March 19, 2016 *Don't Fear The Sleeper* American Legion Post 84 Orono
November 19, 2016 *Hogwash* American Legion Post 84 Orono

Da Hoodz: Kris Pyro *"The Heat"*
5' 6" 161lbs New Bedford, Massachusetts

Record: 1 – 3
Shows wrestled on:

November 15, 2015 ***Killin' & Thrillin*** American Legion Post 84 Orono
January 30, 2016 ***Under Fire*** American Legion Post 84 Orono
March 19, 2016 ***Don't Fear The Sleeper*** American Legion Post 84 Orono
November 19, 2016 ***Hogwash*** American Legion Post 84 Orono

Davey Cash began wrestling in 1996 as Black Dragon, Pyro debuted in 2004, they started teaming as Da Hoodz in 2009. Together they have been one of New England's top tag teams winning tag team championships in NWA-On Fire, NECW, and PWF Northeast. Holding both the NECW & PWF titles for over a year. In 2014, Da Hoodz had an outstanding match with The Young Bucks and in 2015 with Death By Elbow: Chris Hero & JT Dunn. Both matches took place with Beyond Wrestling.

Dan Barry *"Everyone's Favorite Wrestler"*
5' 11" 210lbs The Isle of Manhattan

Record: 0 – 1
Shows wrestled on:
April 28, 2017 ***Can We Kick It?*** Portland Club

Trained by Mikey Whipwreck, Barry debuted in 2001. In his career Barry has formed two tag teams called Team Tremendous, the first with Ken Scampi from 2005 – 2013 and then Bill Carr from 2013 – present. With Carr, Barry has had his most successful run as a tag team winning championships in PWR, ISW, CZW, and NYWC. Barry was seen on the WWE Network show Holey Foley! as the trainer of Noelle Foley.

Dan Maff *"The Bayonne Bad Ass" "The Boricua Beast"*
5' 7" 305lbs Bayonne, New Jersey

Record: 1 – 1
Shows wrestled on:

September 06, 2019 ***Know Your Enemy*** Portland Expo
October 25, 2019 ***Fresh Blood*** AMVets Hall Yarmouth

Maff was trained by Homicide and debuted in 1999 with Monster Mack as Da Hit Squad. The duo won numerous tag team championships in the northeast. Maff took a 3.5-year hiatus from wrestling between 2005 & 2008. In 2019, he resigned with Ring of Honor. In his two matches with Limitless Wrestling Maff commanded the crowd leaving them wanting more.

Dan Terry *"The Fittest Man in Wrestling"*
5' 8" 216lbs Boston, Massachusetts
Record: 0 – 1
Shows wrestled on:
September 08, 2018 ***2018 Litchfield Fair***

Trained at the Bell Time Club, he debuted in 2013 with NCW: Northeast Championship Wrestling and has made this his home promotion. With Verne Vicallo he is a former NCW Tag Team Champion holding the titles for 462 days.

Danjerhawk
5' 4" 139lbs

Record: 1 – 0
Shows wrestled on:
May 11, 2018 ***Feed The Need*** Portland Club

A product of the Wrestle Factory he debuted in 2018 and now goes by Mach-10.

Danhausen
5' 9" 185lbs Montreal, Quebec, Canada

Record: 0 – 3
Shows wrestled on:

March 09, 2019 *Welcome to the Dance* Westbrook Armory
October 25, 2019 *Fresh Blood* AMVets Hall Yarmouth
January 24, 2020 *Flirtin' With Disaster* AMVets Hall Yarmouth

Trained by Jimmy Jacobs and Truth Martini, Danhausen debuted in 2013 as "Kid Gorgeous" Donovan Danhausen. In 2016 he won the FIP Florida Heritage Champion. In 2019, Donovan began to make the changes evolving to the Danhausen we know today. Since these changes his career has launched him into another level that appears to have no ceiling.

Daniel Garcia *"Red Death"*
5' 11" 187lbs Buffalo, New York

Record: 6 – 4
Shows wrestled on:
August 11, 2018 *2018 Hollis Pirate Festival* Hollis Fire Department
September 21, 2018 *Pretenders Beware* Westbrook Armory

November 30, 2018 *No Control* Portland Club
July 12, 2019 *2019 Vacationland Cup* Portland Club
October 25, 2019 *Fresh Blood* AMVets Hall Yarmouth
January 24, 2020 *Flirtin' With Disaster* AMVets Hall Yarmouth
February 22, 2020 *Practice What You Preach* AMVets Hall Yarmouth
December 19, 2020 *2020 Vacationland Cup* AMVets Hall Yarmouth

Garcia began his training in 2017 with Pepper Parks, now known as The Blade, having his in-ring debut also in 2017. He has wrestled in the Northeastern United States and in Canada for SMASH and C*4 Wrestling where he is the reigning C*4 Champion having captured the title on November 29, 2019 from "Walking Weapon" Josh Alexander. This title victory is Garcia's favorite moment in wrestling so far in his young career. He has held the Empire State Wrestling championship since June 29, 2019. On January 6, 2019, he was involved in a vehicle crash along with Kevin Bennett, Kevin Blackwood and Puf that took Garcia out of action for six months with two broken legs. In September 2020 he appeared in two episodes of AEW Dark. On January 27, 2021 he wrestled Tyler Rust on an episode of NXT under the name Dante Rios. On March 19, 2021 at *Double Vision* he defeated Christian Casanova to win the Limitless Wrestling World Championship.

Danny Miles *"Dynamite" "The Distance"*
5' 7" 196lbs Palmer, Massachusetts

Record: 2 – 2
Shows wrestled on:
May 28, 2016 *No Dropkicks in the Living Room* American Legion Post 84 Orono
October 07, 2016 *Risk It For The Biscuit* Westbrook Armory
October 29, 2016 *Who Watches the Watchmen?* The Field House at University of Maine Orono

February 25, 2017 ***Do What You Love, Fuck The Rest-Fest***
American Legion Post 84 Orono

Trained by Tony Roy, Rush, Kevin Landry, & Antonio Thomas, Miles made his wrestling debut in 2006. Wrestling primarily in New England, Miles became a regular with Big Time Wrestling traveling with them as they ran shows across the country. In February 2015 with BTW he wrestled against the Rock n' Roll Express in West Virginia and Tennessee.

Darby Allin
5' 8" 180lbs Seattle, Washington

Record: 2 – 4
Shows wrestled on:
November 03, 2017 ***Hybrid Moments*** Portland Club
January 19, 2018 ***The World Is Ours*** Westbrook Armory
March 30, 2018 ***Only Fools Are Satisfied*** Westbrook Armory
May 11, 2018 ***Feed The Need*** Portland Club
November 30, 2018 ***No Control*** Portland Club
March 09, 2019 ***Welcome to the Dance*** Westbrook Armory

Allin was trained by John Carlos making his in-ring debut in 2015. In 2016, Allin signed with WWN appearing at Evolve 59 starting a feud with Ethan Page. In Evolve, Darby's popularity rose with his never say die style of wrestling. 2018 saw him travel to Mexico for AAA and Progress Wrestling's US tour. In 2019, he traveled to the United Kingdom to compete in the Super Strong Style 16 tournament. He signed with All Elite Wrestling in 2019 and has become one of the most popular wrestlers in the promotion. On November 7, 2020 he defeated Cody Rhodes to win the AEW TNA Championship. In Limitless Wrestling he wowed the fans in his matches with Ace Romero, Jeff Cobb, Zachary Wentz, Teddy Hart, and MJF.

Darius Carter *"The Debonair Millionaire" "Wrestling's Richest Prize"*
6' 1" 187lbs Palm Beach, Florida

Record: 1 – 0
Shows wrestled on:
July 23, 2016 ***Hook, Line, & Sinker*** American Legion Post 84 Orono

Carter debuted in 2009 and wrestled in the New York & New Jersey area. He was a regular in Beyond Wrestling early in his career and has been with Warriors of Wrestling since the beginning winning both the Heavyweight and No Limits Championship. Carter defeated Johnny Torres in his only Limitless match to date.

Dave Dyer *"Belfast Bulldog"*
5' 10" 227lbs Belfast, Maine

Record: 1 - 1
Shows wrestled on:
The Road Season 1 *Episodes 6 & 9* American Legion Post 84, Orono

Began training at the Limitless Dojo in December 2018, only intended to stay for one class but never stopped going. Dyer chronicled his training in a series of articles in the Kennebec Journal, the local newspaper. His first match was in June 2019 at Speedway 95 in Hermon, Maine for NAWA: North Atlantic Wrestling Association. His favorite moment in wrestling to date was on February 26, 2021 where he main evented the first Limitless Dojo Showcase show against his teacher and mentor DangerKid.

Davey Boy Smith Jr. *"Bulldog"*
6' 5" 264lbs Calgary, Alberta, Canada

Record: 2 – 0
Shows wrestled on:
May 10, 2019 ***Hooked on a Friedman*** Westbrook Armory
September 06, 2019 ***Know Your Enemy*** Portland Expo

This third-generation star from the famous Hart family began training to be a wrestling at the age of 8. He had his first real match 1999 at the age of 14 for Stampede Wrestling. He made his first tour of New Japan in 2005, signed with the WWE in 2006 competing on house shows before being sent to OVW and then Deep South Wrestling and later FCW. He made his main roster debut in 2009 teaming with Tyson Kidd and Natayla as the Hart Dynasty capturing the tag team championships twice. After leaving the WWE in 2011 Smith has traveled the US Indies, wrestled around with world with stints in New Japan, NOAH, MLW, & All Japan Pro Wrestling.
Smith's two appearances with Limitless were part of The New Hart Foundation teaming with Teddy Hart to defeat the Maine State Posse and Work Horsemen.

Davis Starr *"The Product"*
5' 11" 211lbs Bishop's Stortford, England

Record: 1 – 3
Shows wrestled on:
January 27, 2017 ***Unreal*** Westbrook Armory
April 28, 2017 ***Can We Kick It?*** Portland Club
January 19, 2018 ***The World Is Ours*** Westbrook Armory
July 27, 2018 ***Vacationland Cup*** Westbrook Armory

A former collegiate wrestler, he made his professional wrestling debut in February 2012 after training with the Wild Samoans. He toured the US Indies becoming a bigger name in the United

Kingdom wrestling scene, also wrestling in other European countries.

Davienne *"Not America's Sweetheart"*
5' 0" Rutland, Massachusetts

Record: 7 – 4
Shows wrestled on:
September 24, 2016 ***Past Your Bedtime*** American Legion Post 84 Orono
November 19, 2016 ***Hogwash*** American Legion Post 84 Orono
November 03, 2017 ***Hybrid Moments*** Portland Club
August 11, 2018 ***2018 Hollis Pirate Festival*** Hollis Fire Department
September 08, 2018 ***2018 Litchfield Fair***
September 21, 2018 ***Pretenders Beware*** Westbrook Armory
June 22, 2019 ***La Kermesse Festival Night 1*** St. Louis Field Biddeford
June 23, 2019 ***La Kermesse Festival Night 2*** St. Louis Field Biddeford
The Road Season 1 *Episodes 4, 9, & 10* American Legion Post 84, Orono

Davienne debuted in 2013 after training with Brian Fury. She has wrestled primarily in the New England area but has also wrestled in Canada and a 2015 tour with Marvelous in Japan. A mainstay with Lucky Pro Wrestling where she held the Women's Championship for 791 days while simultaneously holding the Chaotic Wrestling Women's Championship for 395 days. She became the first ¡Let's Wrestle! Champion by winning the 2019 ¡Let's Wrestle! Rumble.

Delilah Doom
5' 0" 120lbs Los Angeles, California

Record: 0 – 1

Shows wrestled on:
November 30, 2018 *No Control* Portland Club

Doom was trained by Sho Funaki and debuted in 2014. She has wrestled primarily on the West Coast but is a regular with Rise and Shimmer. She wrestled two enhancement matches in the WWE in 2016 & 2017. She is a former Shimmer tag team champion and has held multiple championships in the Texas based Inspire Pro Wrestling.

Delmi Exo *"Just One of the Boys" "The Galaxy DelmiGod"*
5' 7" 145lbs Providence, Rhode Island

Record: 3 – 4
Shows wrestled on:
August 11, 2018 *2018 Hollis Pirate Festival* Hollis Fire Department
June 22, 2019 *La Kermesse Festival Night 1* St. Louis Field Biddeford

The Road Season 1 *Episodes 1, 2, 4, & 11* American Legion Post 84, Orono
December 19, 2020 *2020 Vacationland Cup* AMVets Hall Yarmouth

Delmi trained with Doug Summers and debuted in May 2015. Shortly after her debut she and her sister Ashley Vox formed the tag team The Sea Stars. The duo would go onto capture the Shimmer, Battle Club Pro, and Sabotage tag team championships. With Kasey Catal, she holds the Women Superstars Uncensored tag team championships. She also held the New Brunswick, Canada based Next Wrestling Entertainment Women's Championship for 517 days.
In January 2020 Delmi started a near three-month residency in Japan training and wrestling for Marvelous.
In 2020 The Sea Stars were featured in the Pro Wrestling Illustrated 500 wrestlers, the PWI Female 100, and the PWI Top 50 Tag Teams. This was the first year that PWI released the tag team ratings making this the first year this could be accomplished. Ashley Vox ranked 471 in the 500 and 66 in the Female 100, Delmi Exo ranked 477 in the 500 and 75 in the Female 100, while the team was ranked 26th in the tag team rankings. They are the only two people to be ranked in all three listings. In 2020 the Sea Stars competed for Impact Wrestling and in 2021 for AEW.

Demorest
5' 10" 268lbs Trenton, New Jersey

Record: 0 – 1
Shows wrestled on:
February 22, 2020 *Practice What You Preach* AMVets Hall Yarmouth

Demorest was a celebrated backyard wrestler prior to having his first pro match in October 2009. He considers himself self-trained but did train with Fire Ant in 2018 at the Wrestle Factory. Considered by many to have innovated many moves used today, Demorest is one everyone should be watching.

Deonna Purrazzo *"The Virtuosa"*
5' 3" 138lbs Hackettstown, New Jersey

Record: 0 – 1
Shows wrestled on:
January 19, 2018 ***The World Is Ours*** Westbrook Armory

Purrazzo trained at the D2W Pro Wrestling Academy making her in-ring debut in 2013. She has competed in-ring of Honor, TNA, RevPro in the United Kingdom, World of Stardom in Japan, NXT, and is currently signed with Impact wrestling defeating Jordynne Grace for the Knockouts Championship on July 18, 2020.

Dick Justice *"Supercop"*
5' 10" 299lbs Rochester, New York

Record: 2 – 4
Shows wrestled on:
March 17, 2017 ***Hysteria*** Westbrook Armory
April 28, 2017 ***Can We Kick It?*** Portland Club
January 19, 2018 ***The World Is Ours*** Westbrook Armory
March 30, 2018 ***Only Fools Are Satisfied*** Westbrook Armory
July 27, 2018 ***Vacationland Cup*** Westbrook Armory
September 21, 2018 ***Pretenders Beware*** Westbrook Armory

Trained by Colin Delaney, Dick Justice started wrestling in 2008 as Richard Venice. Dick Justice first appeared in 2012 at 2CW and over the next several years his popularity grew coming to a crescendo in 2018. In October 2019 Dick Justice posted on his Twitter that he was stepping away from wrestling indefinitely.

DJ Z
5' 7" 169lbs Chicago, Illinois

Record: 1 – 1
Shows wrestled on:
September 21, 2018 *Pretenders Beware* Westbrook Armory
November 30, 2018 *No Control* Portland Club

Formerly known as Zema Ion and currently known as Joaquin Wilde he was trained by Super Hentia, Shirley Doe, and Taz El Ferroz in Pittsburgh, Pennsylvania making his ring debut in August 2004. He would work the US Indies and make trips to Mexico until he was signed by Impact Wrestling in 2011. He would remain with the promotion on and off through 2018. In Impact he would win the X-Division Championship twice and hold the Tag Team Championships with partner Andrew Everett. He signed with the WWE in 2019 working for NXT.

DL Hurst *"Dark Horse"*
5' 11" 189lbs Billerica, Massachusetts

Record: 5 – 4
Shows wrestled on:
January 19, 2018 *The World Is Ours* Westbrook Armory
March 30, 2018 *Only Fools Are Satisfied* Westbrook Armory
March 09, 2019 *Welcome to the Dance* Westbrook Armory
May 10, 2019 *Hooked on a Friedman* Westbrook Armory
June 22, 2019 *La Kermesse Festival Night 1* St. Louis Field Biddeford
June 23, 2019 *La Kermesse Festival Night 2* St. Louis Field Biddeford
July 12, 2019 *2019 Vacationland Cup* Portland Club
September 06, 2019 *Know Your Enemy* Portland Expo
October 25, 2019 *Fresh Blood* AMVets Hall Yarmouth

WRESTLEBROOK PHOTO

Hurst trained at the New England Pro Wrestling Academy making his in-ring debut in 2017. He made his first appearance in Limitless Wrestling at *Hybrid Moments*, November 3, 2017 at the Portland Club with Brett Domino as part of Anthony Greene's entourage. AG would replace Domino and Hurst with the Platinum Hunnies. Hurst wrestled in both the 2018 & 2019 CHIKARA Young Lions Cup tournaments. An injury in July 2018 kept Hurst out of the ring until February 2019.

When he returned to Limitless in March 2019, he got a huge ovation when he defeated "Smart" Mark Sterling. Later that night when Brett Domino lost a handicapped match to the Platinum Hunnies he appeared to come to their rescue after Domino attacked the Hunnies post-match, instead Hurst bent his crutch over the back of Ava Everett. Their reunion didn't last long though and by September at *Know Your Enemy,* Hurst was back on the fan favorite side picking up an impressive win in the Scramble Match over Harlow O'Hara, Jody Threat, John Silver, and Puf. On August 30, 2019 Hurst captured the Chaotic Wrestling New England Championship.

Dominic Garrini *"The Bone Collector"*
5' 11" 207lbs North Canton, Ohio

Record: 0 – 1
Shows wrestled on:
November 29, 2019 *Twilight Zone* AMVets Hall Yarmouth

With a background in Judo and Brazilian Jiu-Jitsu Garrini trained at the AIW Training Center making his pro wrestling debut in 2016. His offensive repertoire relies heavily on his Judo and BJJ training and has served him well in his short career. With Kevin Ku he formed the tag team Violence is Forever capturing the SUP: Southern Underground Pro, PWF: Pro Wrestling Freedom, and BLP: Black Label Pro tag team championships.

Dominik Dijakovic
6' 7" 260lbs Worcester, Massachusetts

Record: 4 – 4
Shows wrestled on:
March 19, 2016 *Don't Fear The Sleeper* American Legion Post 84 Orono
May 28, 2016 *No Dropkicks in the Living Room* American Legion Post 84 Orono
July 23, 2016 *Hook, Line, & Sinker* American Legion Post 84 Orono
September 24, 2016 *Past Your Bedtime* American Legion Post 84 Orono
October 07, 2016 *Risk It For The Biscuit* Westbrook Armory
January 27, 2017 *Unreal* Westbrook Armory
April 28, 2017 *Can We Kick It?* Portland Club
June 23, 2017 *La Kermesse Festival Night 1* St. Louis Field Biddeford
July 21, 2017 *Nothing Gold Can Stay* Westbrook Armory
The former Donovan Dijak debuted in 2013 after training with Brian Fury and Todd Hanson (Ivar of the Viking Raiders). A

mainstay of the New England region he signed with Ring of Honor in 2014 winning the Top Prospect tournament in 2015. He stayed with the promotion until early 2017. On the Indies he captured all the titles in Chaotic Wrestling and on September 3, 2017 Keith Lee defeated Dijak in the Quarter Finals of the 2017 PWG Battle of Los Angeles in a match that was rated five stars by Dave Meltzer's Wrestling Observer. This would be Dijak's final match on the Indies before reporting the WWE's NXT brand.

Dorian Graves
5' 9" 180lbs New York City

Record: 2 – 1
Shows wrestled on:
April 28, 2017 *Can We Kick It?* Portland Club
September 22, 2017 *Question The Answers* Westbrook Armory
January 19, 2018 *The World Is Ours* Westbrook Armory

Began wrestling in 2012 wrestling primarily in the New York region. In 2015 formed the tag team Massage NV with VSK breaking up in 2019. Together they held the Create A Pro Wrestling Tag Team Championships for 362 days from 2016 - 2017. Held the VPW: Victory Pro Wrestling Tag Team Championships with Kevin Tibbs for 322 days from 2015 - 2016, losing the VPW titles the day before he won the CAP titles.

Doug Wyzer *"Vagrant Freedom Fighter"*
6' 0" 180lbs Union Station, Portland, Maine

Record: 0 – 4
Shows wrestled on:
June 22, 2019 *La Kermesse Festival Night 1* St. Louis Field Biddeford
June 23, 2019 *La Kermesse Festival Night 2* St. Louis Field Biddeford

The Road Season 1 *Episodes 5 & 6* American Legion Post 84, Orono

He initially started training in 2017 at the New England Pro Wrestling Academy but didn't conclude his training until November 2018 at the Limitless Dojo. He made his in-ring debut in 2019 at ¡Let's Wrestle! show *Curl of the Burl* in a tag team match against The Stigma with his tag team partner Jacob Drifter in the Dirty Drifters. One of Wyzer's favorite moments was his tag match against the Maine State Posse at the ¡Let's Wrestle! Mark Godfrey Benefit Show and wrestling in front of his whole family near his hometown at an NAWA: North Atlantic Wrestling Association event. On that show he wrestled a singles match in the opening bout and in a tag team in the main event against "Mr. USA" Tony Atlas.

Dozer *"The Rabid Dog"*
5' 6" 245lbs from The Dog Pound

Record: 0 – 1
Shows wrestled on:
The Road Season 1 *Episode 4* American Legion Post 84, Orono

Began training with Eric Johnson and Champ Mathews, then Larry Huntley in 2010. In 2012 he defeated Champ Mathews in a scaffold match in Waterville, Maine. He formed the tag team The Leatherheads with Ace Romero, the duo won the IWE Tag Team Championships twice holding them for 77 combined days.

Dylan Nix *"Dweller of the Deep"*
5' 10" 280lbs Amnesty Bay

Record: 1 – 2
Shows wrestled on:
The Road Season 1 *Episodes 3, 9, & 11* American Legion Post 84, Orono

A student of the Limitless Dojo he began his training in 2019. Still very early in his career he has wrestled or other promotions in Maine. He and partner Konner Hex picked up an upset victory over The Competition: Champ Mathews and Conner Murphy.

Eddie Kingston *"Mad King"*
5' 11" 240lbs Yonkers, New York

Record: 0 – 1
Shows wrestled on:
January 19, 2018 ***The World Is Ours*** Westbrook Armory

Trained primarily at the CHIKARA Wrestle Factory by Mike Quackenbush and Chris Hero Kingston made his in-ring debut October 12, 2002. Kingston would wrestle for CHIKARA until 2016, holding the CHIKARA Grand Championship for 924 days including a title defense in Maine on July 29, 2012 against Sara Del Rey in Portland. During this time, he also wrestled all over the US Indies including Combat Zone Wrestling, PWG, IWA Mid-South, Jersey All Pro and more. He also had stints in-ring of Honor and Impact Wrestling. In 2019, he had a run in NWA with Homicide. Kingston's talent in the ring also led him to international tours including Canada, Japan, and the United Kingdom. Long known as one of the best unsigned wrestlers in the world today he finally got the national exposure he long deserved wrestling Cody Rhodes for the TNT Championship on the July 22, 2020 episode of AEW Dynamite, a week later it was announced that he has signed with the promotion.

Eli Everfly *"The Fly"*
5' 4" Angelic Wasteland

Record: 1 – 3
Shows wrestled on:
May 11, 2018 ***Feed The Need*** Portland Club

July 27, 2018 *Vacationland Cup* Westbrook Armory
November 30, 2018 *No Control* Portland Club

Trained by Joey Kaos and Robby Phoenix, Everfly debuted in 2013. Wrestling primarily on the West Coast he also made trips to Canada and Mexico. He is a former SBW Submission Champion holding the title for 189 days in 2017. On November 20, 2018 Everfly wrestling as Dane Bryant teamed with Wayne Bryant on WWE SmackDown Live to defeat The Miz & Shane McMahon when Everfly pinned Miz with a small package.

Eric Johnson *"Maine's Mutant Mastodon" "Brewer Bulldozer"*
6' 0" 452lbs Brewer, Maine

Record: 7 – 0
Shows wrestled on:
June 22, 2019 *La Kermesse Festival Night 1* St. Louis Field Biddeford

June 23, 2019 *La Kermesse Festival Night 2* St. Louis Field Biddeford
The Road Season 1 *Episodes 1, 3, 5, 7, & 8* American Legion Post 84, Orono

Johnson started training under Larry Huntley and New Wrestling Horizons in 2003. He then went on to train with "Mr. USA" Tony Atlas and had his debut match in 2004 using the name Eric Lash. When he returned to NWH he became "Too Fit" Eric Atlas, years later he would team with Tony Atlas as American Muscle. While booking NAWA events in Brewer Johnson decided to start his own promotion, the IWE: Independent Wrestling Entertainment in January 2008. He promoted shows monthly in Brewer at City Side Restaurant and in Fairfield at the Community Center, as well as spot shows around the State until he sold the promotions to John Bryar in December 2016.
Johnson has worked for nearly every promotion in Maine since his debut, he's also held championships in most of them as well. On April 30, 2010 Johnson teamed with Savio Vega at the Fairfield Community Center to defeat Sonny Roselli and Mark Moment with Joey Eastman. This weekend of matches led to Johnson being booked by Vega in IWA Puerto Rico for two tours. Known most for working in New England, Johnson has also wrestled in five Canadian Provinces and experienced three winter death tours. Some of Johnson's favorite matches include teaming with Atlas and Vega but also a series of matches with Champ Mathews in IWE and his CHIKARA debut in the 2012 Young Lions Cup. Johnson's contributions to Maine wrestling are undeniable.

Eric Spicely
6' 2" 185lbs Olneyville, Providence, Rhode Island

Record: 0 – 1
Shows wrestled on:
November 15, 2015 *Killin' & Thrillin* American Legion Post 84 Orono

An MMA fighter with a record of 17 – 5 he turned pro in 2013 with CES MMA. In 2016 he was on the cast of The Ultimate Fighter 23, he failed to win the competition however he was signed by the UFC he last fought for them in June 2019. He was trained to be a wrestler by Oney Lorcan and wrestled mostly in Beyond teaming with Matt Riddle and Chuck O'Neil.

Ethan Page *"All Ego"*
6' 2" 214lbs Hamilton, Ontario, Canada

Record: 3 – 5
Shows wrestled on:
November 19, 2016 *Hogwash* American Legion Post 84 Orono
March 17, 2017 *Hysteria* Westbrook Armory
April 28, 2017 *Can We Kick It?* Portland Club
June 23, 2017 *La Kermesse Festival Night 1* St. Louis Field Biddeford
November 03, 2017 *Hybrid Moments* Portland Club
January 19, 2018 *The World Is Ours* Westbrook Armory
May 10, 2019 *Hooked on a Friedman* Westbrook Armory
January 24, 2020 *Flirtin' With Disaster* AMVets Hall Yarmouth

Debuting in-ring in 2006 Page is also the owner and promoter of Alpha-1 Wrestling which began operations in 2010. Page has a passion for wrestling and is an excellent self-promoter with his YouTube vlog, social media, and Highspots show Ego's Amigos. From my experience both in person and online he is genuine and a wicked nice guy.
Page wrestled across Canada making his first US appearances in 2008 for IWA Mid-South, CHIKARA and other promotions. In 2011 Page and Alexander teamed up for the first time and formed the very formidable tag team Monster Mafia and are still teaming today as The North. Together the duo captured championships in IWL, FPW, PWG, A1W, IWC, PWR, and held the Impact Wrestling Tag Team Championships for over a year.

Page wrestled for ROH in 2014, Evolve in 201, the same year he first toured England. In 2018 he made his first tour of Japan with DDT-Pro. He started his stint with Impact wrestling in 2017 – 2018, but in 2019 when Josh Alexander returned to wrestling is when Page's best run with the promotion started.

Flex Rumblecrunch *"The Supreme Talent" "Golden"*
6' 3" 255lbs Agawam, Massachusetts

Record: 1 – 2
Shows wrestled on:
July 23, 2016 **Hook, Line, & Sinker** American Legion Post 84 Orono
September 24, 2016 **Past Your Bedtime** American Legion Post 84 Orono
October 07, 2016 **Risk It For The Biscuit** Westbrook Armory

Also known as Sean Burke, he was trained by Antonio Thomas and debuted in June 2010. In 2013 he and partners Blaster McMassive and Max Smashmaster became the trio Devastation Corporation primarily in CHIKARA and a few other promotions. At the same time, he would wrestle in other promotions as Sean Burke, primarily in the New England area. As Burke he became a two-time NECW and Chaotic Wrestling heavyweight champion as well as capturing the Chaotic New England title. In 2016 he and McMassive joined Evolve as the Gatekeepers. Flex first retired in March 2017 but came back in April 2018 wrestling five matches in as many months.

Flip Gordon *"The Mercenary"*
5' 10" 208lbs Kalispell, Montana

Record: 1 – 4
Shows wrestled on:
November 15, 2015 **Killin' & Thrillin** American Legion Post 84 Orono

September 24, 2016 *Past Your Bedtime* American Legion Post 84 Orono
January 27, 2017 *Unreal* Westbrook Armory
May 13, 2017 *Problematic* Westbrook Armory
July 21, 2017 *Nothing Gold Can Stay* Westbrook Armory

Training at the New England Pro Wrestling Academy, Gordon debuted in 2015 with Chaotic Wrestling. In the short 5 years Flip had been wrestling he toured Mexico with CMLL and The Crash, England with multiple promotions, and Japan with NJPW. He signed with Ring of Honor in 2017 and has been a top start with them.

Foxx Vinyer *"The Vindicator"*
5' 10" 246lbs Albany, New York

Record: 0 – 1
Shows wrestled on:
February 25, 2017 *Do What You Love, Fuck The Rest-Fest* American Legion Post 84 Orono

Debuting in 2009 he is best known to Maine fans from his matches in NWA On-Fire and IWE where he is a former IWE Heavyweight and Tag Team Champion. In recent years he has been a regular for PPW: Pennsylvania Premiere Wrestling.

Francis Kipland Stevens *"One Tough Nerd"*
6' 2" 227lb New York, New York

Record: 1 – 1
Shows wrestled on:
November 19, 2016 *Hogwash* American Legion Post 84 Orono
June 24, 2017 *La Kermesse Festival Night 2* St. Louis Field Biddeford

Trained by Mikey Whipwreck he debuted in 2008 for NYWC where he was a regular for several years. He has primarily stayed in the New York area making the occasional shots outside the region. With CPA held the Create-A-Pro Tag Team Championships as the Breakfast Club for 274 days. In late 2019 wrestled a few enhancement matches for the WWE on Raw & Smackdown.

Franco Varga *"Born to Standout" "Biggest Wrestler Ever"*
6' 0" 275lbs San Juan, Puerto Rico

Record: 0 – 1
Shows wrestled on:
February 25, 2017 ***Do What You Love, Fuck The Rest-Fest***
American Legion Post 84 Orono

Varga debuted in 2016 and wrestled mostly in the Delaware and New York area. He toured Canada with the CWE 9th Anniversary Tour. In 2019 he traveled to England with Preston City Wrestling.

Frank Jaeger *"Frisky"*

Record: 2 – 3
Shows wrestled on:
The Road Season 1 *Episodes 2, 3, 5, 6, & 8* American Legion Post 84, Orono

Fred Yehi *"Bonafide" "Savageweight" "The Resurrector of Wrestling"*
5' 9" 185lbs Georgia

Record: 0 – 2
Shows wrestled on:
January 19, 2018 **The World Is Ours** Westbrook Armory
October 25, 2019 **Fresh Blood** AMVets Hall Yarmouth

Trained by Jay Fury & Steve Platinum he debuted in 2012. An excellent mat technician Yehi has wrestled across the United States, United Kingdom, and Germany. He is a former FIP heavyweight champion and Evolve tag team champion with Tracy Williams.

Gangrel
6' 0" 240lbs The Other Side of Darkness

Record: 1 – 0
Shows wrestled on:
October 25, 2019 *Fresh Blood* AMVets Hall Yarmouth

He debuted in 1988 after training with The Great Boris Malenko wrestling in the Florida area. He then traveled to Stampede Wrestling in Canada. He traveled around the United States wrestling shots in the WWF, WCW, & ECW as well as winning and losing the USWA Heavyweight Championship to Jeff Jarrett. He made his WWE debut as Gangrel in 1998 forming The Brood with Edge & Christian and later the Hardy Boys. He was released in 2001 and has continued to wrestle around the world since then.

Geno Bauer *"Big"*
6' 2" 265lbs From Anywhere He Damn Well Pleases

Record: 0 – 1
Shows wrestled on:
October 07, 2016 *Risk It For The Biscuit* Westbrook Armory

Bauer began training with NWA New England, finished training with IWE. He wrestled in the New England area, primarily Maine.

George Gatton
5' 6" 178lbs Syracuse, New York

Record: 0 – 1
Shows wrestled on:
March 19, 2016 *Don't Fear The Sleeper* American Legion Post 84 Orono

Trained by Drew Gulak he debuted in 2014 wrestling mostly with CZW and their Dojo Wars events. Wrestling mostly in the New York & New Jersey area he has also wrestled a few matches in Canada.

Good Hank Flanders
6' 2" 12 Stone Maspeth Queens City of New York

Record: 1 – 0
Shows wrestled on:
September 12, 2015 *Stage One* City Side Restaurant, Brewer

Trained by Amazing Red he debuted in 2012 with House of Glory his home wrestling promotion. Now wrestling as Hank Flanagan, his favorite match to date is from Stage One vs. Anthony Greene.

GPA *"The Academic Standard"*

Record: 0 – 1
Shows wrestled on:
March 17, 2017 *Hysteria* Westbrook Armory

GPA or Geoffrey Percival Austere began wrestling in 2011 and had wrestled primarily in the Chicago region with occasional shots outside of Illinois. He is a two-time Freelance Underground Heavyweight Champion with his first reign lasting 594 days. He held the Chicago Style Wrestling Metra Division Championship for 491 days.

Green Ant *"The Resilient Rookie"*
6' 0" 161lbs The Colony

Record: 2 – 0
Shows wrestled on:
May 11, 2018 *Feed The Need* Portland Club
November 30, 2018 *No Control* Portland Club

This is the second Green Ant, trained at The Wrestle Factory debuting in 2017 wrestling mostly in Pennsylvania and the Northeast Region. Lost in the finals of the 2020 CHIKARA Young Lions Cup to Ricky South. Toured Michinoku Pro in Japan in October & November 2019.

Harlow O'Hara *"The Priestess"*
Atlanta, Georgia

Record: 3 – 1
Shows wrestled on:
July 27, 2018 *Vacationland Cup* Westbrook Armory
November 30, 2018 *No Control* Portland Club
January 11, 2019 *Snakebitten* Westbrook Armory
September 06, 2019 *Know Your Enemy* Portland Expo

Trained by Robert Gibson, O'Hara debuted in 2017. She is a former Anarchy Women's Champion and a two-time Battle Club Pro Icon Champion.

Hermit Crab
5' 10" 180lbs Rocky Beach, Maine

Record: 0 – 1
Shows wrestled on:
May 11, 2018 *Feed The Need* Portland Club

Trained at The Wrestle Factory he debuted in 2015 and has wrestled primarily for CHIKARA the majority of his career. He is a former Young Lions Cup title holder.

Jacob Drifter
5' 11" 207lbs from Trash Mountain on Garbage Island

Record: 1 – 3
Shows wrestled on:
June 23, 2019 *La Kermesse Festival Night 2* St. Louis Field Biddeford
The Road Season 1 *Episodes 5, 7, & 10* American Legion Post 84, Orono

Drifter started training in 2016 with Eric Johnson. He had his first singles match in February 2018. He scored an upset victory over Ace Romero on Episode 10 on season 1 of The Road pinning Acey Baby. He is a member of the Dirty Drifters.

Jake Hager *"All-American American" "The Savage"*
6' 7" 275lbs Perry, Oklahoma

Record: 1 – 0
Shows wrestled on:
September 22, 2017 *Question The Answers* Westbrook Armory

An NCAA Division 1 All-American from the University of Oklahoma he signed with the WWE in 2006. He started in the developmental territory Deep South Wrestling before moving to Ohio Valley Wrestling in 2007. Later in the same year he was assigned to Florida Championship Wrestling where he would go on to win the Southern & Florida Heavyweight Championships. He made his WWE main roster debut on the ECW brand in 2008 as Jack Swagger, he was released in 2017. In the WWE he captured the WW-ECW Heavyweight Championship, the United States Championship, and the World Heavyweight

Championship. He then traveled around the Indies, as well as MLW: Major League Wrestling and Lucha Underground. In 2019 he signed with All Elite Wrestling.

In 2019 he also signed with Bellator MMA fighting three times in 2019 winning his first two fights in the first round with an arm-triangle submission, and his third fight was ruled a no contest after an accidental groin strike.

Jake Something
6' 2" 235lbs Michigan

Record: 1 – 2
Shows wrestled on:
March 09, 2019 *Welcome to the Dance* Westbrook Armory
November 29, 2019 *Twilight Zone* AMVets Hall Yarmouth
February 22, 2020 *Practice What You Preach* AMVets Hall Yarmouth

A product of the ROH dojo, Something debuted in 2014 and has been touring the US & Canadian Indies. He is currently signed with Impact wrestling as Cousin Jake or Jake Deaner. He has won titles in AAW, Border City Wrestling, Black Label Pro and others. He was a body double for Bruiser Brody in the Dark Side of The Ring episode on Brody.

James Limits
6' 1" 246lbs Pleasant Valley, New York

Record: 0 – 2
Shows wrestled on:
February 25, 2017 *Do What You Love, Fuck The Rest-Fest* American Legion Post 84 Orono
June 24, 2017 *La Kermesse Festival Night 2* St. Louis Field Biddeford

Better known to Maine fans as Jimmy Limits, he began his in-ring career in 2015 and is a former IWE Champion. His current home promotion is Truly Independent Wrestling based out of Pittsfield, Massachusetts. Has done tours in Nova Scotia and Ontario Canada.

Jaxon Stone *"Youth Gone Wild"*
6' 1" 224lbs Plano, Texas

Record: 0 – 1
Shows wrestled on:
January 19, 2018 *The World Is Ours* Westbrook Armory

Trained at MPX Wrestling School, Jaxon debuted in 2015 wrestling primarily in the Texas and Oklahoma region. In late 2016 he spent a month at the wXw Wrestling Academy in Germany, and a three-month stint in the Spring and Autumn of 2017. In February 2019, he spent time wrestling in the United Kingdom for various promotions.

Jay Freddie
5' 8" 198lbs Syracuse, New York

Record: 7 – 6
Shows wrestled on:
March 17, 2017 *Hysteria* Westbrook Armory
April 28, 2017 *Can We Kick It?* Portland Club
September 22, 2017 *Question The Answers* Westbrook Armory
November 03, 2017 *Hybrid Moments* Portland Club
January 19, 2018 *The World Is Ours* Westbrook Armory
March 30, 2018 *Only Fools Are Satisfied* Westbrook Armory
May 11, 2018 *Feed The Need* Portland Club
July 27, 2018 *Vacationland Cup* Westbrook Armory
September 21, 2018 *Pretenders Beware* Westbrook Armory
November 30, 2018 *No Control* Portland Club
January 11, 2019 *Snakebitten* Westbrook Armory

March 09, 2019 *Welcome to the Dance* Westbrook Armory
May 10, 2019 *Hooked on a Friedman* Westbrook Armory

Debuted in 2008 cutting his teeth with Squared Circle Wrestling. For the next several years he would wrestle primarily in the Northeast region for 2CW, Top Rope Promotions and other promotions. In May 2015 he would make his first of many tours of Japan, this one would be a near four-month stint with The Great Muta's Wrestle 1 promotion. He would return every year including early 2020. In 2017 he held the UWA World Trios Championship with Jiro Kuroshio & Kumagoro.
In Limitless Wrestling he became a member of the Thick Boys with John Silver & Puf. His biggest singles victory was over Chris Dickinson at Can We Kick It?

Jaylen Bradyn
5'8" 139lbs from Your Baby Momma's Day Dream

Record: 2 – 1
Shows wrestled on:
The Road Season 1 *Episodes 1, 7, 8, & 9* American Legion Post 84, Orono

Bradyn trained with Matt Taven & Vinny Marseglia, he is one half of Waves and Curls with Traevon Jordan. His favorite moment in wrestling is the Usos vs. The New Day from WWE Hell in a Cell 2017.

JD Drake *"Blue Collar Bad Ass" "New Age Enforcer"*
6' 2" 302lbs Shelby, North Carolina

Record: 3 – 7
Shows wrestled on:
July 21, 2017 *Nothing Gold Can Stay* Westbrook Armory
January 19, 2018 *The World Is Ours* Westbrook Armory
March 30, 2018 *Only Fools Are Satisfied* Westbrook Armory

May 11, 2018 *Feed The Need* Portland Club
July 12, 2019 *2019 Vacationland Cup* Portland Club
September 06, 2019 *Know Your Enemy* Portland Expo
October 25, 2019 *Fresh Blood* AMVets Hall Yarmouth
November 29, 2019 *Twilight Zone* AMVets Hall Yarmouth
January 24, 2020 *Flirtin' With Disaster* AMVets Hall Yarmouth
December 19, 2020 *2020 Vacationland Cup* AMVets Hall Yarmouth

Trained by the legendary "Mr. Number 1" George South, he debuted in 2002. For the next 15 years he wrestled primarily in the Mid-Atlantic region capturing numerous championships. In 2017, he and Anthony Henry, the Work Horsemen, made their Evolve debut and defeated Catch Point: Jaka & Chris Dickinson to win the Evolve Tag Team Championships. They would hold the championships for 76 days losing them to ACH & Ethan Page. On October 28, 2018, Drake would win the World Wrestling Network Championship in a ladder match defeating Anthony Henry, AR Fox, Austin Theory, Darby Allin and Harlem Bravado. He would lose the title in July 2019 to Austin Theory when he unified it with the Evolve Championship. In early 2020 Drake would get a win at an NXT house show in Tampa, Florida

and he would also make his United Kingdom debut at Progress Chapter 103.
Known for his rough house style, in Limitless Wrestling Drake has become a fan favorite having outstanding matches with Brian Pillman Jr., Alec Price, Maine State Posse and more.

Jeff Cannonball *"Deathmatch Vegan"*
5' 11" 400lbs Highland Park, New Jersey

Record: 4 – 2
Shows wrestled on:
June 23, 2017 *La Kermesse Festival Night 1* St. Louis Field Biddeford
June 24, 2017 *La Kermesse Festival Night 2* St. Louis Field Biddeford
September 22, 2017 *Question The Answers* Westbrook Armory
May 11, 2018 *Feed The Need* Portland Club
July 27, 2018 *Vacationland Cup* Westbrook Armory
September 21, 2018 *Pretenders Beware* Westbrook Armory

Trained by Corey Havoc, Cannonball debuted in 2008. Overtime he developed a reputation for being a deathmatch wrestler battling with and against Matt Tremont in several of them. He competed in the 2016 CZW Cage of Death, won the OPW Survival of the Sickest 2 tournament, and competed in several more deathmatch tournaments. He is a former two-time H20 Heavyweight Champion defeated "Franchise" Shane Douglas in 2017 for his first reign, and current ISW Falls Count Anywhere champion. He is the host of Short Soda Reviews on his twitter @JeffCannonball

Jeff Cobb *"Mr. Athletic"*
5' 10" 262lbs Honolulu, Hawaii

Record: 1 – 1
Shows wrestled on:

May 28, 2016 *No Dropkicks in the Living Room* American Legion Post 84 Orono
January 19, 2018 *The World Is Ours* Westbrook Armory

Before entering professional wrestling, Cobb was an amateur wrestler that represented Guam at the 2004 Summer Olympics in Athens, Greece in the 84kg weight class. Training with Oliver John he made his pro debut in 2009 in Hawaii. His first big exposure came in 2015 under a mask as The Monster Matanza Cueto for Lucha Underground where he held the LU Championship. In 2016 he debuted for PWG and made his first tour in the UK and Mexico. In 2017 he debuted in Canada and in Germany for wXw, made it to the finals of the 2017 PWG Battle of Los Angeles and debuted for New Japan Pro Wrestling teaming with Michael Elgin in the World Tag League. Cobb has held several championships and is a former NJPW NEVER Openweight Champion, ROH Television Champion, and PWG World Champion. He is currently signed with Ring of Honor and New Japan Pro Wrestling.

Jeremy Leary *"Dirt Dawg" "The Best Hair in Wrestling"*
5' 9" 215lbs From The Other Side Of The Tracks

Record: 6 – 12
Shows wrestled on:
November 15, 2015 *Killin' & Thrillin* American Legion Post 84 Orono
March 19, 2016 *Don't Fear The Sleeper* American Legion Post 84 Orono
May 28, 2016 *No Dropkicks in the Living Room* American Legion Post 84 Orono
July 23, 2016 *Hook, Line, & Sinker* American Legion Post 84 Orono
October 07, 2016 *Risk It For The Biscuit* Westbrook Armory
October 29, 2016 *Who Watches the Watchmen?* The Field House at University of Maine Orono

November 19, 2016 *Hogwash* American Legion Post 84 Orono
January 27, 2017 *Unreal* Westbrook Armory
February 25, 2017 *Do What You Love, Fuck The Rest-Fest* American Legion Post 84 Orono
March 17, 2017 *Hysteria* Westbrook Armory
April 28, 2017 *Can We Kick It?* Portland Club
May 13, 2017 *Problematic* Westbrook Armory
June 23, 2017 *La Kermesse Festival Night 1* St. Louis Field Biddeford
June 24, 2017 *La Kermesse Festival Night 2* St. Louis Field Biddeford
June 22, 2019 *La Kermesse Festival Night 1* St. Louis Field Biddeford
June 23, 2019 *La Kermesse Festival Night 2* St. Louis Field Biddeford
July 12, 2019 *2019 Vacationland Cup* Portland Club
September 06, 2019 *Know Your Enemy* Portland Expo

Trained by Kevin Landry, and partially by Antonio Thomas at the Pro Wrestling Combine, Leary debuted in 2009. Held the Revival Pro Wrestling championship 328 days, his reign included a Falls Count Anywhere match with Brian Myers which he considers one of his favorite matches. Debuted in CHIKARA in 2016 and competed at the 2018 King of Trios.

Leary is best known in Limitless Wrestling for two very memorable moments. The first at *Who Watches The Watchmen* when he led the audience on a sing-along of Journey's *Don't Stop Believing* and secondly losing his precious hair when he and Skylar lost to Ashley Vox and Kris Statlander at *Know Your Enemy*, Bradford the Barber had the honor of shaving Leary's head. He retuned to Limitless Wrestling on *The Road* Season 2 as the leader of the heel faction The Hive.

Jessica Troy
5' 7" Newcastle, New South Wales, Australia

Record: 1 – 0
Shows wrestled on:
June 24, 2017 *La Kermesse Festival Night 2* St. Louis Field Biddeford

Trained by Adam Hoffman and Jack Bonza she debuted in 2014. Her first tour in the United States was from May to August 2017 when she made her stop in Maine for Night 2 of La Kermesse Festival. She is a two-time PWWA Champion and Former Wrestling GO! Champion. She is a regular with SHIMMER Women Athletes.

Jessicka Havok *"The Havok Death Machine"*
6' 0" 264lbs Defiance, Ohio

Record: 0 – 2
Shows wrestled on:
November 03, 2017 *Hybrid Moments* Portland Club
September 21, 2018 *Pretenders Beware* Westbrook Armory

Havok debuted in 2004 after training in her home state of Ohio. She traveled the Independents eventually signing with TNA

Wrestling in 2014. She was only with the promotion for a year but captured the Knockouts Championship during that run. She had her first tour of Japan with World of Stardom in 2016. She returned to Impact in 2019.

JGeorge *"Thunderheart"*
6' 0" 215lbs, New Bridge, New Jersey

Record: 0 – 1
Shows wrestled on:
January 30, 2016 ***Under Fire*** American Legion Post 84 Orono

He debuted in March 2014; however, he is currently training at Create-A-Pro Wrestling Academy. His favorite match to date was for Warriors of Wrestling *Ultimate Survival 2017* on July 8, 2017 in New York City where he defeated Simon Grimm in a singles match.

Jimmy Jacobs *"Zombie Princess"*
5' 7" 180lbs Grand Rapids, Michigan

Record: 1 – 0
Shows wrestled on:
March 30, 2018 ***Only Fools Are Satisfied*** Westbrook Armory

Trained by Truth Martini and others, Jacobs debuted in-ring in 1999, although he had been involved in wrestling since 1998. He first appeared with Ring of Honor in 2003 and spent six years with the promotion. He returned in 2011 for another four-year run. From 2015 – 2017 Jacobs worked for the WWE on the creative team. He was released in April 2017 and signed with Impact Wrestling at the end of 2017. He won numerous championships in his career including being a five-time Ring of Honor World Tag Team Champion.

Jimmy Lloyd *"Different Boy"*
5' 10" 200lbs New Jersey

Record: 0 – 2
Shows wrestled on:
April 28, 2017 *Can We Kick It?* Portland Club
September 22, 2017 *Question The Answers* Westbrook Armory

Trained at the OTW Pro Wrestling Academy making his in-ring debut in 2014. In 2016 he started appearing regularly for CZW Dojo Wars. Now known as a prolific Deathmatch Wrestler, he had his first in 2016 with Nate Hatred for Game Changer Wrestling. Won the 2018 CZW Tournament of Death 17 defeating Rickey Shane Page in the finals. Has had a multiyear feud with Brandon Kirk that is destined to never end.

Jody Threat *"The Wild Child"*
5' 4" 160lbs Hailing from Your Local Skate Park

Record: 0 – 5
Shows wrestled on:
September 06, 2019 ***Know Your Enemy*** Portland Expo
October 25, 2019 ***Fresh Blood*** AMVets Hall Yarmouth
November 29, 2019 ***Twilight Zone*** AMVets Hall Yarmouth
January 24, 2020 ***Flirtin' With Disaster*** AMVets Hall Yarmouth
February 22, 2020 ***Practice What You Preach*** AMVets Hall Yarmouth

Debuted in October 2017 in her hometown of Toronto, Ontario after training with "Walking Weapon" Josh Alexander, she quickly became a standout on the Canadian Indies. She made her US debut in 2018 and in the summer of 2019 traveled across the pond for a tour of the United Kingdom. She was the first ever Women's Champion for the Ontario based Barrie Wrestling holding the title for 455 days. She has also held both Michigan based CLASH Women's Championship and Devine Women's Championship for over a year. In Limitless Wrestling, even though she has yet to pick up a victory in the promotion she has developed a huge following of loyal fans that are excited to see her at every show.

Joe Quick

Record: 0 – 1
Shows wrestled on:
September 12, 2015 ***Stage One*** City Side Restaurant, Brewer

Trained at the House of Glory under Brian XL & Amazing Red. With Adam Falcon he comprised the team The Falcon Corps. Has the distinction in being in the first ever Limitless Wrestling match.

Joey Janela *"The Bad Boy"*
5' 8" 183lbs Ashbury Park, New Jersey

Record: 1 – 2

Shows wrestled on:
May 28, 2016 *No Dropkicks in the Living Room* American Legion Post 84 Orono
April 28, 2017 *Can We Kick It?* Portland Club
September 22, 2017 *Question The Answers* Westbrook Armory

Debuting in 2006 Janela would primarily wrestle in National Wrestling Superstars as his home promotion for the first several years of his career capturing the Cruiserweight Championship three times. In 2011 he would start branching out more regularly to other promotions. In 2014 he debuted in CZW: Combat Zone Wrestling capturing the Wired Championship three times. In 2016 in GCW at Zandig's Tournament of Survival Janela was defeated by Zandig in a deathmatch where Zandig performed a sit-out slam off the roof of a building through light tubes, barbed wire, and fire into the back of a pick-up truck. Janela is currently signed with All Elite Wrestling but still wrestles for Game Changer Wrestling and Beyond Wrestling.

Joey Ryan
5' 10" 209lbs Los Angeles, California

Record: 1 – 0
Shows wrestled on:
September 22, 2017 *Question The Answers* Westbrook Armory

Debuting in the year 2000, he was a founding member of Pro Wrestling Guerilla winning their World Championship and a 4-time tag team champion. He would wrestle around the world including being a multi-time holder of the Japan based DDT Iron Man Heavy Metal Weight Champion. He had stints in-ring of Honor, Impact Wrestling, and Lucha Underground. Formed a very successful tag team with Candice LaRae as the World's Cutest Tag team winning several tag team championships together.

John Silver *"Raw Dog" "Meat Man"*
5' 4" 180lbs Long Island, New York

Record: 6 – 12
Shows wrestled on:
March 19, 2016 ***Don't Fear The Sleeper*** American Legion Post 84 Orono
July 23, 2016 ***Hook, Line, & Sinker*** American Legion Post 84 Orono
January 27, 2017 ***Unreal*** Westbrook Armory
April 28, 2017 ***Can We Kick It?*** Portland Club
July 21, 2017 ***Nothing Gold Can Stay*** Westbrook Armory
September 22, 2017 ***Question The Answers*** Westbrook Armory
November 03, 2017 ***Hybrid Moments*** Portland Club
January 19, 2018 ***The World Is Ours*** Westbrook Armory
March 30, 2018 ***Only Fools Are Satisfied*** Westbrook Armory
May 11, 2018 ***Feed The Need*** Portland Club
September 21, 2018 ***Pretenders Beware*** Westbrook Armory
November 30, 2018 ***No Control*** Portland Club

January 11, 2019 ***Snakebitten*** Westbrook Armory
May 10, 2019 ***Hooked on a Friedman*** Westbrook Armory
September 06, 2019 ***Know Your Enemy*** Portland Expo
October 25, 2019 ***Fresh Blood*** AMVets Hall Yarmouth
November 29, 2019 ***Twilight Zone*** AMVets Hall Yarmouth
January 24, 2020 ***Flirtin' With Disaster*** AMVets Hall Yarmouth

Silver debuted in 2007 training with Mikey Whipwreck wrestling primarily for NYWC the first few years of his career. He first began teaming with Alex Reynolds in 2011, eventually calling themselves the Beaver Boys where they captured the PWG & CZW World Tag Team Championships. Silver is a former CZW World Heavyweight Champion holding the crown for 153 days in 2019. Is currently signed with All Elite Wrestling with Alex Reynolds as part of The Dark Order.

Johnny Clash
6' 1" 216lbs North Massapequa, New York

Record: 0 – 1
Shows wrestled on:
March 19, 2016 ***Don't Fear The Sleeper*** American Legion Post 84 Orono
Trained at Create-A-Pro Wrestling Academy he debuted in 2015. Has wrestled mostly in the New York and New Jersey area. He held the CAP Tag titles with Liam Davis and is a two-time CAP Champion holding the title for a combined 391 days.

Johnny Torres *'The Concept"*
5' 10" 170lbs Rockville, Connecticut

Record: 3 – 2
Shows wrestled on:
March 19, 2016 ***Don't Fear The Sleeper*** American Legion Post 84 Orono

July 23, 2016 *Hook, Line, & Sinker* American Legion Post 84 Orono
September 24, 2016 *Past Your Bedtime* American Legion Post 84 Orono
October 07, 2016 *Risk It For The Biscuit* Westbrook Armory
October 29, 2016 *Who Watches the Watchmen?* The Field House at University of Maine Orono

The former Johnny Miyagi has been wrestling since 2008 after training with Kevin Landry, Aaron Morrison, Antonio Thomas, and Johnny Idol. A former five-time IWE Tag Team Champion, three times with Scotty Wild and two-times with Shane Marvel, he also captured the IWE Heavyweight and Junior Heavyweight championships. His favorite moment in wrestling was when he went to his first independent show November 5, 2004 Ring of Honor Weekend of Thunder in Revere, Massachusetts when Jushin Thunder Liger defeated "American Dragon" Bryan Danielson.

Jonathan Gresham *"The Octopus"*
5' 4" 161lbs Atlanta, Georgia

Record: 1 – 2
Shows wrestled on:
July 23, 2016 *Hook, Line, & Sinker* American Legion Post 84 Orono
May 13, 2017 *Problematic* Westbrook Armory
November 03, 2017 *Hybrid Moments* Portland Club

One of the most technically gifted wrestlers in the world he was trained by Mr. Hughes and debuted in 2005. He has wrestled around the world in Mexico, United Kingdom, Germany, Japan, Canada, along the way he won championships in Mexico and Germany and across the United States. He is a former CZW World champion, and ROH Tag Team Champion with Jay Lethal.

Jordan Oliver
6' 0" 176lbs Newburg, New York

Record: 0 – 1
Shows wrestled on:
January 11, 2019 *Snakebitten* Westbrook Armory

Trained at the CZW Academy he debuted in 2016. Held the CZW Wired Championship for 427 days during 2018 – 2019. Has become a mainstay in Game Changer Wrestling and is one to watch in the coming years.

Jodynne Grace *"Thick Momma Pump" "Last Pure Athlete"*
5' 1" 150lbs Austin, Texas

Record: 1 – 1
Shows wrestled on:
November 03, 2017 *Hybrid Moments* Portland Club
July 27, 2018 *Vacationland Cup* Westbrook Armory

Training with Mr. B, Papa Don, and George de la Isla, she debuted in 2011 wrestling in the Texas region. Over the years she has wrestled across the US Indies capturing regional championships. She has toured Mexico, The United Kingdom, winning the Progress Women's Championship and Japan. She signed with Impact Wrestling in 2018 and won the Knockouts Championship in Mexico from Taya Valkyrie in January 2020.

Josh Alexander *"Walking Weapon"*
6'1" 216lbs Bolton, Ontario, Canada

Record: 0 – 1
Shows wrestled on:
January 24, 2020 *Flirtin' With Disaster* AMVets Hall Yarmouth

Trained with he debuted in 2005 wrestling, spending the next several years wrestling across Canada winning several championships. He formed the Monster Mafia tag team with "All Ego" Ethan Page winning the PWG World Tag Team Championships. In July 2015 he left wrestling because of a neck injury, however made a return in April 2016. In February 2019 Alexander signed with Impact Wrestling, again teaming up with Ethan Page this time as The North holding the Impact Tag Team Championships for 383 days.

Josh Briggs
6' 8" 268lbs

Record: 7 – 10
Shows wrestled on:
April 28, 2017 *Can We Kick It?* Portland Club
June 23, 2017 *La Kermesse Festival Night 1* St. Louis Field Biddeford
July 21, 2017 *Nothing Gold Can Stay* Westbrook Armory
September 22, 2017 *Question The Answers* Westbrook Armory
November 03, 2017 *Hybrid Moments* Portland Club
January 19, 2018 *The World Is Ours* Westbrook Armory
March 30, 2018 *Only Fools Are Satisfied* Westbrook Armory
May 11, 2018 *Feed The Need* Portland Club
July 27, 2018 *Vacationland Cup* Westbrook Armory
September 21, 2018 *Pretenders Beware* Westbrook Armory
November 30, 2018 *No Control* Portland Club
January 11, 2019 *Snakebitten* Westbrook Armory
March 09, 2019 *Welcome to the Dance* Westbrook Armory
October 25, 2019 *Fresh Blood* AMVets Hall Yarmouth
January 24, 2020 *Flirtin' With Disaster* AMVets Hall Yarmouth
February 22, 2020 *Practice What You Preach* AMVets Hall Yarmouth

Trained by Mike Hallow and Brian Fury he debuted in December 2016. Quickly made a name for himself in the Northeast United

States signing with Evolve in May 2018 winning the Evolve Championship from Austin Theory in November 2019 until the promotion folded on July 2, 2020.

Joshua Bishop *'The Intense Icon"*
6' 3" 230lbs Rip City

Record: 1 – 0
Shows wrestled on:
October 25, 2019 ***Fresh Blood*** AMVets Hall Yarmouth

Bishop debuted in 2017 in his home state of Ohio with AIW: Absolute Intense Wrestling. He has stayed in the Midwest for most of his career branching out to the Northeast in late 2019. He has held both the AIW Intense and AIW Absolute championships on two occasions. With his partner Wes Barkley they are the Rip City Shooters. Together they held the UXWA Tag Team Championship. Currently he is one half of the Crazy Tough Enemies with Matthew Justice in GCW: Game Changer Wrestling.

JT Dunn *"The Juice"*
5' 10" 176lbs Providence, Rhode Island

Record: 16 – 10 – 1
Shows wrestled on:
May 28, 2016 *No Dropkicks in the Living Room* American Legion Post 84 Orono
July 23, 2016 *Hook, Line, & Sinker* American Legion Post 84 Orono
October 07, 2016 *Risk It For The Biscuit* Westbrook Armory
January 27, 2017 *Unreal* Westbrook Armory
February 25, 2017 *Do What You Love, Fuck The Rest-Fest* American Legion Post 84 Orono
March 17, 2017 *Hysteria* Westbrook Armory
April 28, 2017 *Can We Kick It?* Portland Club
May 13, 2017 *Problematic* Westbrook Armory
June 23, 2017 *La Kermesse Festival Night 1* St. Louis Field Biddeford
July 21, 2017 *Nothing Gold Can Stay* Westbrook Armory
September 22, 2017 *Question The Answers* Westbrook Armory
November 03, 2017 *Hybrid Moments* Portland Club
January 19, 2018 *The World Is Ours* Westbrook Armory
March 30, 2018 *Only Fools Are Satisfied* Westbrook Armory
May 11, 2018 *Feed The Need* Portland Club
July 27, 2018 *Vacationland Cup* Westbrook Armory
September 21, 2018 *Pretenders Beware* Westbrook Armory
November 30, 2018 *No Control* Portland Club
January 11, 2019 *Snakebitten* Westbrook Armory
March 09, 2019 *Welcome to the Dance* Westbrook Armory
May 10, 2019 *Hooked on a Friedman* Westbrook Armory
July 12, 2019 *2019 Vacationland Cup* Portland Club
September 06, 2019 *Know Your Enemy* Portland Expo
October 25, 2019 *Fresh Blood* AMVets Hall Yarmouth
November 29, 2019 *Twilight Zone* AMVets Hall Yarmouth
January 24, 2020 *Flirtin' With Disaster* AMVets Hall Yarmouth
February 22, 2020 *Practice What You Preach* AMVets Hall Yarmouth

Dunn debuted in 2009 after training with David Cole. In 2013 he formed a tag team with David Starr known as the Juicy Product, they captured the WSU, FIP, NYWC, & CZW tag Team Championships. In 2015 he teamed with Chris Hero forming Death by Elbow wrestling primarily in Beyond, however they did challenge The Young Bucks for the PWG World Tag Team Championships at *PWG Thirteen* on July 29, 2016. Later in 2016 Hero and Dunn traveled to Germany for wXw competing in the World Tag Team League 2016 Block B.

In Limitless Wrestling Dunn started out slow with two losses before picking up his first win. He would headline several Limitless Shows including defeating Cody Rhodes at *Unreal*. He won the *2018 Vacationland Cup* and competed in the match to crown the first Limitless Wrestling Champion with his Death by Elbow giving MJF the pin on Greene to win the title. Dunn has won several matches since then, but he has yet to challenge to the Limitless Wrestling World Championship.

Kai Katana
5' 10" 200lbs The Land of the Rising Sun

Record: 0 – 1
Shows wrestled on:
April 28, 2017 *Can We Kick It?* Portland Club

Debuted in 2012 and is currently wrestling under the name Kyler Kahn. Spent the first part of his career in Victory Pro Wrestling in New York winning the New Work State Championship and a two-time VPW Heavyweight Champion. Under the name Wani he captured the CHIKARA Young Lions Cup in 2017 holding it for 64 days.

Kaitlin Diemond *"Canadian Rockstar" "Anti-Diva"*
5' 8" 147lbs Toronto, Ontario, Canada

Record: 0 – 2
Shows wrestled on:
June 23, 2017 *La Kermesse Festival Night 1* St. Louis Field Biddeford
June 24, 2017 *La Kermesse Festival Night 2* St. Louis Field Biddeford

Diemond debuted in 2005 after training with Mike Shea in Ontario. She wrestled across the Canadian Indies capturing multiple championships including holding the Ontario based Crossfire Wrestling Women's Championship for 472 days. From November 2013 to April 2014 she lived in Mexico training with Gran Apache, Jennifer Blake, Fenix, & Super Crazy. She traveled to Japan in January 2016 for World of Stardom where she trained with Io Shirai and wrestled for the promotion until April 2016. She has also wrestled in China, Germany, Ireland, and England totaling eight different countries, living in five of them. However, her greatest achievement from the world of professional wrestling is that it brought her to her wife, former wrestler Jawsolyn.

Kalvin Strange *"Classic"*
6' 0" 190lbs Veazie, Maine

Record: 2 – 2
Shows wrestled on:
January 19, 2018 *The World Is Ours* Westbrook Armory
August 11, 2018 *2018 Hollis Pirate Festival* Hollis Fire Department
September 08, 2018 *2018 Litchfield Fair*
June 23, 2019 *La Kermesse Festival Night 2* St. Louis Field Biddeford

Began his training in 2016 at Storm Wrestling Academy in Calgary, Alberta, Canada. He has competed in Maine in IWE and ¡Let's Wrestle! defeating Davienne to win the ¡Let's Wrestle! Championship on May 31, 2019. Strange would defend the title at *La Kermesse Festival Night 2* that June. He would hold the title for 226 losing it to "Masshole" Mike McCarthy on January 11, 2020 in a Fans Bring the Weapons Match.

Kasey Catal
5' 1" 120lbs Poughkeepsie, New York

Record: 0 – 1
Shows wrestled on:
September 21, 2018 *Pretenders Beware* Westbrook Armory

Trained at Create-A-Pro Wrestling Academy she debuted in-ring 2017, and also has acted as a valet. Wrestling primarily in the Northeast region of the United States she has held the WSU Tag Team Championships with Delmi Exo, and the New Jersey based Empower Wrestling champion holding the title since October 24, 2019. On November 27, 2020 she defeated TJ Crawford to win the Synergy Wrestling Cruiserweight Crown Championship. She is married to wrestler Branon Kirk.

Keith Lee *"Limitless"*
6' 2" 340lbs Wichita Falls, Texas

Record: 0 – 2
Shows wrestled on:
May 28, 2016 ***No Dropkicks in the Living Room*** American Legion Post 84 Orono
March 17, 2017 ***Hysteria*** Westbrook Armory

Trained by "Killer" Tim Brooks, Lee debuted in 2005. In his career he has wrestled across the United States and in Mexico, Canada, Germany, Ireland, and England. He is currently signed with the WWE where is a former NXT North American and NXT Champion. In PWG he is a former World Champion and on September 2nd at the 2017 Battle of Las Angeles he defeated Dijak in a quarterfinal match that was awarded five stars by The Wrestling Observer.

Ken Broadway *"Cashflow" "The Crown Jewel"*
6' 0" 220lbs New York City

Record: 0 – 1
Shows wrestled on:
January 30, 2016 ***Under Fire*** American Legion Post 84 Orono

Trained by Brian XL & Amazing Red, Broadway debuted in 2013. Wrestling mostly in the New York & New Jersey region, he is a former House of Glory Elite and Crown Jewel Champion.

Kennedi Copeland
5' 4" 120lbs of angst, from Upstate, New York

Record: 2 – 1
Shows wrestled on:
November 03, 2017 ***Hybrid Moments*** Portland Club

The Road Season 1 *Episodes 3 & 9* American Legion Post 84, Orono

Copeland began her training in 2011 taking a hiatus for four years before returning in 2015. Her first match was September 12, 2015 in Montgomery, Vermont for Slam All-Star Wrestling, she defeated PJ Gonzalez. As a fan her favorite moment in wrestling was when she attended WWE *New Year's Revolution* January 8, 2006 in Albany, New York when Edge defeated John Cena for the WWE Championship, cashing in his Money in the Bank.

Kevin Bennett
6' 0" 180lbs Buffalo, New York

Record: 0 – 1
Shows wrestled on:
March 30, 2018 ***Only Fools Are Satisfied*** Westbrook Armory

Was trained by The Blade having his first match August 7, 2010. He has wrestled primarily in the Northeastern United States and Ontario, Canada. On January 6, 2019 he was involved in a serious vehicle crash along with Daniel Garcia, Kevin Blackwood and Puf. He has held the Ontario based SMASH wrestling heavyweight championship since June 2, 2019. In his home promotion Empire State Wrestling he held the Interstate Championship for 889 days! His favorite moment in wrestling was winning the ESW Heavyweight Championship, it was a title he dreamed about holding since he was a kid, "when the referee counted to three tears ran down my face in an instant."

Kevin Blackwood
5' 10" 175lbs Buffalo, New York

Record: 4 – 8
Shows wrestled on:
March 30, 2018 ***Only Fools Are Satisfied*** Westbrook Armory

July 27, 2018 *Vacationland Cup* Westbrook Armory
August 11, 2018 *2018 Hollis Pirate Festival* Hollis Fire Department
September 21, 2018 *Pretenders Beware* Westbrook Armory
November 30, 2018 *No Control* Portland Club
July 12, 2019 *2019 Vacationland Cup* Portland Club
September 06, 2019 *Know Your Enemy* Portland Expo
October 25, 2019 *Fresh Blood* AMVets Hall Yarmouth
January 24, 2020 *Flirtin' With Disaster* AMVets Hall Yarmouth
February 22, 2020 *Practice What You Preach* AMVets Hall Yarmouth
December 19, 2020 *2020 Vacationland Cup* AMVets Hall Yarmouth

Blackwood began training in 2016 in Buffalo at Grapplers Anonymous with Pepper Park, now known as the Blade in AEW. He had his first match 2016 for ESW: Empire State Wrestling. In January 2017 he made his Canadian debut for Toronto, Ontario based SMASH. He also wrestles for C*4 and

FLQ: Fédération de Lutte Québécoise spending almost more time competing in Canada than he does in the states. Stateside he spends most of his time in the Northeast region. On January 6, 2019 he was involved in a serious vehicle crash along with Daniel Garcia, Kevin Bennett and Puf driving home from a show in Montreal. Blackwood's injuries kept him out of action for nearly six months, he made his return to the ring at the *2019 Vacationland Cup* winning his first-round match and being eliminated in the finals. On November 29, 2019 he captured the C*4 Underground Championship from Jonathan Rukin and still holds the title.

Kevin Ku
5' 11" 205lbs Nashville, Tennessee

Record: 0 – 3
Shows wrestled on:
May 11, 2018 *Feed The Need* Portland Club
October 25, 2019 *Fresh Blood* AMVets Hall Yarmouth
November 29, 2019 *Twilight Zone* AMVets Hall Yarmouth

Trained at the New England Pro Wrestling Academy Ku debuted in 2014 having his first match under the name Kevin Park for IWE: Independent Wrestling Entertainment in Brewer, Maine against Ace Romero. He would stay in the Northeast until relocating to Georgia in mid-2015. He competed in the region branching out to the Midwest in 2017. In 2018 with partner Dominic Garrini he formed the tag team Violence is Forever capturing the SUP: Southern Underground Pro, PWF: Pro Wrestling Freedom BLP: Black Label Pro tag team championships. As a single he held the Dojo Pro White Belt Championship and was the PWF Heavyweight Champion for 115 days.

Kid Curry

Record: 0 – 1
Shows wrestled on:

June 23, 2019 *La Kermesse Festival Night 2* St. Louis Field Biddeford

A third-generation wrestler, his father wrestled as "Flying" Fred Curry and his grandfather was Bull Curry. His brother also wrestles as Fred Curry Jr.

Kikotaru
5' 7" 245lbs Osaka, Japan

Record: 0 – 1
Shows wrestled on:
March 17, 2017 *Hysteria* Westbrook Armory

Kikotaru debuted in 1994 in FMW and W*ING as a hardcore wrestler under his birth name. He wrestled in various promotions in Japan before taking up residency in DDT. In 2016 he moved to Las Vegas, Nevada where he currently resides.

Kimber Lee
5' 4" 126lbs Seattle, Washington

Record: 0 – 1
Shows wrestled on:
May 11, 2018 *Feed The Need* Portland Club

She trained with Drew Gulak at the Combat Zone Wrestling Academy debuting in late 2011. She wrestled around the U.S. Indies having a notable feud with "Dirty Daddy" Chris Dickinson in Beyond Wrestling. She captured the CHIKARA Grand Championship holding the title for 177 days in 2015. She signed with WWE in 2016 spending two years with the promotion with the NXT brand, her most notable exposure being in the 2017 Mae Young Classic where she advanced to the third round before being defeated by Mercedes Martinez. After leaving NXT she returned to the Indies and is currently signed with Impact Wrestling.

Kirby Wackerman

Record: 0 – 2
Shows wrestled on:
The Road Season 1 *Episodes 1 & 7* American Legion Post 84, Orono

Kobe "The Ram" Durst *"Diamond Tiger"*
5' 9" 194lbs Toronto, Ontario, Canada

Record: 0 – 1
Shows wrestled on:
November 19, 2016 **Hogwash** American Legion Post 84 Orono

Trained by Marcus Marquez he debuted in 2013 and has wrestled in the Canadian Indies and Chicago area of the United States. He held the C*4 Championship for 412 days, C*4 Underground Championship for 385 days, and is a three time Alpha-1 Champion holding the title a combined 784 days.

Konnor Hex

Record: 0 – 1
Shows wrestled on:
The Road Season 1 *Episode 3* American Legion Post 84, Orono

Kris Statlander *"The Galaxy's Greatest Alien"*
5' 9" 143lbs Andromeda Galaxy

Record: 11 – 3
Shows wrestled on:
January 19, 2018 ***The World Is Ours*** Westbrook Armory
March 30, 2018 ***Only Fools Are Satisfied*** Westbrook Armory
August 11, 2018 ***2018 Hollis Pirate Festival*** Hollis Fire Department
September 21, 2018 ***Pretenders Beware*** Westbrook Armory
November 30, 2018 ***No Control*** Portland Club
January 11, 2019 ***Snakebitten*** Westbrook Armory
March 09, 2019 ***Welcome to the Dance*** Westbrook Armory
May 10, 2019 ***Hooked on a Friedman*** Westbrook Armory
July 12, 2019 ***2019 Vacationland Cup*** Portland Club
September 06, 2019 ***Know Your Enemy*** Portland Expo

October 25, 2019 *Fresh Blood* AMVets Hall Yarmouth
November 29, 2019 *Twilight Zone* AMVets Hall Yarmouth
January 24, 2020 *Flirtin' With Disaster* AMVets Hall Yarmouth
February 22, 2020 *Practice What You Preach* AMVets Hall Yarmouth

After training to be a stuntwoman, Statlander was trained in wrestling by Pat Buck & Curt Hawkins at Create-A-Pro Wrestling Academy. She debuted in the ring in November 2016 and in just a few short years has made a tremendous name for herself. In Limitless Wrestling she is known for her on again and off again friendship and feud with Ashley Vox culminating in two no holds barred style matches where Vox got the best of Statlander both times. She has held numerous championships and is currently signed with All Elite Wrestling. She is one of the most popular wrestlers in Limitless Wrestling.

KTB *"Kyle The Beast"*
6' 1" 273lbs New Jersey

Record: 0 – 1
Shows wrestled on:
November 30, 2018 *No Control* Portland Club

KTB was trained in New Jersey by Gino Caruso at the ECPW school. He had his first match December 18, 2004. In ECPW he held the Junior Division Championship and held the Jersey Championship Wrestling Tag Team Championship. In Game Changer Wrestling he held the tag team championship with Monsta Mack and was the Heavyweight Champion for 350 days. His favorite moment in wrestling was on August 22, 2019 when he battled Daisuke Sekimoto at 1st Ring in Tokyo, Japan.

Lee Moriarty *"The Apex of Combat"*
6' 0" 183lbs Pittsburg, Pennsylvania

Record: 0 – 1
December 19, 2020 *2020 Vacationland Cup* AMVets Hall Yarmouth

Trained by Dean Raford and Brandon K he debuted in late 2015. He was a regular with the Pennsylvania based PWX: Pro Wrestling eXpress winning multiple championships in the promotion. He captured the Heavyweight Championships, Tag Team Championship, and is a two-time Three Rivers Champion. Has wrestled mostly in the Eastern United States building a steady following through 2019 - 2020. On March 6, 2021 in Hanceville, Alabama Moriarty defeated Warhorse ending his 532 day reign as the IWTV Independent Wrestling Champion.

Leyla Hirsch *"Legit"*
5' 0" 125lbs Moscow, Russia

Record: 1 – 1
Shows wrestled on:

September 06, 2019 ***Know Your Enemy*** Portland Expo
October 25, 2019 ***Fresh Blood*** AMVets Hall Yarmouth

Trained at the CZW Academy, she debuted in late 2017 at the CZW Dojo Wars. She wrestled primarily for CZW through mid-2019 when she made her Beyond debut at *Uncharted Territory* episode 14. In September 2019, one week after *Know You Enemy*, she traveled to Germany to wrestle for wXw spending over a month with the promotion competing in the *Femme Fatales 2019* tournament losing in the finals in an outstanding match with Lufisto. January 2020 saw her make her Japanese debut with World of Stardom spending two months with the promotion until the Corona Virus halted everything. In early 2021 she signed with AEW after appearing on *Dark* & *Dynamite*.

Lil Blay
5' 11" 180lbs Windsor, Nova Scotia, Canada

Record: 0 – 1
Shows wrestled on:
July 12, 2019 ***2019 Vacationland Cup*** Portland Club

Debuted in 2014 and has wrestled mostly in the Canadian Maritimes for Nova Scotia based Ultimate Championship Wrestling. Has had a few matches in Maine but has yet to break out in the United States. Is a former UCW Junior Heavyweight Tag Team and Atlantic Canada Champion.

Lince Dorado
5' 7" 170lbs San Juan, Puerto Rico

Record: 1 – 0
Shows wrestled on:
September 24, 2016 ***Past Your Bedtime*** American Legion Post 84 Orono

Dorado began training in Mexico in 2007 with El Pantera making his US debut at CHIKARA King of Trios 2007 teaming with El Pantera and Sicodelico Jr. He then trained at the Wrestle Factory. Although he wrestled across the US Indies, he stayed primarily in CHIKARA until he signed with the WWE in July 2016 after competing in the Cruiserweight Classic Tournament. His victory of Flip Gordon at *Past Your Bedtime* was Dorado's final independent match to date before going full time with the WWE.

Lio Rush
5' 6" 160lbs Washington D.C.

Record: 0 – 1
Shows wrestled on:
April 28, 2017 ***Can We Kick It?*** Portland Club

Entered the Maryland Championship Wrestling training center in 2014 and made his in-ring debut in October of that year under the name Lil Green. He had his first singles match with Joey Janela on May 6, 2015 at CZW *Dojo Wars* under the name Lennon Duffy. On December 12, 2015 at *Cage of Death XVII* Rush would defeat Janela for the CZW Wired Championship, he would pin Janela two weeks later at MCW *Season's Beatings*. In February 2016 Janela would reclaim the Wired Championship in a two out of three falls match only to drop it to Rush in a fatal four way the following month. September 10, 2016 would see Janela once again defeat Rush, this time in a ladder match for the Wired Championship. 2017 would see the two face off several more times with Rush coming out on top before he signed with the WWE and the NXT brand. He would spend 2.5 years with the company winning the Cruiserweight Championship. He was released in April 2020 and returned to the Indies losing to Janela at GCW *Homecoming* July 26, 2020 in Atlantic City, New Jersey.

Logan Black *"The King of Chaos"*
5' 11" 229lbs New York City

Record: 1 – 0
Shows wrestled on:
July 23, 2016 **Hook, Line, & Sinker** American Legion Post 84 Orono

Black began wrestling in 2010 as one half of American Nightmare with Matt Kaplan, the duo would hold the Warriors of Wrestling tag team championship for 175 days. Black has held the championships two more times with Chris Benne and Jason Sinclair as The Apostles of Chaos. A middle school teacher during the week Black wrestling primarily in the New York and Northeast region.

Love Doug
5' 6" weighing 160 Valentines hailing From the City of Love

Record: 0 – 6
Shows wrestled on:
The Road Season 1 *Episodes 2, 8, 9, & 10* American Legion Post 84, Orono

Love Doug began training June 10, 2019 with Matt Taven and Vinny Marseglia. He debuted in a pre-show triple threat match for Top Rope. When asked about his favorite moment in wrestling he responded, "wrestling Thrill Ride and having the opportunity to express my love!"

Luke Robinson *"Finely Tuned Athletic Machine" "Golden Boy"*
6' 1" 210lbs Auburn, Maine

Record: 2 – 0
Shows wrestled on:

July 23, 2016 *Hook, Line, & Sinker* American Legion Post 84 Orono
September 22, 2017 *Question The Answers* Westbrook Armory

Trained with "Mr. USA" Tony Atlas making his in-ring debut in 2005. On August 22, 2009 he defeated Apolo for the NWA OnFire Heavyweight Championship holding the title for 547 days. He wrestled primarily in Maine and New Brunswick until 2011 when he started branching out. Also, in 2011 he was cast in season 5 of WWE *Tough Enough* where he finished as the runner up, in my opinion he was robbed and should have won. After *Tough Enough* Robinson would return to the Indies leaving wrestling in December 2012. A successful personal trainer Robinson has only returned to the ring a few times for IWE, Limitless Wrestling and ¡Let's Wrestle!

M1nute Men
Record 1 - 4
Tommy Trainwreck *"Terrific"*
5' 11" 268lbs Philadelphia, Pennsylvania

Devin Blaze *"Delicious"*
5' 10" 147lbs Philadelphia, Pennsylvania

Shows wrestled on:
September 12, 2015 *Stage One* City Side Restaurant, Brewer
January 30, 2016 *Under Fire* American Legion Post 84 Orono
March 19, 2016 *Don't Fear The Sleeper* American Legion Post 84 Orono
May 28, 2016 *No Dropkicks in the Living Room* American Legion Post 84 Orono
October 29, 2016 *Who Watches the Watchmen?* The Field House at University of Maine Orono

Both men debuted in 2010 wrestling primarily in the New England region and only wrestling occasionally as a singles wrestler. They first teamed together in November 2010 winning the NWA Onfire Tag Team Championships in June 2012 holding the titles for 183 days, the duos only tag team gold. Both would leave wrestling in 2017, last teaming together in Lucky Pro Wrestling in April 2017. Blaze returned to the ring in January 2020.

Mac Daniels *"The Main Attraction"*
6' 3" 225lbs Boca Raton, Florida

Record: 1 – 2
Shows wrestled on:
June 22, 2019 ***La Kermesse Festival Night 1*** St. Louis Field Biddeford
December 19, 2020 **2020 VACATIONLAND CUP** AMVets Yarmouth, Maine

Daniels began training at the Limitless Dojo in November 2018. He made his in-ring debut in March 2019 in a battle royal and his singles debut in April 2019. He took on Jon Alba as an adviser in

May 2019. He recently scored a victory over Love Doug during the *Double Vision* pre-show. Has a very bright future in the world of professional wrestling.

Maddison Miles
5' 5" 141lbs Halifax, Nova Scotia, Canada

Record: 1 – 0
Shows wrestled on:
March 30, 2018 ***Only Fools Are Satisfied*** Westbrook Armory

Trained by Gary Williams, Miles debuted while still in high school in 2015. Began her career primarily in the Canadian Maritimes for the first couple years. Made her first UK tour in February 2018, and her US debut March 30, 2018 at *Only Fools Are Satisfied*. Was on the 2018 Canadian Wrestling Elite Spring Death Tour wrestling 20 matches in 21 days in 20 different towns. In September 2018 she debuted in Mexico with LLF and returned to the UK in October. Returned to CWE for their 10th anniversary Death Tour in 2019 wrestling 31 matches in 31 days in 31 different towns.
In May 2019 she traveled to England for two months making her wrestling debut in Germany and Austria during that time. She moved to England in October 2019 returning to Canada in mid-2020. She is a two-time Dynamic Over The Top Action Wrestling Women's champion holding the title for all but one day since October 27, 2018. She is also a former Maritime Women's Champion, CWF Champion, and co-holder of the Germany based Power of Wrestling Women's Tag Team Championship. In April 2020 she was honored as the Cauliflower Alley Club Rising Star Award.

Maine State Posse: DangerKid
5' 11" 180lbs The Great State of Maine

Record: 23 – 17

Shows wrestled on:
January 30, 2016 *Under Fire* American Legion Post 84 Orono
March 19, 2016 *Don't Fear The Sleeper* American Legion Post 84 Orono
May 28, 2016 *No Dropkicks in the Living Room* American Legion Post 84 Orono
July 23, 2016 *Hook, Line, & Sinker* American Legion Post 84 Orono
September 24, 2016 *Past Your Bedtime* American Legion Post 84 Orono
October 07, 2016 *Risk It For The Biscuit* Westbrook Armory
October 29, 2016 *Who Watches the Watchmen?* The Field House at University of Maine Orono

November 19, 2016 *Hogwash* American Legion Post 84 Orono
January 27, 2017 *Unreal* Westbrook Armory
February 25, 2017 *Do What You Love, Fuck The Rest-Fest* American Legion Post 84 Orono
March 17, 2017 *Hysteria* Westbrook Armory
April 28, 2017 *Can We Kick It?* Portland Club
May 13, 2017 *Problematic* Westbrook Armory

June 23, 2017 *La Kermesse Festival Night 1* St. Louis Field Biddeford
July 21, 2017 *Nothing Gold Can Stay* Westbrook Armory
September 22, 2017 *Question The Answers* Westbrook Armory
November 03, 2017 *Hybrid Moments* Portland Club
January 19, 2018 *The World Is Ours* Westbrook Armory
March 30, 2018 *Only Fools Are Satisfied* Westbrook Armory
July 27, 2018 *Vacationland Cup* Westbrook Armory
August 11, 2018 *2018 Hollis Pirate Festival* Hollis Fire Department
September 08, 2018 *2018 Litchfield Fair*
September 21, 2018 *Pretenders Beware* Westbrook Armory
November 30, 2018 *No Control* Portland Club
January 11, 2019 *Snakebitten* Westbrook Armory
March 09, 2019 *Welcome to the Dance* Westbrook Armory
May 10, 2019 *Hooked on a Friedman* Westbrook Armory
June 22, 2019 *La Kermesse Festival Night 1* St. Louis Field Biddeford
July 12, 2019 *2019 Vacationland Cup* Portland Club
September 06, 2019 *Know Your Enemy* Portland Expo
October 25, 2019 *Fresh Blood* AMVets Hall Yarmouth
November 29, 2019 *Twilight Zone* AMVets Hall Yarmouth
January 24, 2020 *Flirtin' With Disaster* AMVets Hall Yarmouth
February 22, 2020 *Practice What You Preach* AMVets Hall Yarmouth
The Road Season 1 *Episodes 1, 3, 4, & 11* American Legion Post 84, Orono
December 19, 2020 *2020 Vacationland Cup* AMVets Hall Yarmouth

DangerKid's wrestling career began in October 2014 when he started training with Eric Johnson and IWE: Independent Wrestling Entertainment. He had his first match in April 2015 under a mask as Skully, one half of the tag team the Fog in Island Falls, Maine against the tag team The Defiance. The other man under the hood in The Fog was none other than Aiden Aggro, known as

Humerus. They began training together and naturally fit as a tag team together. As The Fog they held the IWE Tag Team Championships for 90 days from May to August 2016. In IWE he

also competed under the name Levi Lexington capturing the Juniorweight Championship holding it for 188 days in 2016, the same time he held the tag titles. Incidentally Aggro was wrestling as Aumon Jordan in IWE and held the Maine State Championship while they held the tag championships. He also held the IWE Heavyweight Championship.

He made his Limitless debut as a cameraman at *Killin' & Thrillin'* accidentally costing Alexander Lee the Scramble Match. His feud with Lee involved them teaming together, then breaking up with Lee bringing Aggro in as Lee's partner. At *Hook, Line, & Sinker* Kid defeated Lee in a Fans Bring the Weapons Match that solidified Kid's and Aggro's partnership as the Maine State Posse. Lee would join them, and the trio would stay together until Lee turned on them at the *2019 Vacationland Cup*.

The Maine State Posse have traveled to promotions in the Northeast Region of the United States becoming two-time tag team champions in both Chaotic Wrestling and Northeast Championship Wrestling. January 17, 2020, they made their Canadian debut challenging Le Tabarnak de Team for the C*4 Tag team Championships in Ottawa, Ontario, Canada. In February they returned to Canada for SMASH in Toronto, Ontario. As a team their biggest victory to date came on January 24, 2020 at Limitless Wrestling *Flirtin' With Disaster* they defeated the Impact Wrestling World Tag Team Champions: The North: Ethan Page and Josh Alexander in a non-title match up.

The Posse are staples of Limitless Wrestling and its sister promotion ¡Let's Wrestle! No other tag team has competed in more matches in Limitless than the Maine State Posse.

Maine State Posse: Aiden Aggro *"The Pine Prince"*
5' 11" 207lbs The Great State of Maine

Record: 19 – 13
Shows wrestled on:
March 19, 2016 **Don't Fear The Sleeper** American Legion Post 84 Orono
May 28, 2016 **No Dropkicks in the Living Room** American Legion Post 84 Orono
July 23, 2016 **Hook, Line, & Sinker** American Legion Post 84 Orono
September 24, 2016 **Past Your Bedtime** American Legion Post 84 Orono
October 07, 2016 **Risk It For The Biscuit** Westbrook Armory
October 29, 2016 **Who Watches the Watchmen?** The Field House at University of Maine Orono
November 19, 2016 **Hogwash** American Legion Post 84 Orono
January 27, 2017 **Unreal** Westbrook Armory
February 25, 2017 **Do What You Love, Fuck The Rest-Fest** American Legion Post 84 Orono
March 17, 2017 **Hysteria** Westbrook Armory

April 28, 2017 *Can We Kick It?* Portland Club
May 13, 2017 *Problematic* Westbrook Armory
June 23, 2017 *La Kermesse Festival Night 1* St. Louis Field Biddeford
July 21, 2017 *Nothing Gold Can Stay* Westbrook Armory
September 22, 2017 *Question The Answers* Westbrook Armory
January 19, 2018 *The World Is Ours* Westbrook Armory
March 30, 2018 *Only Fools Are Satisfied* Westbrook Armory
July 27, 2018 *Vacationland Cup* Westbrook Armory
August 11, 2018 *2018 Hollis Pirate Festival* Hollis Fire Department

September 08, 2018 *2018 Litchfield Fair*
September 21, 2018 *Pretenders Beware* Westbrook Armory
November 30, 2018 *No Control* Portland Club
January 11, 2019 *Snakebitten* Westbrook Armory
March 09, 2019 *Welcome to the Dance* Westbrook Armory
May 10, 2019 *Hooked on a Friedman* Westbrook Armory
June 22, 2019 *La Kermesse Festival Night 1* St. Louis Field Biddeford
July 12, 2019 *2019 Vacationland Cup* Portland Club
September 06, 2019 *Know Your Enemy* Portland Expo

October 25, 2019 *Fresh Blood* AMVets Hall Yarmouth
November 29, 2019 *Twilight Zone* AMVets Hall Yarmouth
January 24, 2020 *Flirtin' With Disaster* AMVets Hall Yarmouth
February 22, 2020 *Practice What You Preach* AMVets Hall Yarmouth
December 19, 2020 *2020 Vacationland Cup* AMVets Hall Yarmouth

He began his training in 2014 with Eric Johnson and the IWE: Independent Wrestling Entertainment. He debuted as Humerus one half of the tag team The Fog with his partner Skully, now known as DangerKid. While competing in the IWE the duo held the Tag Team Championships as The Fog. He also wrestled for the promotion as Aumon Jordan where he was managed by Jon Alba and held the Maine State Championship for 189 days. He held the Tag Team and Maine State Championships simultaneously while his partner was the Juniorweight Champion. As Aiden Aggro he held the IWE Heavyweight Championship for 133 days.

He made his Limitless Wrestling debut as the partner of Alexander Lee who was feuding with DangerKid. However, at *Hook, Line, & Sinker* he showed his allegiance to DangerKid aiding him in his Fans Bring The Weapons Match with Alexander Lee.

The Maine State Posse have traveled to promotions in the Northeast Region of the United States becoming two-time tag team champions in both Chaotic Wrestling and Northeast Championship Wrestling. January 17, 2020, they made their Canadian debut challenging Le Tabarnak de Team for the C*4 Tag team Championships in Ottawa, Ontario, Canada. In February they returned to Canada for SMASH in Toronto, Ontario. As a team their biggest victory to date came on January 24, 2020 at Limitless Wrestling *Flirtin' With Disaster* they defeated the Impact Wrestling World Tag Team Champions: The North: Ethan Page and Josh Alexander in a non-title match up.

The Posse are staples of Limitless Wrestling and its sister promotion ¡Let's Wrestle!. No other tag team has competed in more matches in Limitless than the Maine State Posse.

Mance Warner
6' 1" 215lbs Bucksnort, Tennessee

Record: 0 – 1
Shows wrestled on:
May 10, 2019 **Hooked on a Friedman** Westbrook Armory

Trained by Billy Roc he debuted in 2015 mostly wrestling in the Indiana area including IWA-Mid South where he captured the Heavyweight Championship twice and held the tag team titles. He made his CZW debut in May 2018 losing in the Tournament of Death semifinals to Jimmy Lloyd. In December 2018 at Cage of Death XX he defeated Rickey Shane Page for the vacant CZW World championship in the Cage of Death. He would hold the title for 125 days losing it at Best of the Best 18 in a fatal four way to

Anthony Greene. He is now a regular for Game Changer Wrestling.

Manny Martinez *"Macho" "El Jefe"*
5' 8" 170lbs Tijuana, Mexico

Record: 0 – 3
Shows wrestled on:
February 25, 2017 ***Do What You Love, Fuck The Rest-Fest*** American Legion Post 84 Orono
April 28, 2017 ***Can We Kick It?*** Portland Club
August 11, 2018 ***2018 Hollis Pirate Festival*** Hollis Fire Department

Record show matches for Martinez as far back as 2009 for NYWC: New York Wrestling Connection. He has wrestled primarily in New York but has spent time in the Carolina's where he captured the NWA Mid-Atlantic Junior Heavyweight Championship for 29 days in 2017. In 2019 he held the New Jersey based Star-Pro Wrestling Junior Heavyweight Championships for 42 days.

Marcus Hall *"Mourning Star"*
5' 11" 235lbs Bridgeport, Connecticut

Record: 0 – 1
Shows wrestled on:
September 12, 2015 ***Stage One*** City Side Restaurant, Brewer

Trained at Rampage Pro Wrestling in Maine and debuted with the company. He was the first ever Rampage Pro Wrestling champion defeating Psycho Mike in a tournament final. He would go on to hold the title three times for a combined 569 days. He wrestled extensively in Maine for various promotions and in Vermont for Slam All-Star Wrestling. Moved to Florida in 2006 for two years before returning to Maine. While he was there, he won the ACE Tag Team titles with Legion Cage and won the FPWA

Heavyweight Championship. It appears his final match was at Stage One in a losing effort to Christian Casanova.

Mark Moment *"Tower of Power"*
6' 1" 205lbs Miami Beach

Record: 0 – 0 – 1
Shows wrestled on:
October 29, 2016 ***Who Watches the Watchmen?*** The Field House at University of Maine Orono
A Maine native, Moment trained at the Chaotic Wrestling Center debuting in 2005. Shortly after his debut he had his first tour of Nova Scotia, Canada for MainStream Wrestling. Wrestled on the NWA 57th Anniversary Show at the Tennessee State Fairgrounds in Nashville losing to Jason Rumble. He wrestled for nearly every promotion in Maine winning championships in the NAWA, NWH, IWE, Maine Event Wrestling and more. As the MEW Champion he wrestled AJ Styles to a time limit draw. In 2010, 2011, & 2012 he wrestled three matches against Eddie Edwards coming up short in 2010 for the Ring of Honor World Championship, and in 2011 for the Ring of Honor World Television Championship. However, in 2012 Moment defeated Edwards in a Fans Bring the Weapons Match. All three of these matches took place in Fairfield, Maine at the Community Center for IWE. His last match to date is a no contest at *Who Watches The Watchmen* against Champ Mathews.

Mark Sterling *"Smart"*
5' 11" 200lbs Long Island, New York

Record: 3 – 5
Shows wrestled on:
November 19, 2016 ***Hogwash*** American Legion Post 84 Orono
June 24, 2017 ***La Kermesse Festival Night 2*** St. Louis Field Biddeford
September 22, 2017 ***Question The Answers*** Westbrook Armory
January 19, 2018 ***The World Is Ours*** Westbrook Armory

March 09, 2019 *Welcome to the Dance* Westbrook Armory
June 22, 2019 *La Kermesse Festival Night 1* St. Louis Field Biddeford
July 12, 2019 *2019 Vacationland Cup* Portland Club
February 22, 2020 *Practice What You Preach* AMVets Hall Yarmouth

Sterling debuted in 2001 and has trained and been affiliated with the Create-A-Pro Wrestling Academy since its inception. He even held the CAP Championship for 280 days in 2017. He has wrestled or managed in the Northeast region for the majority of his career. Is a co-host on the Major Figure Podcast with Matt Cardona and Brian Myers. Most recently was featured on AEW as MJF's lawyer and was defeated by Jon Moxley in five minutes on the September 2, 2020 edition of Dynamite.

Martin Stone *"The Enforcer" "The Guvnor"*
6' 0" 189lbs London, England

Record: 1 – 1
Shows wrestled on:
January 19, 2018 *The World Is Ours* Westbrook Armory
March 30, 2018 *Only Fools Are Satisfied* Westbrook Armory

Now known as Danny Burch in the WWE, Stone debuted in 2002 after training at the FWA Academy. For the next several years he wrestled across Europe until he was signed by the WWE in 2011 assigned to Florida Championship Wrestling in 2012. He was released in 2014 and returned to the UK scene. In 2014 he was on the second season of TNA British Boot Camp but did not win. In April 2018 he returned full time to NXT. He has won numerous championships around the world including the wXw Tag Team Championships for 371 days, 1PW Heavyweight Championship for 681 days and more.

Masha Slamovich *"Russian Dynamite"*
5' 3" 136lbs Moscow, Russia

Record: 1 – 1
Shows wrestled on:
October 25, 2019 **Fresh Blood** AMVets Hall Yarmouth
November 29, 2019 **Twilight Zone** AMVets Hall Yarmouth

Trained by Johnny Rodz and Amazing Red she debuted in 2016. She also trained in Japan with Chigusa Nagayo during her time there. She has wrestled primarily in the Eastern United States and in Canadian Maritimes. She has been in Japan since February 2020 wrestling for Marvelous, Wave, Ice Ribbon, Sendai Girls and other joshi promotions. She returned to the States after a year abroad returning to Limitless Wrestling for Season 3 of The Road.

Matt Cross *"M-Dogg 20"*
5' 7" 183lbs Cleveland, Ohio

Record: 1 – 2
Shows wrestled on:
November 03, 2017 **Hybrid Moments** Portland Club
January 19, 2018 **The World Is Ours** Westbrook Armory
September 21, 2018 **Pretenders Beware** Westbrook Armory

Trained by JT Lightning he debuted in 1999. Won the IWA Mid-South Heavyweight Championship in 2002 defeating Chris Hero. Cross has wrestled around the world in over two dozen countries winning championships along the way too numerous to mention them all. He has competed in promotions such as PWG, Ring of Honor, Lucha Underground, AIW and more. He was cast in the 2011 WWE *Tough Enough* series but was eliminated early on in the competition.

Matt Knicks *"Marvelous"*
5' 8" 165lbs Bridgeview, Illinois

Record: 0 – 1
Shows wrestled on:
March 17, 2017 *Hysteria* Westbrook Armory

Debuted in March 2010 and has trained with several people including Steve Boz. Has wrestled mostly in the Midwest region for various, specifically Illinois, for the majority of his career winning a few tag team championships.

Matt Sydal *"Air" "Reborn"*
5' 9" 165lbs St. Louis, Missouri

Record: 1 – 0
Shows wrestled on:
March 17, 2017 *Hysteria* Westbrook Armory

Sydal debuted in October 2000 and has wrestled around the world for some of the biggest promotions in the world winning championships in the WWE, Ring of Honor, Impact, New Japan Pro Wrestling and other promotions. Considered to be one of the most innovative highflyers in wrestling and a master of the shooting star press.

Matthew Justice *"Thrash" "One Man Militia"*
6' 0" 220lbs Middlefield, Ohio

Record: 0 – 1
Shows wrestled on:
October 25, 2019 *Fresh Blood* AMVets Hall Yarmouth

Justice debuted in 2006 after training with JT Lightning in Ohio. He wrestled across the US Indies until he was signed by the WWE in March 2011. He was assigned to Florida Championship Wrestling until he was released in September of the same year. Justice returned to the Indies winning championships in

NYWC, PWX, and AIW amongst others. In recent years he has adopted the hardcore style of wrestling and attempts to jump off the highest point he can during is matches. He is also not a believer in CTE's.

Max Caster *"The Tweener"*
5' 11" 224lbs Long Island, New York

Record: 1 – 2
Shows wrestled on:
August 11, 2018 *2018 Hollis Pirate Festival* Hollis Fire Department
March 09, 2019 *Welcome to the Dance* Westbrook Armory
June 23, 2019 *La Kermesse Festival Night 2* St. Louis Field Biddeford

A product of the Create-A-Pro Academy, he debuted in 2015. He is one third of The Shook Crew with Bryce Donovan & Bobby Orlando. He held the CAP Tag Team Champion with Bobby Orlando. He also held the CAP Championship on two occasions holding the title for a combined 355 days. The trio is well known for their Diss Tracks about upcoming opponents. In late 2020 he signed with AEW and has made several appearances on AEW Dark. In AEW he formed the tag team The Acclaimed with Anthony Bowens.

Max Smashmaster *"Personification of Annihilation"*
6' 4" 352lbs Boston, Massachusetts

Record: 1 – 2
Shows wrestled on:
November 15, 2015 *Killin' & Thrillin* American Legion Post 84 Orono
July 23, 2016 *Hook, Line, & Sinker* American Legion Post 84 Orono
January 27, 2017 *Unreal* Westbrook Armory

Smashmaster debuted in 2004 after being trained by Steve Bradley wrestling under the name The Shane and then later Sebastian Reese. In 2012 now known as Max Smashmaster, he and Blaster McMassive teamed up to form Devastation Corporation with manager Sydney Bakabella. In 2013 Flex Rumblecrunch joined the group. The group would win CHIKARA's Campeonatos de Parejas holding the titles for 295 days. Smashmaster took a hiatus from wrestling in 2017 but only in the ring. Through 2019 you can hear his voice providing commentary on the Limitless Wrestling home video releases.

Maximum Mecca
5' 2" 110lbs Waterbury, Connecticut

Record: 1 – 0
Shows wrestled on:
November 15, 2015 ***Killin' & Thrillin*** American Legion Post 84 Orono

Trained by Kevin Landry she debuted in wrestling in 2011 outside the ring as a valet and then later stepped in the ring in 2015. Wrestling in the New England region she feuded with Davienne over the LPW Women's Championship but was unable to capture the championship.

Megabyte Ronnie
6' 4" 225lbs Buffalo, New York

Record: 1 – 0
December 19, 2020 ***2020 Vacationland Cup*** AMVets Hall Yarmouth

Ronnie Hartman is a veteran and former competitive eater. He started training in Buffalo in 2018. He has quickly made a name for himself on the Northeast Indie scene, even making his AEW debut in September 2020 against Brian Cage. In the world of competitive eating he has participated in several events including appearing multiple times in the World Famous 4th of July Nathan's Famous Franks Hot Dog Eating Contest. In 2019 he finished in 11th place with 28.5 hotdogs and buns in ten minutes. In 2018 he finished 21st with 21 hotdogs and buns in ten minutes.

Michael Elgin *"Unbreakable"*
5' 11" 245lbs Oshawa, Ontario, Canada

Record: 0 – 1
Shows wrestled on:
April 28, 2017 ***Can We Kick It?*** Portland Club

Debuted in 2004 trained with Joe E. Legend, Tyson Dux, and others. Has wrestled around the world and across the US Indies with runs in-ring of Honor, Impact, CMLL, New Japan Pro Wrestling and Pro Wrestling NOAH. He is a former ROH World Champion as well as holding the IWGP Intercontinental and NEVER Openweight championships as well as several other titles.

Mick Moretti *"The Rapscallion"*
5' 11" 187lbs Australia

Record: 1 – 1
Shows wrestled on:
June 24, 2017 ***La Kermesse Festival Night 2*** St. Louis Field Biddeford
September 21, 2018 ***Pretenders Beware*** Westbrook Armory

Debuted in 2009 and wrestles primarily in his native Australia however he has had a couple extended tours of the United States. Former two-time Pro Wrestling Australia heavyweight and tag team champion. Held the tag titles for a combined 859 days.

Mike Bennett
5' 11" 224lbs Boston, Massachusetts

Record: 1 – 0
Shows wrestled on:
September 24, 2016 *Past Your Bedtime* American Legion Post 84 Orono

Trained by Steve Bradley and "Brutal" Bob Evans, Bennett began his in-ring career in 2002. He wrestled across the US Indies making his ROH debut in 2008. He along with Matt Taven and his wife Maria would form The Kingdom and in 2015 captured both the ROH and IWGP World Tag Team Championships. He joined Impact Wrestling in 2016 for about a year then signed with WWE in April 2017. His three years with the promotion were lackluster at best starting on Raw brand then moving to 205 live, he is a two-time WWE 24/7 Champion.

Mike Gamble *"American Sumo"*
6' 0" 352lbs Hilo, Hawaii

Record: 2 – 1
Shows wrestled on:
January 27, 2017 *Unreal* Westbrook Armory
June 24, 2017 *La Kermesse Festival Night 2* St. Louis Field Biddeford
September 22, 2017 *Question The Answers* Westbrook Armory

Began his training with Mike Bennett, Matt Taven, & Vinny Marseglia on October 12, 2015. Got his start in Limitless Wrestling managing Tyler Nitro at *Past Your Bedtime* making his in-ring debut. He is a two-time Pioneer Valley Promotions tag team champion, his first reign with Dexter Loux and second with "Cold Steel" Chuck O'Neil. His favorite moment in wrestling came on July 14, 2018 in Troy, New York for Northeast Wrestling when he had the opportunity to wrestle one of his heroes "Hacksaw" Jim Duggan.

Mike Graca *"The Mind Eraser"*
6' 0" 202lbs Cranston, Rhode Island

Record: 3 – 8
Shows wrestled on:
July 23, 2016 ***Hook, Line, & Sinker*** American Legion Post 84 Orono
September 24, 2016 ***Past Your Bedtime*** American Legion Post 84 Orono
October 07, 2016 ***Risk It For The Biscuit*** Westbrook Armory
October 29, 2016 ***Who Watches the Watchmen?*** The Field House at University of Maine Orono
November 19, 2016 ***Hogwash*** American Legion Post 84 Orono
January 27, 2017 ***Unreal*** Westbrook Armory
February 25, 2017 ***Do What You Love, Fuck The Rest-Fest*** American Legion Post 84 Orono
March 17, 2017 ***Hysteria*** Westbrook Armory
May 13, 2017 ***Problematic*** Westbrook Armory
June 23, 2017 ***La Kermesse Festival Night 1*** St. Louis Field Biddeford
July 21, 2017 ***Nothing Gold Can Stay*** Westbrook Armory

Debuted in 2011 and spent the majority of his career in the New England territory. Made a grand entrance at *Unreal* entering the Westbrook Armory out of the back of an ambulance in a straitjacket.

Mike Law *"The Colossal"*
6' 7" 163lbs Ozone Park, New York

Record: 0 – 1
Shows wrestled on:

August 11, 2018 ***2018 Hollis Pirate Festival*** Hollis Fire Department

Trained with Lowlife Louie and others he debuted in 2001 wrestling in the New York and Northeast region. Held the World-1 Television Championship for 350 days.

Mike McCarthy *"Masshole"*

Record: 0 – 1
Shows wrestled on:
August 11, 2018 ***2018 Hollis Pirate Festival*** Hollis Fire Department

Mikey Webb
5' 10" 207lbs Clinton, Massachusetts

Record: 0 – 3
Shows wrestled on:
October 07, 2016 ***Risk It For The Biscuit*** Westbrook Armory
January 27, 2017 ***Unreal*** Westbrook Armory
April 28, 2017 ***Can We Kick It?*** Portland Club

Based in New England his first match of record I can find was in 2011, his last in 2018. He was a regular for Chaotic Wrestling winning the New England and Tag Team Championship with Donovan Dijak as The American Destroyers. In Lucky Pro Wrestling he won the Heavyweight Championship holding it for 294 days.

Mistress Belmont
5' 6" 135lbs Portland, Maine

Record: 0 – 1
Shows wrestled on:

March 19, 2016 *Don't Fear The Sleeper* American Legion Post 84 Orono

Belmont debuted in 2004 after training with Steve Bradley had stayed primarily in the New England territory where, for a time, she was the top women's wrestler. She is a three-time NECW Women's Champion holding the crown for 960 combined days, three-time IWE Women's Champion for a combined 884 days, two-time Chaotic Wrestling Women's champion, and she has held other championships as well.

MJF: Maxwell Jacob Friedman
5' 11" 226lbs Plainview, Long Island, New York

Record: 8 – 2
Shows wrestled on:
March 17, 2017 *Hysteria* Westbrook Armory
July 21, 2017 *Nothing Gold Can Stay* Westbrook Armory
September 22, 2017 *Question The Answers* Westbrook Armory
November 03, 2017 *Hybrid Moments* Portland Club
January 19, 2018 *The World Is Ours* Westbrook Armory
March 30, 2018 *Only Fools Are Satisfied* Westbrook Armory

January 11, 2019 *Snakebitten* Westbrook Armory
March 09, 2019 *Welcome to the Dance* Westbrook Armory
May 10, 2019 *Hooked on a Friedman* Westbrook Armory
September 06, 2019 *Know Your Enemy* Portland Expo

Trained at Create-A-Pro Wrestling Academy MJF debuted in 2015 and in the last five years has become one of the fastest rising stars in all of wrestling. He has wrestled across the US Indies in the United Kingdom and Canada. Some of the championships he has won include the CZW Wired and World Championship, MLW Tag Team & Middleweight Champion, and was the first Limitless Wrestling World Champion. He held the championship for 181 days defending it successfully twice, once in London, England against "Superbad" Kid Sabian. MJF is currently signed with All Elite Wrestling and is in the faction Pinnacle.

Mr. Grim *"Hitman for Hire"*
5' 10" 270lbs Washington D.C.

Record: 3 – 5
Shows wrestled on:
February 25, 2017 ***Do What You Love, Fuck The Rest-Fest*** American Legion Post 84 Orono
March 17, 2017 ***Hysteria*** Westbrook Armory
April 28, 2017 ***Can We Kick It?*** Portland Club
May 13, 2017 ***Problematic*** Westbrook Armory
July 21, 2017 ***Nothing Gold Can Stay*** Westbrook Armory
September 22, 2017 ***Question The Answers*** Westbrook Armory
January 19, 2018 ***The World Is Ours*** Westbrook Armory
January 11, 2019 ***Snakebitten*** Westbrook Armory

Trained by Matt Wyld, Grim debuted in 2013 wrestling up and down the Eastern seaboard ever since. He's known for placing his defeated opponents in a body bag and carrying them to the back after the match. He recently wrestled a match on AEW Dark losing to Wardlow by referee's decision.

Myron Reed *"Hot Fire"*
6' 0" 172lbs Louisville, Kentucky

Record: 0 – 3
Shows wrestled on:
May 11, 2018 ***Feed The Need*** Portland Club
November 29, 2019 ***Twilight Zone*** AMVets Hall Yarmouth
February 22, 2020 ***Practice What You Preach*** AMVets Hall Yarmouth

Began his in-ring career in Ohio Valley Wrestling and has wrestled mostly in the Mid-Western United States region. Held the MLW Middleweight Championship for 355 days, a former two-time IWA-Midsouth Tag Team champion and has held numerous other titles. He is a member of the Rascalz with Trey Miguel, Desmond Xavier, and Zachary Wentz

Nick McKenna *"Flash"*
5' 7" 203lbs Scarborough, Maine

Record: 1 – 0
Shows wrestled on:
October 07, 2016 ***Risk It For The Biscuit*** Westbrook Armory

McKenna began his wrestling journey training with wrestling veteran "Cousin" Larry Huntley in the summer of 2001 in the former Maine based Eastern Wrestling Alliance. He had his first match on December 8, 2001 in Saco, Maine wrestling in fatal four way against Tim Kilgore, Romeo St. Clair, and the winner of the match Johnny Curtis, now known as Fandango in the WWE. In the EWA he held the Tag Team Championships with Cueball for 140 days. He also held the Maine based PWA: Pro Wrestling America New England Championship on two occasions. He has wrestled for most of the Maine wrestling promotions over his 19-year career. His favorite moment to date was in 2014, he made his return to the ring after a five-year hiatus "I received an overwhelming response from the crowd. It was a moment I'll never forget."

Nick Stapp *"Baby Girl"*

Record: 2 – 4
Shows wrestled on:
June 24, 2017 ***La Kermesse Festival Night 2*** St. Louis Field Biddeford
June 23, 2019 ***La Kermesse Festival Night 2*** St. Louis Field Biddeford
The Road Season 1 *Episodes 3, 7, 9, & 11* American Legion Post 84, Orono

Formerly known as CPA, Stapp trained at Create-A-Pro Wrestling Academy, holding their tag team championship with Francis

Kipland Stevens for 274 days. Began wrestling in 2013 and has stayed in the Northeast region.

Nico Silva *"Rhode Island Lion"*
5' 10" 234lbs Newport, Rhode Island

Record: 0 – 3
Shows wrestled on:
July 27, 2018 ***Vacationland Cup*** Westbrook Armory
September 08, 2018 ***2018 Litchfield Fair***
June 22, 2019 ***La Kermesse Festival Night 1*** St. Louis Field Biddeford

New England based grappler that was a regular in Top Rope Promotions from 2016 to 2017. He is also a long standing regular in Pioneer Valley Pro wrestling.

Oleg the Usurper
6' 4" 249lbs Mt. Pulpit Haven

Record: 0 – 1
Shows wrestled on:
March 17, 2017 ***Hysteria*** Westbrook Armory

Making his start in 2008 with CLASH Wrestling in Michigan as Josh Thor. Joined up with CHIKARA's Wrestling is…. division in 2012 as Oleg the Usurper. Joined The Wrecking Crew with Jaka and Blaster McMassive. Has challenged for the Grand Championship on multiple occasions coming up short each time.

Ophidian *"Master of Snake Style"*
5' 7" 165lbs The 36th Chamber

Record: 0 – 1
Shows wrestled on:
January 11, 2019 ***Snakebitten*** Westbrook Armory

Trained at the CHIKARA Wrestle Factory he debuted in 2007 and primarily stayed in the promotion until he started branching out in earnest in 2019. Challenged Warhorse for the IWTV Independent Wrestling Championship in December 2019. Defeated Mike Quackenbush on February 29, 2020 at Stem The Hemorrhaging Of Polka at CHIKARA's last event.

Oswald Project
Height (Holds up hand) this tall, over 100lbs from A Petri Dish in Wyoming

Record: 0 – 3
Shows wrestled on:
November 29, 2019 ***Twilight Zone*** AMVets Hall Yarmouth
January 24, 2020 ***Flirtin' With Disaster*** AMVets Hall Yarmouth
February 22, 2020 ***Practice What You Preach*** AMVets Hall Yarmouth

Self-taught in the art of dancing his first match was Pizza Party Wrestling April 3, 2019 defeating Ezekiel James. December 21, 2019 Project wrestled Demorest with the stipulation that if Demorest won, Project would not be allowed to contact or even look at Demorest again. If Project won, Demorest would become his friend forever. They are now known as the tag team Good Friends Forever.

Owen Brody *"The O Bro"*
5' 9" 205lbs

Record: 1 – 2
Shows wrestled on:
September 12, 2015 ***Stage One*** City Side Restaurant, Brewer
October 07, 2016 ***Risk It For The Biscuit*** Westbrook Armory
April 28, 2017 ***Can We Kick It?*** Portland Club

The O Bro began training part time in 2004 but didn't have his first match until 2007. In Maine he's a regular with NAWA and ¡Let's Wrestle! with his Syndicate Partner B.A. Tatum. His favorite moment in wrestling was a Hair vs. Hair match against DangerKid at Geno's in Portland, Maine, "at one point the crowd was screaming so loud that my ears rang."

Paris Van Dale
5' 5" 135lbs Newport, Rhode Island

Record: 0 – 4
Shows wrestled on:
The Road Season 1 *Episodes 2, 6, 7, & 10* American Legion Post 84, Orono

Van Dale began training in mid-2018 at the New England Pro Wrestling Academy. She had her first match on March 15, 2020 at the WSU: Women's Superstars United *13th Anniversary Show* in Voorhees Township, New Jersey. With Basic Becca in her corner she scored a victory over Doink The Clown. Her favorite moment in wrestling today was teaming with Armani Kayos as The Higher Society against Anthony Greene and Ava Everett on Episode 6 in Season one of The Road.

Pat Buck *"The Buzzkiller"*
6' 0" 221lbs Queens, New York

Record: 0 – 2
Shows wrestled on:
March 09, 2019 *Welcome to the Dance* Westbrook Armory
May 10, 2019 *Hooked on a Friedman* Westbrook Armory

Debuting in 2003 with NYWC and later NECW he moved to Ohio in 2005 to train at OVW. He wrestled exclusively for OVW for the next four years capturing the OVW Southern Tag Team Championships twice. In 2009 he returned to NYWC however worked as a referee for Florida Championship Wrestling into 2010. In 2012 he opened Create-A-Pro Wrestling Academy and has trained some of the current top stars in wrestling including MJF & Kris Statlander. He is currently a road agent for the WWE.

Paul London
5'10" 180lbs Austin, Texas

Record: 1 – 0
Shows wrestled on:
May 13, 2017 ***Problematic*** Westbrook Armory

Trained at Shawn Michaels Texas Wrestling Academy along with Daniel Bryan, Lance Cade, Brian Kendrick, Milano Collection AT and others, he debuted in 2000. London has wrestled around the world and across the US Indies. He is a former three-time WWE Tag Team Champion and also held the Cruiserweight championships. He is an innovative highflyer known for his 450 splash and dropsault. He is currently working as a road agent for Impact Wrestling.

Penelope Ford *"The Bad Girl"*
5' 4" 119lbs Philadelphia, Pennsylvania

Record: 0 – 2
Shows wrestled on:
March 30, 2018 ***Only Fools Are Satisfied*** Westbrook Armory
November 30, 2018 ***No Control*** Portland Club

Trained at the CZW Dojo she debuted in 2014. She wrestled in the New York and New Jersey region until 2017 when she started branching out. Worked as the valet and sometimes partner of Joey Janela but is now with Kip Sabian. Signed with All Elite Wrestling in January 2019.

Pepper Parks *"The Blade"*
6'0" 220lbs Buffalo, New York

Record: 2 – 3
Shows wrestled on:
January 11, 2019 **Snakebitten** Westbrook Armory
March 09, 2019 **Welcome to the Dance** Westbrook Armory
July 12, 2019 **2019 Vacationland Cup** Portland Club
September 06, 2019 **Know Your Enemy** Portland Expo
October 25, 2019 **Fresh Blood** AMVets Hall Yarmouth

Trained by Less Thatcher he debuted in 2000 for the Heartland Wrestling Association wrestling with the promotion through 2006 capturing their Tag Team, Cruiserweight, and two-time Heavyweight Champion. Wrestled for Ring of Honor and Combat Zone wrestling on and off for a few years. Signed with Impact Wrestling competing as Braxton Sutter from 2015 to 2018. In November 2019 he and partner The Butcher signed with All Elite Wrestling.

Perry Von Vicious
6' 2" 215lbs Silicon Valley, California

Record: 1 – 0
Shows wrestled on:
June 23, 2019 **La Kermesse Festival Night 2** St. Louis Field Biddeford

Got his start in the New England region training with Antonio Thomas, he debuted in January 2008. Relocated to California wrestling for Big Time Wrestling out of Newark and All Pro Wrestling out of Hayward winning the APW Worldwide Internet Championship. Coming back to New England in 2017 he won the Pioneer Valley Pro championship. In 2018 he made his Canadian debut with Next Wrestling Entertainment.

Petey Williams *"Maple Leaf Muscle"*
5' 7" 179lbs Windsor, Ontario, Canada

Record: 1 – 0
Shows wrestled on:
November 03, 2017 **Hybrid Moments** Portland Club

Trained at the Can-Am Wrestling School by Scott D'Amore Williams debuted in 2002 with Border City Wrestling. A TNA Original he debuted with the company in 2004 as part of Team Canada and spent the next five years with the promotion. While there he captured the X-Division twice holding it a combined 310 days. After leaving Impact he wrestled in All Japan Pro Wrestling, Ring of Honor, and across the US Indies. He retired from wrestling in 2014, returning three years later. This match at Hybrid Moments was his sixteenth match back in the ring. Williams is best known as being the innovator of the Canadian Destroyer, a front flip piledriver.

Pierre Carl Ouellet *"PCO"*
6' 1" 300 lbs Montreal, Quebec, Canada

Record: 0 – 1
Shows wrestled on:
July 27, 2018 **Vacationland Cup** Westbrook Armory

Debuting in 1987 in Montreal he trained with Edouard Carpentier among many others. He debuted in the WWE in 1993 with Jacques Rougeau as the Quebecers. The duo would team together for two years and win the Tag Team Championship three times. In 1995 he was repackaged at Jean-Pierre Lafitte and feuded with Bret Hart after stealing the Hitman's ring jacket. The theft took place on the August 26, 1995 episode of WWF Superstars which was taped on August 15th at the Cumberland Country Civic Center in Portland, Maine. I was at that show and remember this event,

Bret was wrestling Rad Radford (Louie Spicolli) when it happened.
PCO left the WWF in 1995, went to WCW, then ECW, then back to WWF, then back to WCW before wrestling on the Indies until he retired in 2011. He came out of retirement in 2016 and had a career changing match with Walter at *Joey Janela's Spring Break 2* in April 2018 launching to the highest point of his career. Currently signed with Ring of Honor he won their World Championship in December 2019 holding the title for 78 days.

Pinkie Sanchez *"El Presidente"*
5' 11" 169lbs New York, New York

Record: 0 – 1
Shows wrestled on:
November 29, 2019 *Twilight Zone* AMVets Hall Yarmouth

Debuted in 2004 after training with EC Negro and others, wrestling in the Northeast region. In 2008 he joined CHIKARA as Pinkie Sanchez, but in 2009 became the masked Carpenter Ant for the promotion. In Beyond Wrestling became a member of Team Pazuzu.

Private Party
Isiah Kassidy
6' 0" 215lbs New York City

Record: 1 – 4
Shows wrestled on:
September 12, 2015 *Stage One* City Side Restaurant, Brewer
November 15, 2015 *Killin' & Thrillin* American Legion Post 84 Orono
January 30, 2016 *Under Fire* American Legion Post 84 Orono
May 28, 2016 *No Dropkicks in the Living Room* American Legion Post 84 Orono
January 11, 2019 *Snakebitten* Westbrook Armory

Marc Quen
5' 10" 210lbs New York City

Record: 1 – 2
Shows wrestled on:
January 30, 2016 *Under Fire* American Legion Post 84 Orono
May 28, 2016 *No Dropkicks in the Living Room* American Legion Post 84 Orono
January 11, 2019 *Snakebitten* Westbrook Armory

Both Kassidy & Quen debuted in July 2015 and trained at the House of Glory wrestling school. They first teamed together in August 2015 and have remained a team for the last five years. In that time, they have won numerous tag team championships including the HOG, GCW, FTW, and more. They signed with AEW in April 2019 scoring a victory over the Young Bucks in the first round of the AEW Tag Team Championship Tournament.

Puf
5' 10" 418lbs Buffalo, New York

Record: 6 – 2
Shows wrestled on:
August 11, 2018 *2018 Hollis Pirate Festival* Hollis Fire Department
November 30, 2018 *No Control* Portland Club
January 11, 2019 *Snakebitten* Westbrook Armory
March 09, 2019 *Welcome to the Dance* Westbrook Armory
May 10, 2019 *Hooked on a Friedman* Westbrook Armory
July 12, 2019 *2019 Vacationland Cup* Portland Club
September 06, 2019 *Know Your Enemy* Portland Expo
January 24, 2020 *Flirtin' With Disaster* AMVets Hall Yarmouth
December 19, 2020 *2020 Vacationland Cup* AMVets Hall Yarmouth

Trained by Pepper Parks he debuted in 2017 and has wrestled in the Northeast United States and Canada. Struggled to be accepted by Jon Silver of the Thick Boys and finally was welcomed into the group after defeating Silver at *Flirtin' With Disaster.*

Rachael Ellering
5' 6" 141lbs St. Paul, Minnesota

Record: 0 – 1
Shows wrestled on:
May 11, 2018 *Feed The Need* Portland Club

This second-generation wrestler trained with Lance Storm at the Storm Wrestling Academy in Calgary, (dramatic pause) Alberta, Canada debuting in 2015. In 2016 she had her first matches with WWE at NXT. In 2017 she made a couple appearances in Impact Wrestling, later in 2017 she entered the Mae Young Classic as Rachael Evers being eliminated in the second round. She made her Stardom debut in Japan on Christmas Eve 2017 touring with the company through the end of January. In 2018 she competed in both the Mae Young Classic and the Stardom 5Star Grand Prix. In 2019 she signed with WWE assigned to NXT until she tore her ACL in May that put her out for a year, when she was released by WWE. She recently has wrestled in AEW.

Rembrandt Lewis
6' 0" 190lbs Pennsylvania

Record: 0 – 1
Shows wrestled on:
January 30, 2016 *Under Fire* American Legion Post 84 Orono

Made his first appearances in Maine in 2014 with IWE, is a regular with Excellence Pro Wrestling and House of Glory. Most recently wrestled on AEW Dark teaming with Fuego Del Sol in a loss to Stu Grayson and Evil Uno of the Dark Order

Rene Dupree
6' 3" 250lbs Moncton, New Brunswick, Canada

Record: 0 – 1
Shows wrestled on:
March 17, 2017 *Hysteria* Westbrook Armory

Trained by his father Emile Dupree, legendary wrestler and promoter of Martine Wrestling, Rene debuted in 1997. Signed with WWE in 2002 he was with the promotion until 2007 and captured two Tag Team Championships one with Sylvain Grenier as La Resistance the other with Kenzo Suzuki. From 2007 to 2014 he wrestled in Japan for Hustle, All Japan Pro Wrestling, and Wrestle-1. For the next several years he wrestled mostly in Canada and select US Indies. He returned to Japan for Wrestle-1 in September 2019 losing in the finals of the Wrestle-1 Tag League. In April 2020 he debuted in Pro Wrestling NOAH teaming with El Hijo del Dr. Wagner Jr to win the Global Tag League and the next day the GHC Tag Team Championships.

Rex Lawless *"Pectoral Poseidon"*
6' 3" 284lbs Bellmore, New York

Record: 0 – 2
Shows wrestled on:
November 19, 2016 *Hogwash* American Legion Post 84 Orono
March 17, 2017 *Hysteria* Westbrook Armory

Trained by Pat Buck he debuted in 2010 and is a regular for NYWC while branching out into other Northeastern promotions like CZW, Beyond, IWC, and more. He is a four-time NYWC Tag Team Champion and two-time Heavyweight champion.

Rey Fenix
5' 9" 185lbs Mexico City, Mexico

Record: 1 – 0
Shows wrestled on:
July 21, 2017 **Nothing Gold Can Stay** Westbrook Armory

Trained with Gran Apache, and many others, making his debut in Mexico in 2005. He wrestled across Mexico in the Indies and CMLL and Lucha Libre AAA. He also toured Japan for NOAH in 2013 and made his US debut with Lucha Underground in 2014. His career exploded at this time along with brother Pentagon Jr. becoming worldwide superstars and holding numerous tag team championships. In 2018 he signed with Impact Wrestling, and later MLW before signing with AEW in 2019. He is a former AAA Mega Champion, holding the title for 420 days, and with Pentagon Jr. the current AAA World Tag Team Champions since June 16, 2019.

Ric King *"The Kick"*
Margaretville, Georgia

Record: 0 – 1
Shows wrestled on:
July 23, 2016 **Hook, Line, & Sinker** American Legion Post 84 Orono

I can't find much on Ric King, he has matches dating back to 2008 in Alabama for Great Championship Wrestling where he held the Interstate Championship for 201 days in 2010. Most recent matches in ECPW in 2019.

Richard Holliday *"The Most Marketable Man in Wrestling" "The Airpod God"*
6' 3" 238 lbs New Haven, Connecticut

Record: 1 – 0
Shows wrestled on:
September 08, 2018 **2018 Litchfield Fair**

Trained by Mario Mancini & Paul Roma at Paradise Alley Pro Wrestling he debuted in 2015 and has wrestled primarily in the Northeast Region. Signed with MLW in 2018 formed the tag team The Dynasty with MJF. Made his Mexico debut with MLW defending the Tag Team Championships against LA Parka Jr. and El Hijo de LA Park.

Ricky Archer
6' 0" 185lbs Saugus, Massachusetts

Record: 1 – 2
Shows wrestled on:
The Road Season 1 *Episodes 2 & 6* American Legion Post 84, Orono
December 19, 2020 **2020 VACATIONLAND CUP** AMVets Yarmouth, Maine

Began training in December 2018 at the New England Pro Wrestling Academy having his first match in May 2019 against Christian Casanova in Chaotic Wrestling. Favorite moment in wrestling to date is his debut against Casanova and his match with Ace Romero on The Road.

Ricochet *"King" "Future of Flight" "The One and Only"*
5' 9" 187lbs Paducah, Kentucky

Record: 0 – 1
Shows wrestled on:
March 17, 2017 ***Hysteria*** Westbrook Armory

Trained by Brandon Walker and Chuck Taylor he debuted in 2003. One of the most innovative highflyers in all of wrestling he has wrestled all over the world holding championships in Japan, England, and the United States. Had a tremendous series of matches with Will Ospreay, their first in 2013, but the May 27,

2016 Best of the Super Juniors tournament match that main evented Korakuen Hall is their most famous. He is currently signed with the WWE where has held the NXT North American and United States Championships.

Rip Byson *"Iron"*
5' 10" 235lbs Killdevil Hills, North Carolina

Record: 4 – 4
Shows wrestled on:
June 23, 2019 ***La Kermesse Festival Night 2*** St. Louis Field Biddeford
February 22, 2020 ***Practice What You Preach*** AMVets Hall Yarmouth
The Road Season 1 *Episodes 2, 3, 5, 7, & 9* American Legion Post 84, Orono
December 19, 2020 ***2020 Vacationland Cup*** AMVets Hall Yarmouth

Began his training in 2012 with the New England Pro Wrestling Academy. Had his first match in 2013 with Chaotic Wrestling under the name Tomahawk in celebration of his Native American heritage. Made his first appearances in Maine for NWA Onfire and later MainEvent Wrestling. In IWE he won the Maine State Championship holding the title for 167 days. He's been a three-time Pioneer Valley Promotions Tag Team Champion and held their Heavyweight championship at the same time he was the NCW New England Champion. He also held tag titles in NCW: Northeast Championship Wrestling and LPW: Lucky Pro Wrestling.

Through-out his career he has wrestled primarily in the Northeast and New Brunswick, Canada with shots in Texas. In 2019 he transitioned from Tomahawk into Rip Byson unleashing his Japanese strong style inspired offense on his opponents. He challenged for the IWTV Independent Wrestling Championship at Practice What You Preach, coming up short but giving Warhorse more than a run for his money. Byson defeated DL Hurst to become the number one contender and challenged Limitless Wrestling World Champion: Anthony Greene at Pandemic at the Dojo episode six. At the 2020 Vacationland Cup he defeated Big Beef in a stiff hard-hitting match.

Rob Marsh
5' 9" 235lbs Cambridge, Massachusetts

Record: 0 – 1
Shows wrestled on:
September 08, 2018 *2018 Litchfield Fair*

Got his start in 2006 with "Lobsterman" Jeff Costa. Held the IWE Tag Team Championship with Bill Vaux. Competed at the 2017 IWA Mid-South *So You Wanna Be A Deathmatch Star? Tournament* in Memphis, Indiana. Defeated JP O'Reilly and Drew Chaos on his way to the finals where he came up short against JC Rotten.

Rob Matter
5' 7" 165lbs Davenport, Iowa

Record: 0 – 1
Shows wrestled on:
March 17, 2017 *Hysteria* Westbrook Armory

Very little information available on Matter. I found matches starting back in 2012 with Iowa based Scott County Wrestling. Formed a tag team with Stevie Fierce as Beauty and the Beast winning tag team championships in Freelance Wrestling twice the first time back when it was called Underground Wrestling. Most recent match results I can find is from 2018.

Rude Boy Riley
6' 1" 209lbs New York, New York

Record: 0 – 2
Shows wrestled on:
July 23, 2016 ***Hook, Line, & Sinker*** American Legion Post 84 Orono
March 17, 2017 ***Hysteria*** Westbrook Armory

Started out as a referee before transitioning to a wrestler in 2007 and wrestling in the Northeast territory. Wrestled only one other match after *Hysteria* before being arrested on March 29th for possession of child pornography. In March 2018 he pled guilty receiving two years interim-supervision probation, five days in jail, and must register as a sex offender.

Sami Callihan *"The Callihan Death Machine" "The New Horror"*
5' 9" 209lbs Dayton, Ohio

Record: 0 – 4
Shows wrestled on:

February 25, 2017 ***Do What You Love, Fuck The Rest-Fest***
American Legion Post 84 Orono
July 21, 2017 ***Nothing Gold Can Stay*** Westbrook Armory
November 03, 2017 ***Hybrid Moments*** Portland Club
September 21, 2018 ***Pretenders Beware*** Westbrook Armory

Trained by Les Thatcher, Cody Hawk, & others he debuted in 2006. Found success in CZW and IWA-Midsouth in 2008. Made his first tour of Germany and England in 2009. Signed with WWE in 2013 spending two years in NXT as Solomon Crowe wrestled on many live events and was seen on TV with a hacker gimmick, but only wrestled in four televised matches, all losses. Was featured in an excellent Kenny Johnson documentary available on YouTube "They Came For the Stiff". Returned to the Indies with a vengeance, wrestled for Lucha Underground, teamed with Juice Robinson in the 2017 New Japan Pro Wrestling World Tag League finishing second in their block. Signed with Impact Wrestling in 2018 becoming a major player with the company bringing in his Ohio Versus Everything crew. He captured the Impact Wrestling World Championship from Brian Cage in a steel cage holding the title for 79 days.

Santana & Ortiz
Santana: 5' 10" 198lbs
Ortiz: 5' 8" 191lbs
New York City

Record: 3 – 2
Shows wrestled on:
March 19, 2016 ***Don't Fear The Sleeper*** American Legion Post 84 Orono
May 28, 2016 ***No Dropkicks in the Living Room*** American Legion Post 84 Orono
July 23, 2016 ***Hook, Line, & Sinker*** American Legion Post 84 Orono

Whether you call them LAX, EYFBO, or Proud and Powerful you can just call them one of the best tag teams in the world. Santana debuted in 2007 and Ortiz a year later in 2008, they first teamed together on March 9, 2012 and have remained a team ever since. The duo have wrestled in promotions across the United States, Mexico, Canada, United Kingdom, Germany and more. They have captured ten different tag team championships including being four-time Impact Wrestling tag team champions. They signed with AEW debuting in August 2019.

Sasha Jenkins *"Bad Mama Jama"*
5' 9" 188lbs The Bronx, New York

Record: 0 – 1
Shows wrestled on:
March 19, 2016 ***Don't Fear The Sleeper*** American Legion Post 84 Orono

Trained at House of Glory with Amazing Red and Brian XL, he debuted in 2013. Wrestles mostly in New York but is a regular with the Connecticut based Blitzkrieg Pro where he is a former Bedlam Champion.

Scott Wild *"The White Delight"*
6' 0" 218lbs Feeding Hills, Massachusetts

Record: 5 – 5
Shows wrestled on:
September 12, 2015 *Stage One* City Side Restaurant, Brewer
November 15, 2015 *Killin' & Thrillin* American Legion Post 84 Orono
January 30, 2016 *Under Fire* American Legion Post 84 Orono
March 19, 2016 *Don't Fear The Sleeper* American Legion Post 84 Orono
May 28, 2016 *No Dropkicks in the Living Room* American Legion Post 84 Orono
July 23, 2016 *Hook, Line, & Sinker* American Legion Post 84 Orono
September 24, 2016 *Past Your Bedtime* American Legion Post 84 Orono
October 07, 2016 *Risk It For The Biscuit* Westbrook Armory
October 29, 2016 *Who Watches the Watchmen?* The Field House at University of Maine Orono
February 25, 2017 *Do What You Love, Fuck The Rest-Fest* American Legion Post 84 Orono

Wild trained with Aaron Morrison having his first match in November 2007. Best known by fans in Maine for his time in IWE where he held the Junior Heavyweight Championship, is a four-time Tag Team Champion, and a two-time Heavyweight Champion. He has also competed for ¡Let's Wrestle! His favorite moment in wrestling on the Warped Tour with Blitzkrieg Pro in 2018.

Scotty Slade
5' 7" 152lbs San Francisco, California

Record: 1 – 1
Shows wrestled on:
September 24, 2016 *Past Your Bedtime* American Legion Post 84 Orono
October 07, 2016 *Risk It For The Biscuit* Westbrook Armory

Slade began wrestling in 2003 with "Brutal" Bob Evans and Steve Bradley making his in-ring debut in January 2004. With Mark Shurman they formed Team Friendship capturing tag team titles in CTWE, twice in NECW and Chaotic Wrestling, and in Northeast Wrestling. His favorite moment in wrestling was wrestling in the main event of Chaotic Wrestling's *Cold Fury 13*, March 21, 2014. Mark Shurman defended his Heavyweight Championship against Brian Fury & Slade in a triple threat match that saw Fury win the title.

Sebastian Cage *"The Litt Superstar"*
5' 11" 165lbs Los Angeles, California

Record: 0 – 1
Shows wrestled on:
February 25, 2017 *Do What You Love, Fuck The Rest-Fest* American Legion Post 84 Orono

Trained with Aztro Negro, Joel Maximo and others he debuted August 20, 2014. Has spent his career in the Northeast region with matches against Brian Myers, Super Crazy and Robbie E. He was the first holder of the FLLL Light Heavyweight Champion, first LAW Dynamite Division Champion, and first Pro Wrestling Magic Junior Heavyweight Champion. He has held numerous other championships.

Shane Marvel *"Your Hero"*
6' 1" 215lbs Gotham City

Record: 0 – 1
Shows wrestled on:
November 15, 2015 **Killin' & Thrillin** American Legion Post 84 Orono

Started training in 2008 with Antonio Thomas and Kevin Landry making his in-ring debut in late 2008. First came to Maine with IWE where he captured the tag team championship twice and held the IWE Heavyweight championship two-times for a combined 112 days. He won his first IWE Championship pinning for ECW World Champion Justin Credible. After *Killin' & Thrillin'* he relocated to the West Coast and currently wrestles for Party Hard Wrestling.

Shane Sabre *"All Confidence"*
6' 0" 210lbs The Great White North

Record: 1 – 0
Shows wrestled on:
November 19, 2016 **Hogwash** American Legion Post 84 Orono

Trained by Rob Feugo and "All Ego" Ethan Page, Sabre debuted in 2012. He states his favorite part about wrestling is that it has allowed him to travel all over North America and Europe. With his Space Pirates partner Space Monkey, they have captured multiple tag team championships including holding the Alpha-1 tag titles for 308 days.

Shane Strickland *"Swerve"*
6' 1" 201lbs Tacoma, Washington

Record: 0 – 1
Shows wrestled on:
March 30, 2018 *Only Fools Are Satisfied* Westbrook Armory

Started training in 2008 with Ground Xero Wrestling Academy making his in-ring debut in 2009. He wrestled across the US Indies for the next several years winning the CZW Wired Championship two-times and the CZW World Championship for 126 days. He signed with Lucha Underground in 2014 as the masked Killshot. He also wrestled in Evolve winning the Heavyweight Championship. In 2019 he signed with the WWE adopting the name Isiah Scott in NXT.

Shawn Spears *"The Chairman" "Perfect 10"*
6' 3" 223lbs Niagara Falls, Ontario, Canada

Record: 0 – 1
Shows wrestled on:
July 12, 2019 *2019 Vacationland Cup* Portland Club

Trained at the Hart Wrestling School with Smith Hart and at WrestlePlex with Eric Young debuting in-ring in 2002. He bombed around the Canadian Indies and Northeastern United States and even popped up at WWE Cyber Sunday in 2006 playing Stan who was superkicked by Shawn Michaels. He signed with the WWE in 2006 going to OVW and then wrestling as Gavin Spears on WW-ECW. Released in 2009 he returned to the Indies, debuted in Mexico and won the WWC Tag Team Titles. He returned to the WWE for NXT in 2013 as the "Perfect 10" Tye Dillinger. At the height of his popularity in NXT he was brought up to the Smackdown Brand and spent the next two years in obscurity being released in 2019. He signed with AEW in 2019 and is currently being managed by Tully Blanchard for the promotion. He is currently a member of the faction Pinnacle with MJF, Wardlow, FTR, and Tully Blanchard.

Shazza McKenzie *"Heartcore"*
5' 3" 125lbs Sydney, New South Wales, Australia

Record: 0 – 1
Shows wrestled on:
May 10, 2019 **Hooked on a Friedman** Westbrook Armory

Trained with Madison Eagles and several others debuting in 2008. Has spent the majority of her career in her native Australia holding the PWWA championship twice for a combined 1182 days. She made her first US tour in March 2012 and has returned to the States each year since then until the pandemic. She competed in the AEW All Out Casino Battle Royal in 2019.

Sierra *"Picture Perfect"*
5' 2" 120lbs Warwick, Rhode Island

Record: 1 – 0
Shows wrestled on:
June 23, 2019 **La Kermesse Festival Night 2** St. Louis Field Biddeford

Trained by Matt Taven and Mike Bennett she had her first match in 2018. She has wrestled primarily in the New England area.

Simon Grimm
6' 1" 220lbs Hoboken, New Jersey

Record: 0 – 1
Shows wrestled on:
January 11, 2019 **Snakebitten** Westbrook Armory

Trained with Donovan Morgan, Harley Race, and others he debuted in 2002. In 2013 he signed with WWE and the NXT brand, and formed the tag team the Vaudevillians with Aiden English capturing the NXT Tag Team Championships at NXT

Takeover Brooklyn. He was released in 2017 returning to the Indies. He signed with MLW in 2018 where he is the leader of the Contra Unit.

Skylar *"Hot Scoop"*
5' 3" 130lbs

Record: 8 – 11
Shows wrestled on:
October 07, 2016 ***Risk It For The Biscuit*** Westbrook Armory
October 29, 2016 ***Who Watches the Watchmen?*** The Field House at University of Maine Orono
November 19, 2016 ***Hogwash*** American Legion Post 84 Orono
January 27, 2017 ***Unreal*** Westbrook Armory
February 25, 2017 ***Do What You Love, Fuck The Rest-Fest*** American Legion Post 84 Orono
March 17, 2017 ***Hysteria*** Westbrook Armory
April 28, 2017 ***Can We Kick It?*** Portland Club
May 13, 2017 ***Problematic*** Westbrook Armory
June 23, 2017 ***La Kermesse Festival Night 1*** St. Louis Field Biddeford
June 24, 2017 ***La Kermesse Festival Night 2*** St. Louis Field Biddeford
September 22, 2017 ***Question The Answers*** Westbrook Armory
November 03, 2017 ***Hybrid Moments*** Portland Club
May 11, 2018 ***Feed The Need*** Portland Club
May 10, 2019 ***Hooked on a Friedman*** Westbrook Armory
June 22, 2019 ***La Kermesse Festival Night 1*** St. Louis Field Biddeford
June 23, 2019 ***La Kermesse Festival Night 2*** St. Louis Field Biddeford
July 12, 2019 ***2019 Vacationland Cup*** Portland Club
September 06, 2019 ***Know Your Enemy*** Portland Expo
October 25, 2019 ***Fresh Blood*** AMVets Hall Yarmouth

Skylar debuted in 2016 and has wrestled primarily in the New England area. She started out in Limitless Wrestling as the manager of Jeremy Leary at *Don't Fear the Sleeper* transitioning to an in-ring competitor at *Risk it for the Biscuit*. In 2018 she made her CHIKARA debut in the Young Lions Cup XIV as Blanche Babish. She won her first round fatal four-way match before being eliminated in the semi-finals by Cam Zagami. She stayed with the promotion through early 2019. In Chaotic Wrestling she is a two-time Women's Champion holding the title for a combined 210 days. In Blitzkrieg Pro she held the Bedlam Championship for 489 days. At *Hooked on a Friedman* she scored a pinfall over former WWE and Impact Women's Champion Victoria. Victoria would only wrestle three more matches before retiring. At *Know Your Enemy* she would team with Jeremy Leary coming up short in a Hair vs. Career match against Ashley Vox & Kris Statlander. However only Leary's hair was on the line that night.

Slyck Wagner Brown
6' 2" 220lbs Kingston, Jamaica

Record: 0 – 1
Shows wrestled on:
October 29, 2016 *Who Watches the Watchmen?* The Field House at University of Maine Orono

SWB began his career in 1997 training at Killer Kowalski's wrestling school in Massachusetts. With fellow Kowalski graduates Jason Rage, Beau Douglas, and Damon D'Archangelo they formed the tWo: true World order. He has held numerous championships including being a three-time NECW Heavyweight Champion and two-time 2CW Heavyweight Champion. He formed a tag team with April Hunter and in 2004 the duo held the JAPW: Jersey All Pro Wrestling and 3PW Tag Team Championships. With Bobby Ocean they teamed as the Black Talented Wrestlers winning the Big Time Wrestling Tag Team Championships. He wrestled three matches in the WWE, in 2002 a dark match victory over The Inferno Kid, in 2003 a loss to Mike Awesome on *Velocity*, and in 2005 he and Johnny Heartbreaker lost to Rosey and the Hurricane on *Sunday Night Heat*. He made a couple appearances for TNA in 2003 & 2011. Most recently he has been wrestling for the New York based Immortal Championship Wrestling.

Sonny Defarge
6' 2" 216lbs Pennsylvania
Record: 0 – 1
Shows wrestled on:
June 24, 2017 *La Kermesse Festival Night 2* St. Louis Field Biddeford

Trained at the Wrestle Factory, Defarge debuted in 2016. He and Cornelius Crummels have formed a successful tag team winning the Premier Championship Wrestling tag team championships twice and the CHIKARA Campeonatos de Parejas.

Sonya Strong
5' 4" 134lbs New York, New York

Record: 2 – 2
Shows wrestled on:
November 15, 2015 ***Killin' & Thrillin*** American Legion Post 84 Orono
January 30, 2016 ***Under Fire*** American Legion Post 84 Orono
March 19, 2016 ***Don't Fear The Sleeper*** American Legion Post 84 Orono
May 28, 2016 ***No Dropkicks in the Living Room*** American Legion Post 84 Orono

Trained by Amazing Red and Brian XL she debuted in 2015. She has wrestled primarily in the Northeast territory PWM and HOG women's championships. Her match with Gangone at Under Fire has over 34 million views on the Limitless Wrestling YouTube page.

Space Monkey
5' 9" 175lbs Sailing the Great Blue North

Record: 0 – 1
Shows wrestled on:
November 19, 2016 ***Hogwash*** American Legion Post 84 Orono

Trained with Ashley Sixx debuting in 2014 and has wrestled across the Canadian and United States Indies. Made his Japan debut in January 2019 with DDT and spent two months with the promotion. Formed the tag team Space Pirates with Shane Sabre capturing tag titles in Alpha-1, C*4, Black Label Pro, and other promotions.

Sully Banger

Record: 0 – 2
Shows wrestled on:
September 24, 2016 *Past Your Bedtime* American Legion Post 84 Orono
October 07, 2016 *Risk It For The Biscuit* Westbrook Armory

Super Crazy *"Extreme Luchadore"*
5' 8" 209lbs Tulancingo, Hidalgo, Mexico

Record: 0 – 1
Shows wrestled on:
July 21, 2017 *Nothing Gold Can Stay* Westbrook Armory

Super Crazy debuted in February 1988 at just 14 years old after training with his brother Ray Pantera. He wrestled on the Mexican Indie scene until he signed with Lucha Libre AAA in 1996. He signed with ECW in 1998 staying with the promotion until it folded in 2001 holding the ECW World Television Championship. He had a tremendous feud with Yoshihirio Tajiri, and Little Guido Maritato highlighted in singles matches and three-way dances at several Pay-Per-Views. After ECW he toured the Indies, spent time in New Japan and then signed with the WWE in 2005. He appeared at the first *One Night Stand* PPV and then as a member of the Mexicools. He left the promotion in 2008 and has been touring the world ever since.

Super Savages:
Caveman *"Prehistoric Savage"*
5' 6" 175 Stones from 10,000 BC

Mantequilla *"The Smooth Superhero"*
5' 11" 185lbs New York, New York

Record: 0 – 2
Shows wrestled on:
November 15, 2015 **Killin' & Thrillin** American Legion Post 84 Orono
July 23, 2016 **Hook, Line, & Sinker** American Legion Post 84 Orono

Caveman was trained by Bronco International and The Amazing Red in 2011. He had his first match in April 2012 against Bobby Venom. The duo captured the New Jersey based Superstars of Wrestling Federation Tag Team Championship. Caveman's favorite moment was competing on a segment for MTV's *Total Request Live* hosted by the Miz where he won the TRL Championship. Mantequilla began wrestling back in 2014, the duo first teamed up in 2015. He has also wrestled in the New York region for the majority of his career. Mantequilla is a former HOG: House of Glory Crown Jewel Championship. The duo held the New Jersey based SWF: Superstars of Wrestling Federation Tag Team Championships.

Swoggle
4' 4" 141lbs Dublin, Ireland

Record: 1 – 2
Shows wrestled on:
March 17, 2017 **Hysteria** Westbrook Armory
September 22, 2017 **Question The Answers** Westbrook Armory
July 12, 2019 **2019 Vacationland Cup** Portland Club

Debuting in 2004 in his native Wisconsin, he signed with the WWE in 2006 as Little Bastard, the sidekick of Fit Finlay. He spent 10 years with the promotion working as both a wrestler and manager holding the WWE Cruiserweight Championship for 65 days. Had a fantastic match on the 2014 Extreme Rules Pre-Show with EL Torito, a WeeLC match. If you are assuming this was a pure comedy match, you'd be wrong, they went all out.

Taeler Hendrix *"Poison Princess"*
5' 7" 125lbs New Bedford, Massachusetts

Record: 0 – 1
Shows wrestled on:
March 17, 2017 ***Hysteria*** Westbrook Armory

Debuted in 2008 after initial training with "Mad Dog" Matt Storm and Brickhouse Baker, in the New England territory for NECW and Top Rope Promotions. August 13, 2011, she lost a Loser Leaves Town Match to Mistress Belmont at PWF Northeast in Providence, Rhode Island. She relocated to Kentucky continuing her training with Ohio Valley Wrestling winning the Women's Championship three times over the next 17 months holding it for 307 days. Was a participant in the TNA Gut Check Challenge at the time when OVW was a developmental territory for TNA. Has also worked for Ring of Honor, Queens of Combat, Shimmer, and appeared as a Rosebud on WWE TV.

Tasha Steelz
5' 4" 130lbs Brick City, New Jersey

Record: 0 – 1
Shows wrestled on:
January 24, 2020 ***Flirtin' With Disaster*** AMVets Hall Yarmouth

Trained with Kevin Knight and debuted in 2015. Held the IWF Women's Championship for 439 days and the Chaotic Wrestling Women's title for 329 days. Appeared on NWA *Powerrr* amassing a 2 - 2 record. Signed with Impact Wrestling in May 2020. On January 16, 2021 with Kiera Hogan as Fire and Flava the duo won a tournament final over Havok and Nevaeh to win the vacant Impact Wrestling Knockout's Tag Team Championships.

Tabarnak de Team
Mathieu St. Jacques
5' 10" 220 lbs St-Eustache, Quebec, Canada

Thomas Dubois
6' 2" 244lbs St-Eustache, Quebec, Canada

Record: 2 – 1
Shows wrestled on:
May 13, 2017 *Problematic* Westbrook Armory
June 23, 2017 *La Kermesse Festival Night 1* St. Louis Field Biddeford
July 21, 2017 *Nothing Gold Can Stay* Westbrook Armory

St. Jacques was trained by Dru Onyx and Lufisto debuting in 2007, while Dubois was trained by Jacque Rougeau debuting in 2009. Perhaps the best Canadian tag team of the last decade they first teamed together in 2010 for Montreal based Combat Revolution Wrestling where they captured the tag team titles three for over 1500 days. They have also held the C*4 Wrestling titles four times for 1304 days and tag team championships for North

Shore Pro Wrestling, Acclaim Pro Wrestling, Internet Wrestling Syndicate, BATTLEWAR, Inter Species Wrestling, and La Descente Du Coude. They both have had singles championships through the years as well with St. Jacques holding the C*4 Championship for 735 days and Dubois has held to BATTLEWAR Pro Champion for 954 days since March 25, 2018.

Teddy Hart *"Loose Cannon" "The Past, Present, & Future of Professional Wrestling"*
6' 0" 187lbs Calgary, Alberta, Canada

Record: 4 – 2
Shows wrestled on:
September 22, 2017 ***Question The Answers*** Westbrook Armory
March 30, 2018 ***Only Fools Are Satisfied*** Westbrook Armory
May 11, 2018 ***Feed The Need*** Portland Club
March 09, 2019 ***Welcome to the Dance*** Westbrook Armory
May 10, 2019 ***Hooked on a Friedman*** Westbrook Armory
September 06, 2019 ***Know Your Enemy*** Portland Expo

Trained by his Uncles Ross and Bruce Hart he debuted at the age of 15 for Stampede Wrestling. He was first signed by the WWE in 1998 and sent to developmental but was released shortly thereafter. In 2003 he competed in the NWA TNA Super X Cup losing in the second round. In 2003 he made appearances in-ring of Honor and MLW as well. He was part of Team Canada in the 2004 NWA TNA America's Cup. He was re-signed by the WWE and assigned to Ohio Valley Wrestling and Florida Championship Wrestling and was released. In 2007 he signed with Lucha Libre AAA and spent the next three years in Mexico. After several years wrestling across Mexico, Canadian, and US Indies his star started to rise again in 2017 and he formed the New Hart Foundation with Davey Boy Smith Jr. & Brain Pillman Jr. winning the MLW Tag Team Championships, Hart also captured the MLW Middleweight Championship.

Terra Calaway *"The Queen of the Dinosaurs"*
5' 11" 200 lbs Las Vegas, Nevada

Record: 3 – 0
Shows wrestled on:
June 23, 2017 ***La Kermesse Festival Night 1*** St. Louis Field Biddeford
June 24, 2017 ***La Kermesse Festival Night 2*** St. Louis Field Biddeford
November 03, 2017 ***Hybrid Moments*** Portland Club

Trained at Vegas Championship Wrestling and debuted in 2009 competing on the West Coast until May 2015 when she moved to the Northeast region. She held the UPWA: United Pro Wrestling Association Women's Championship for 693 days. She retired from wrestling in December 2019 after losing a match to her husband Jeff Cannonball. On October 31, 2020 she made a surprise return at H20 The Last Extravaganza Weekend winning a gauntlet match for the vacant Inter Species Wrestling Undisputed King of Crazy Championship.

Tessa Blanchard *"The Queen of the Carolinas"*
5' 5" 123lbs Charlotte, North Carolina

Record: 1 – 1
Shows wrestled on:
January 27, 2017 ***Unreal*** Westbrook Armory
January 19, 2018 ***The World Is Ours*** Westbrook Armory

This third-generation wrestler trained with "Mr. No. 1" George South and received guidance from her father Tully Blanchard and stepfather Magnum TA. She debuted in 2014 at the age of 18. Just four months into her career she won the ECWA Super 8 Chickfight Tournament also winning the ECWA Women's Championship defeating Jenny Rose in the finals. In May 2015 she toured the Canadian Maritimes with Atlantic Grand Prix

Wrestling and wrestled twice in China defeating Barbie Hayden both nights. Teaming with Anthony Greene they won the Lucky Pro Wrestling 2015 Kings and Queens Tournament.
In 2016 she made some appearances for NXT and would return in 2017 competing in the Mae Young Classic. She toured Stardom in Japan in 2016 & 2017, Australia in 2017 & 2018, and in 2018 made her Mexico debut. In 2019 she signed with Lucha Libre AAA winning the Reina de Reinas Championship. In 2018 she signed with Impact Wrestling winning the Knockouts Championship and in 2020 she would win the Impact Wrestling World Championship holding the title for 165 days, she was stripped of the title and released from the company.

The Influence:
Jason Devine
5' 9" 165lbs Fall River, Massachusetts

Record: 3 – 1
Shows wrestled on:
September 12, 2015 ***Stage One*** City Side Restaurant, Brewer
November 15, 2015 ***Killin' & Thrillin*** American Legion Post 84 Orono
January 30, 2016 ***Under Fire*** American Legion Post 84 Orono
March 19, 2016 ***Don't Fear The Sleeper*** American Legion Post 84 Orono

Mike Montero *"The Ace"*

Record: 3 – 2 Fall River, Massachusetts
Shows wrestled on:
September 12, 2015 ***Stage One*** City Side Restaurant, Brewer
November 15, 2015 ***Killin' & Thrillin*** American Legion Post 84 Orono
January 30, 2016 ***Under Fire*** American Legion Post 84 Orono
March 19, 2016 ***Don't Fear The Sleeper*** American Legion Post 84 Orono

October 29, 2016 *Who Watches the Watchmen?* The Field House at University of Maine Orono

Both wrestlers based in New England began teaming together in 2013. The duo feuded with Da Hoodz in Beyond Wrestling. Have the distinction of being two of the eight men involved in the first ever match in Limitless Wrestling at *Stage One*.

The Whisper *"The Innovator of Silence"*
5' 10" 172lbs The Realm of the Endless

Record: 0 – 3
Shows wrestled on:
June 24, 2017 *La Kermesse Festival Night 2* St. Louis Field Biddeford
May 11, 2018 *Feed The Need* Portland Club
January 11, 2019 *Snakebitten* Westbrook Armory

Trained at the Wrestle Factory he debuted in 2017 and was a regular with CHIKARA. He won the Young Lions Cup and was co-holder of the Campeonatos de Parejas with Princess Kimber Lee holding the titles for 140 days.

Thief Ant
6'4" 194lbs The Ant Hill

Record: 1 – 1
Shows wrestled on:
May 11, 2018 *Feed The Need* Portland Club
November 30, 2018 *No Control* Portland Club

Trained at the Wrestle Factory he debuted in 2017 and was a regular with CHIKARA. With Green Ant he competed in the CHIKARA 2018 Tag World Grand Prix. Is a member of The Colony with Fire and Green Ant, the trio made it to the Semi Finals of the *2019 King of Trios*.

Tim Donst
5' 10" 196lbs Lancaster, Pennsylvania

Record: 1 – 0
Shows wrestled on:
November 15, 2015 *Killin' & Thrillin* American Legion Post 84 Orono

Donst debuted in 2007 with CHIKARA after training with Chris Hero, Mike Quackenbush and others. He was a regular with the promotions until June 2, 2013 when he lost a Hair vs. Hair match to Gavin Loudspeaker. Started with CZW after feuding with Joe Gacy defeating him for the Wired Championship. Was a regular with AIW holding the Absolute Championship three times for a combined 545 days.

Todo Loco *"Judo Master"*
5' 8" 180lbs Cambridge, Massachusetts

Record: 2 – 0
Shows wrestled on:
October 29, 2016 *Who Watches the Watchmen?* The Field House at University of Maine Orono
September 08, 2018 *2018 Litchfield Fair*

Also known as Benny Jux, Loco made his in-ring debut in 2006. Is one of the original members of the Big Time Wrestling roster he has been with the company since their 2006 resurgence. Also, a regular with NECW winning their Television Championship three times for a combined 295 days. He also has held the NECW Heavyweight Championship winning the title July 2, 2016 and is still technically the champion even though NECW last promoted a show on October 13, 2018.

Tom Lawlor *"Filthy"*
6' 5" 205lbs Las Vegas, Nevada

Record: 0 – 1
Shows wrestled on:
September 06, 2019 **Know Your Enemy** Portland Expo

Started out in Mixed Martial Arts appearing on season 8 of UFC's Ultimate Fighter television show. He debuted in 2007, last fought in 2018 amassing a 10 - 8 record. Lawlor made his wrestling debut in 2005 but stopped in 2008 to focus on MMA. Returned to the squared circle in 2017 and quickly made a name for himself across the US Indies. He joined up with Major League Wrestling holding the World Championship for 154 days in 2019.

Tommaso Ciampa *"Sicilian Psychopath"*
5' 11" 201lbs Milwaukee, Wisconsin

Record: 1 – 0
Shows wrestled on:
May 28, 2016 ***No Dropkicks in the Living Room*** American Legion Post 84 Orono

Trained with Killer Kowalski he debuted in 2005 as Thomas Penmanship. Wrestled on the US Indies becoming a regular with Ring of Honor in 2011 holding the World Television Championship for 111 days from December 2013 - April 2014. He competed in the 2015 *Dusty Rhodes Classic* teaming with Johnny Gargano as DIY but did not sign with WWE until 2016. In NXT he has held the Tag Team and Heavyweight Championships.

Tommy Dreamer *"The Innovator of Violence"*
6' 2" 265lbs Yonkers, New York

Record: 0 – 2
Shows wrestled on:
March 09, 2019 ***Welcome to the Dance*** Westbrook Armory
July 12, 2019 ***2019 Vacationland Cup*** Portland Club

Trained by Johnny Rodz, Dreamer debuted in 1989. One of my all favorite wrestlers he is known as the heart and soul of Extreme Championship Wrestling where he competed from 1993 - 2001. In his career he worked several years for WWE, has wrestled on and off with TNA/Impact Wrestling, wrestled around the world, and runs his own promotion House of Hardcore. In ECW he had a long and violent feud with Raven. Is a former 14-time WWE Hardcore Champion, three-time ECW World Tag Team Champion, ECW World Heavyweight Champion, WW-ECW Heavyweight Champion, and held championships in Canada, Germany, Japan and numerous titles on the US Indies.

Tommy Mack *"Heart Attack"*
5' 10" 229lbs Belmont, New Hampshire

Record: 1 – 0
Shows wrestled on:
October 07, 2016 ***Risk It For The Biscuit*** Westbrook Armory

Trained by Maverick Wild, Mack debuted in 2005. Wrestling in New England he is known to Maine fans for his time in IWE where he held their heavyweight Championship. Unsuccessfully challenged NWA World Champion: Nick Aldis on March 31, 2019 in Concord, New Hampshire. It was the first time the NWA Worlds Championship was defended in New Hampshire.

Tony Deppen
5' 9" 165lbs Shamokin, Pennsylvania

Record: 0 – 1
Shows wrestled on:
May 11, 2018 ***Feed The Need*** Portland Club

Trained at the PCWA Wrestling School, Deppen debuted in 2009. Has wrestled primarily in the North Eastern United States as well as PWG, in Canada for C*4, and in Japan for GCW. He the CHIKARA Campeonatos de Parejas titles with Travis Huckabee for 196 days.

Traevon Jordan
6' 4" 225lbs from Your Baby Momma's Day Dream

Record: 1 – 4
Shows wrestled on:
The Road Season 1 *Episodes 1, 7, 8, & 9* American Legion Post 84, Orono

Jordan was trained by Matt Taven and Vinny Marseglia at the Kingdom Academy. He had his first match in 2019. He is one half of Waves and Curls with his partner Jaylen Bradyn. His favorite moment in wrestling today was December 14, 2008 in Buffalo, New York at WWE *Armageddon* when Jeff Hardy defeated Edge & Triple H in a triple threat match to win the WWE Heavyweight Championship.

Travis Huckabee
5' 8" 180lbs

Record: 1 – 1
Shows wrestled on:
June 24, 2017 **La Kermesse Festival Night 2** St. Louis Field Biddeford
November 30, 2018 **No Control** Portland Club

Trained at the WrestleFactory Huckabee debuted in 2017 for CHIKARA. He made the promotion his home base until its closure winning the Campeonato de Parejas twice, once with Solo Darling and once with Tony Deppen. Huckabee is an excellent and technically sound wrestler.

Trevor Murdoch *"The Outlaw"*
6' 4" 260lbs Waxahachie, Texas

Record: 1 – 0
Shows wrestled on:
February 22, 2020 ***Practice What You Preach*** AMVets Hall Yarmouth

Trained by the legendary Harley Race, Murdoch debuted in 1999 Trevor Rhodes for Race's World League Wrestling winning the promotions Heavyweight Championship five times and Tag Team titles three times. Under the name Stan Dupp with Bo he competed as the Dupps in ECW and TNA. In 2002 he had his first of multiple tours in Japan with Pro Wrestling NOAH. In 2005 he debuted in the WWE with Lance Cade the duo would team together for three years capturing three World Tag Team Championships. Murdoch was released by the WWE in 2008, wrestled in TNA in 2009 as Jethro Holliday. In 2016 he took a two-year hiatus from wrestling retiring in 2018. He returned in 2019 in the revamped NWA and on September 29, 2020 captured the NWA National Championship.

Trey Miguel *"Trigger" "The Fresh Prince of Mid-Air"*
5' 9" 172lbs Toledo, Ohio

Record: 0 – 1
Shows wrestled on:
May 11, 2018 ***Feed The Need*** Portland Club

Miguel trained with Dave Crist making his in-ring debut in August 2009. He has competed in matches in the UK, Ireland, Canada, Mexico, Japan and across the US Indies. He is a member of the Rascalz with Myron Reed, Desmond Xavier, and Zachary Wentz. He has held four different Tag Team Championships with other members of The Rascalz. In 2018 he signed with Impact Wrestling leaving the promotion in November 2020.

Troy Nelson *"Top Shelf"*
6' 0" 215lbs Haverhill, Massachusetts

Record: 11 – 8
Shows wrestled on:
September 12, 2015 **Stage One** City Side Restaurant, Brewer
November 15, 2015 **Killin' & Thrillin** American Legion Post 84 Orono
January 30, 2016 **Under Fire** American Legion Post 84 Orono
May 28, 2016 **No Dropkicks in the Living Room** American Legion Post 84 Orono
July 23, 2016 **Hook, Line, & Sinker** American Legion Post 84 Orono
September 24, 2016 **Past Your Bedtime** American Legion Post 84 Orono
October 29, 2016 **Who Watches the Watchmen?** The Field House at University of Maine Orono
November 19, 2016 **Hogwash** American Legion Post 84 Orono
January 27, 2017 **Unreal** Westbrook Armory
March 17, 2017 **Hysteria** Westbrook Armory
April 28, 2017 **Can We Kick It?** Portland Club

May 13, 2017 *Problematic* Westbrook Armory
July 21, 2017 *Nothing Gold Can Stay* Westbrook Armory
September 22, 2017 *Question The Answers* Westbrook Armory
January 19, 2018 *The World Is Ours* Westbrook Armory
March 30, 2018 *Only Fools Are Satisfied* Westbrook Armory
July 27, 2018 *Vacationland Cup* Westbrook Armory
September 21, 2018 *Pretenders Beware* Westbrook Armory
November 30, 2018 *No Control* Portland Club

Trained with Angel Ortiz and Joel Maximo he debuted in 2013. From 2016 to 2018 he went on a nine-match winning streak in Limitless Wrestling, during this he feuded with Sydney Bakabella who thought "Funny didn't equal money" in pro wrestling and wanted to bring seriousness back to Maine Pro Wrestling. Bakabella brought in challengers Kikutaro, Colt Cabana, WeeBl, Swoggle, and Dick Justice who all fell to Nelson. Nelson stated that wrestling Kikutaro is his favorite moment in the ring. "It was an honor to try my hand at an international and well-travelled competitor, all while making a few people laugh along the way."

Tyler Nitro
5' 9" 161lbs Virginia Beach, Virginia

Record: 3 – 8
Shows wrestled on:
September 24, 2016 *Past Your Bedtime* American Legion Post 84 Orono
October 07, 2016 *Risk It For The Biscuit* Westbrook Armory
October 29, 2016 *Who Watches the Watchmen?* The Field House at University of Maine Orono
November 19, 2016 *Hogwash* American Legion Post 84 Orono
January 27, 2017 *Unreal* Westbrook Armory
February 25, 2017 *Do What You Love, Fuck The Rest-Fest* American Legion Post 84 Orono
March 17, 2017 *Hysteria* Westbrook Armory

April 28, 2017 *Can We Kick It?* Portland Club
May 13, 2017 *Problematic* Westbrook Armory
June 23, 2017 *La Kermesse Festival Night 1* St. Louis Field Biddeford
June 24, 2017 *La Kermesse Festival Night 2* St. Louis Field Biddeford
June 23, 2019 *La Kermesse Festival Night 2* St. Louis Field Biddeford

Tyler debuted in 2013 and was a regular with Pennsylvania based Pro Wrestling Rampage winning the Wild Card Championship and Wild Card Tag Team Championship. In Limitless Wrestling feuded with Cam Zagami.

Tyree Taylor *"Big Boy from Brooklyn" "Tiger"*
5' 10" 330lbs The Crown Heights

Record: 0 – 1
Shows wrestled on:
December 19, 2020 **2020 VACATIONLAND CUP** AMVets Yarmouth, Maine

Trained at the Johnny Rodz World of Unpredictable Wrestling and the New England Pro Wrestling Academy. With Shane Taylor they held the Reality of Wrestling Tag Team Championships for 126 days, held the ACE: American Championship Entertainment Diamond Championship for 168 days and the WOW: Warriors of Wrestling No Limits Championship for 364 days.

Victoria
5' 8" 155lbs Louisville, Kentucky

Record: 0 – 1
Shows wrestled on:
May 10, 2019 *Hooked on a Friedman* Westbrook Armory

Also known as Tara in TNA, Lisa Marie Varon trained to wrestling with Mike Bell and Tom Howard with Ultimate Pro Wrestling debuting in June 2000. She was first seen on WWE TV as a member of the Godfather's Ho Train and was power bombed through a table by Godfather when he turned heel becoming the Goodfather. She won her first of two WWE Women's Championships in a hardcore match defeating Trish Stratus at *Survivor Series* 2002. She left the WWE in 2009 after competing in the Diva Battle Royal at *WrestleMania XXV*. She debuted in TNA in May 2009 she stayed with the promotion until July 2013 winning the Knockouts Championship five times. Over the next six years she competed in about four dozen matches, announcing in January 2019 that this would be her last year as an in-ring competitor. Her final match came on September 21, 2019 competing as Lisa Marie Varon defeating Melina Perez for the vacant More Women's Wrestling Championship in Kenansville, North Carolina. She returned to the ring in 2021 as a surprise entrant in the Women's Royal Rumble Match.

VSK *"The Visionary"*
6' 9" 198lbs Long Island, New York

Record: 3 – 1
Shows wrestled on:
April 28, 2017 **Can We Kick It?** Portland Club
September 22, 2017 **Question The Answers** Westbrook Armory
January 19, 2018 **The World Is Ours** Westbrook Armory

Debuted in 2007 with New York based Victory Pro Wrestling and has stayed primarily in the Northeast region. With Dorian Graves formed the tag team Massage NV. He is a two-time VPW New York State Champion totaling 700 days and a three-time VPW Heavyweight Champion holding the strap for 826 days. He has held the Create-A-Pro Championship since August 23, 2019. Recently wrestled matches for AEW on Dark.

Warbeard Hanson
6' 2" 293lbs Overseas

Record: 2 – 1
Shows wrestled on:
May 28, 2016 *No Dropkicks in the Living Room* American Legion Post 84 Orono
July 23, 2016 *Hook, Line, & Sinker* American Legion Post 84 Orono
January 27, 2017 *Unreal* Westbrook Armory

Now known as Ivar, one half of the The Viking Raiders, in the WWE he began his career in 2002 training with Killer Kowalski and Mike Hallow. He won the NWA New England Tag Team Championship with Beau Douglas just a few months into his start and held the titles for over a year. He was also a three-time Chaotic Wrestling Heavyweight Champion holding the title for 369 days. He also wrestled under the names of Handsome Johnny and the "Duke of Elegance" Don Chesterfield. In 2013 he debuted with Ring of Honor, winning the 2014 Top Prospect Tournament defeating Raymond Rowe in the finals. The two would form the team War Machine a month later competing across the US Indies, the UK, NOAH, New Japan, and signed with the WWE in 2018. In the years since they have captured various titles including the Ring of Honor, two-time IWGP, NXT, and WWE Raw tag team championship.

Warhorse
4000lbs of Heavy Metal

Record: 2 – 1
Shows wrestled on:
May 11, 2018 *Feed The Need* Portland Club
November 29, 2019 *Twilight Zone* AMVets Hall Yarmouth
February 22, 2020 *Practice What You Preach* AMVets Hall Yarmouth

Jake Parnell debuted in 2013 wrestling on the US indie scene. He captured the Zero1 USA Tag Team Championships with Alexandre Rudolph as the Viking War Party. He is also a two-time Zero1 USA World Junior Heavyweight Championships.
In early 2019 he transformed himself into Warhorse, and heavy metal loving headbanger with a painted face that rules ass! On September 21, 2019 in Summit, Illinois Warhorse defeated Erick Stevens capturing the IWTV Independent Wrestling Championship. He was a fighting champion defending it around the Indies for 532 days losing the title to Lee Moriarty on March 6, 2021 in Hanceville, Alabama. On the July 29, 2020 episode of AEW Dynamite Warhorse came up short on his bid for Cody Rhodes' for the TNT Championship.
In Limitless Wrestling Parnell wrestled in a Scramble match at *Feed the Need*, which was won by Ace Austin. He even wrestled on the Dojo Tapings in matches that can be found on YouTube. As Warhorse he defended the IWTV championship at *Twilight Zone* and *Practice What You Preach*.

WeeBL
5' 0" 125lbs Warren, Rhode Island

Record: 0 – 1
Shows wrestled on:
July 21, 2017 *Nothing Gold Can Stay* Westbrook Armory

Rob Araujo was trained by Bob Evans and Dan Freitas debuting in 2007. He was a regular with Eastern Pro Wrestling winning their tag team championships. He is also a regular with Northeast Championship Wrestling winning their New England and Tag Team Championship twice. Although based out of New England he has wrestled across Canada and has appeared in the WWE as JB-Elf and WeeBL.

Wheeler YUTA
6' 0" 189lbs Philadelphia, Pennsylvania

Record: 1 – 0
Shows wrestled on:
March 30, 2018 *Only Fools Are Satisfied* Westbrook Armory

Began training in 2013 with AC Collins in Myrtle Beach, South Carolina. Had his first match May 4, 2013. In CHIKARA he wrestled as Sylverhawk holding the Young Lions Cup for 14 days in 2017. He has wrestled across the US Indies, Canada, Japan, the UK, and Germany. During the pandemic he picked up the pan drum and was seen busking at the showboat in Atlantic City during a Beyond Wrestling event.

Willow Nightingale *"The Girl with the Big Hair and a Bigger Smile"*
5' 6" weighing in at just the perfect amount Long Island, New York

Record: 1 – 3
Shows wrestled on:
September 22, 2017 *Question The Answers* Westbrook Armory
November 03, 2017 *Hybrid Moments* Portland Club
September 21, 2018 *Pretenders Beware* Westbrook Armory
January 11, 2019 *Snakebitten* Westbrook Armory

Trained at the New York Wrestling Connection Training Academy with Mike Mondo and Bull James, she debuted in 2015. Has competed around the United States with the New York and New Jersey region being her home territory. Competes for Women of Wrestling as Eye Candy. She is a former three-time NYWC Starlet Champion holding the title for a combined 908 days. She and Faye Jackson held the Queens of Combat Tag Team Champions for exactly one year and with Solo Darling held the CHIKARA Campeonatos de Parejas Championships for 228 days.

Wrecking Ball Legursky
6' 4" 442lbs Southington, Connecticut

Record: 0 – 1
Shows wrestled on:
March 19, 2016 *Don't Fear The Sleeper* American Legion Post 84 Orono

Trained by Matt Taven & Mike Bennett he has wrestling primarily in New England with matches in the Northeast region. Is a regular with Northeast Wrestling where he held their Heavyweight Championship in 2018. Most recently appeared on Impact Wrestling in a loss to Madman Fulton.

Xavier Bell
5' 10" 185lbs Boston, Massachusetts

Record: 9 – 10
Shows wrestled on:
September 12, 2015 *Stage One* City Side Restaurant, Brewer
November 15, 2015 *Killin' & Thrillin* American Legion Post 84 Orono
January 30, 2016 *Under Fire* American Legion Post 84 Orono
March 19, 2016 *Don't Fear The Sleeper* American Legion Post 84 Orono
May 28, 2016 *No Dropkicks in the Living Room* American Legion Post 84 Orono
July 23, 2016 *Hook, Line, & Sinker* American Legion Post 84 Orono
September 24, 2016 *Past Your Bedtime* American Legion Post 84 Orono
October 07, 2016 *Risk It For The Biscuit* Westbrook Armory

October 29, 2016 ***Who Watches the Watchmen?*** The Field House at University of Maine Orono
November 19, 2016 ***Hogwash*** American Legion Post 84 Orono
January 27, 2017 ***Unreal*** Westbrook Armory
February 25, 2017 ***Do What You Love, Fuck The Rest-Fest*** American Legion Post 84 Orono
March 17, 2017 ***Hysteria*** Westbrook Armory
April 28, 2017 ***Can We Kick It?*** Portland Club
May 13, 2017 ***Problematic*** Westbrook Armory
June 23, 2017 ***La Kermesse Festival Night 1*** St. Louis Field Biddeford
June 24, 2017 ***La Kermesse Festival Night 2*** St. Louis Field Biddeford
July 21, 2017 ***Nothing Gold Can Stay*** Westbrook Armory
January 19, 2018 ***The World Is Ours*** Westbrook Armory

Bell wrestled on the first 18 consecutive Limitless shows, others may have wrestled on more shows, but no one has wrestled on as many consecutive shows as Xavier Bell. He began training with Oney Lorcan, then known as Biff Busick, in August 2014. He had his first match later that year in December. He wrestled primarily in the New England Territory with Top Rope, Beyond, and Limitless Wrestling, he was also a regular with ¡Let's Wrestle! His final match was January 19, 2019 with ¡Let's Wrestle! in Orono, Maine. He competed in a Scramble match and the ¡Let's Wrestle! Rumble being eliminated by Anthony Greene.

Zachary Wentz *"The Sickest Dude in All The Land"*
5' 10" 176lbs Dayton, Ohio

Record: 0 – 1
Shows wrestled on:
May 11, 2018 ***Feed The Need*** Portland Club

Initially trained in Mixed Martial Arts before he debuted in professional wrestling in 2014. He was part of the tag team The

Rascalz with Desmond Xavier. Myron Reed and Trey Miguel. Started out in the Ohio region and branched out across the US Indies. Made his United Kingdom debut in Preston City Wrestling in November 2016, then spent May 2017 touring different promotions in the country. January through March 2018 he toured with Dragon Gate in Japan and in May made his first appearance with Impact Wrestling, where he is currently signed. With Desmond Xavier they have held the PWG World Tag Team Championship since April 20, 2018. He left Impact Wrestling November 2020 signing with the WWE making his NXT debut on January 13, 2021 with Dezmond Xavier in the *Dusty Rhodes Classic*. Wentz, now known as Nash Carter and Xavier, now known as Wes Lee, would team under the name MSK and defeated the Grizzled Young Vets winning the *Dusty Rhodes Classic*.

Zack Sabre Jr *"ZSJ" "Submission Master"*
6' 0" 187lbs Isle of Sheppey, Kent, England

Record: 1 – 0
Shows wrestled on:
January 30, 2016 **Under Fire** American Legion Post 84 Orono

Trained at NWA Hammerlock, Sabre debuted April 20, 2004 at the age of 16. A practitioner of the British Catch style, Sabre is world renowned for his unique and innovative submission maneuvers. He wrestled for all the top promotions in Europe, United States, Japan, and around the world. Multiple times he held more than one championship at a time earning the nicknames Zacky two belts and Zacky three belts. He held the RevPro British Heavyweight Championship 4 times for a combined 1086 days, NWA United Kingdom Junior Heavyweight Championship for 953 days, and the Triple X Wrestling Championship for 882 days. He held the Pro Wrestling Guerrilla World Heavyweight Championship for 489 days and the Evolve Championship for 404 days. On the Tag Team side, he held the RevPro Tag Team

Championship with Minoru Suzuki for 475 days, with Marty Scrull, a two-time IPW: United Kingdom Tag Team Championship twice for 1125 days. He is a former IWGP Heavyweight Tag Team Champion with Taichi.

Zack Sabre Jr. with the Moose State at the Kennebunk, Maine travel plaza

The Managers

Kenneth Banks

Limitless Debut: September 12, 2015 *Stage One* City Side Restaurant Brewer

Banks wrestled under the name Legion "Freaking" Cage getting his start in 2000. His first exposure in wrestling came in Rampage Pro Wrestling based out of Bangor, Maine where he was a two-time Cruiserweight Champion. He would compete in Canada for the Nova Scotia based MainStream Wrestling where he won the Junior Heavyweight Championship. He would win championships from promotions in Florida, Vermont, and Rhode Island as well as the Maine based New Wrestling Horizons. He last competed in 2008 for the NAWA: North Atlantic Wrestling Association in Brewer, Maine. He made his return at Limitless Wrestling managing his former tag team partner Marcus Hall, they are former Florida based ACW: American Combat Wrestling tag team champions. Banks was slated to make his in-ring return at Limitless Wrestling's second event *Killin' & Thrillin'* against Christian Casanova, however he pulled off the show. *Stage One* was his only appearance to date in Limitless Wrestling.

Sidney Bakabella *"King of Managers"*

Limitless Debut: March 17, 2017 *Hysteria* Westbrook Armory

Bakabella got his start in 1976 for Ed McLemore in the Dallas Territory. He eventually moved onto the Pensacola Territory where he was the driver for Andre the Giant. He is responsible for advising Verne Gagne not to put the title on his son Greg. He is a two-time WWE Hall of Famer being inducted in 1992 and again in 2002 to celebrate the tenth anniversary of his first induction. When asked about the honor he stated, "Senior put me in, and Junior kicked me out."

On August 12, 2012 he debuted in CHIKARA with his team Devastation Corporation. He became the Director of Fun until the season 18 finale. He then managed Dasher Hatfield during his run as Grand Champion. Bakabella is the only person to manage the Grand Champion, Campeontas de Parejas, and King of Trios winners. He also provided color commentary staying with the promotion until it folded. At one-point Bakabella faked his own death so Fritz Von Erich would run a benefit show for him.
He arrived in Limitless Wrestling with one goal in mind, to teach Troy Nelson that funny doesn't equal money and to bring seriousness back to Maine Pro Wrestling. Bakabella brought in Kikutaro, Colt Cabana, WeeBL, Dick Justice, Swoggle, and "Smart" Mark Sterling to fight his battle, and they all fell to Nelson. Today Bakabella has returned to his roots and is signed exclusively with Fritz Von Erich and the Dallas Wrestling Office, except when he's managing A Very Good Professional Wrestler.

Jon Alba *"Emmy Award Winning"*

Limitless Debut: May 13, 2017 **Problematic** Westbrook Armory

A lifelong wrestling fan since he was a child, Alba first got involved in wrestling with the Maine based IWE: Independent Wrestling Entertainment. He debuted in 2016 managing Auman Jordan costing Ace Romero the IWE Maine State Championship. He later joined the stable The Station managing Adam Ricker, Jimmy Limits, and Jason Rumble. He debuted in Limitless Wrestling at *Problematic*, May 13, 2017 with Jon Alba's Star Search. His first protege that night was Alex Chamberlain against Mr. Grim, Alba inadvertently cost Chamberlain the match and ended the night being carried out in Grim's body bag. Alba didn't fare well in Limitless Wrestling, returning in March 2018 managing Bear Country to a loss against Whiskey Dick then in July at the *2018 Vacationland Cup* he managed Nico Silva in a scramble match that was won by Kevin Blackwood.

As a result of the loss Alba was banned from Limitless Wrestling. His only other Limitless appearance that year was in

May when he hosted an in-ring segment between Maine State Posse and Joey Eastman.

In May 2019 he first arrived in ¡Let's Wrestle! as the manager of Mac Daniels against Aiden Aggro. In January 2020 he made his ¡Let's Wrestle! in-ring debut enter the ¡Let's Wrestle! Rumble at number 27, he didn't eliminate anyone and was eliminated by The Maine State Posse.

Shortly before the *2020 Vacationland Cup* he was reinstated in Limitless Wrestling and managed Mac Daniels in a four-way qualifying match that was won by CJ Cruz.

Alba has also done commentary for Limitless Wrestling, ¡Let's Wrestle!, and New Jersey based Synergy Pro Wrestling. Alba is the co-host of the Limitless Wrestling Podcast with owner Randy Carver, the first episode aired March 28, 2018 with 76 episodes as of December 24, 2020.

Joey Eastman

Limitless Debut: November 03, 2017 **Hybrid Moments** Portland Club

Eastman began his wrestling journey as a ring announcer in 2003 in the Chicago and Milwaukee area. He was broke into the business by Carmine Despirito and Ed Chuman and along the way he had help from many others. He was the first ring announcer for SHIMMER Women Athletes when they debuted in 2005 and continued the duties for the next decade. Eastman transitioned into a manager with his first charges were Crazy Jack BERZERKER, Tommy Courageous, and Keith Walker. Like many managers in wrestling he eventually found himself competing in the ring with his first match being a six-man tag teaming with Courageous and BERZERKER against Keith Walker, Frankie "The Thumper" Defalco and Jake "The Milkman" Milliman. History was made on July 1, 2006 in Amery, Wisconsin when Eastman defeated "Sweet & Sour" Larry Sweeny to win the ICW/ICWA Tex-Arkana Television Championship. Joey was the 42nd Champion holding the title for one day he lost it on his first defense back to Sweeny in Cottage Grove, Minnesota. On May 22, 2010 in Worcester, Massachusetts at the Juggalo Championship Wrestling Happy Dayz Tour Eastman found himself standing across the ring from Butterbean. Butterbean, who has a combined boxing, kickboxing, and MMA record of 97-24-4 with 68 knockouts, took 53 seconds to dispatch Eastman. That's 18 seconds longer than it took him to defeat Bart Gunn at WrestleMania XV.

Eastman takes responsibility for breaking up the Maine State Posse, he tried to lure DangerKid away from the trio but when that failed, he turned his sights to Alexander Lee. Along with Brandon Kirk they waged war on MSP leading to the Portland Street Fight at *Know Your Enemy* in the Portland Expo. The match ended in the favor of MSP but left Lee and Eastman with a new enemy, Brandon Kirk.

Stokely Hathaway *"Big Stoke"*

Limitless Debut: November 03, 2017 *Hybrid Moments* Portland Club

Hathaway was trained at the Ring of Honor Dojo debuting first as a wrestler in 2014 before transitioning to managing. As a wrestler he competed for Ring of Honor before leaving the promotion in late 2015. In 2016 he arrived in CHIKARA and having trademarked the name Chuck Taylor competed under that name forcing Chuck Taylor to wrestle as Dustin. Competing in Ontario, Canada's Alpha-1 Wrestling he captured the Outer Limits Championship holding the title for 210 days.
He formed the stable The Dream Team with members MJF, Christian Casanova, Faye Jackson, Thomas Sharp, Jonathan Gresham, PB Smooth, Mr. Grim, Austin Theory and others. While in Evolve he was a member of the stable Catch Point and in Major League Wrestling he fronted Black Friday Management. In March 2019 he signed with WWE's NXT Brand where he now goes by Malcolm Bivens.

Ring Announcers

Rich Palladino

Limitless Debut: January 30, 2016 *Under Fire* American Legion Post 84 Orono

Palladino's first foray into professional wrestling came in 1992 when he did commentary for American Wrestling Federation with "Boston Bad Boy" Tony Rumble. It was Rumble that gave Palladino his first break as a ring announcer for Century Wrestling Alliance on October 23, 1993. Palladino served as ring announcer for Extreme Championship Wrestling all around New England from 1996 - 1999 with his first show November 23, 1996 at the Greyhound Wonderland Park in Revere, Massachusetts, the same night as the infamous Mass Transit incident. He would also announce cards in Massachusetts at the Town Hall in Webster, Veterans Memorial Hall in Fall River, IBWE Hall in Waltham, and

The Palladium in Worcester. In Connecticut The Sports Palace and The Sting in New Britain. "The most interesting venue I worked at was the Sting. It was connected to a strip joint and our locker room had access to a balcony that overlooked their stage." He has performed ring announcing duties for many other wrestling promotions including Ring of Honor, the Delaware based ECWA, Beyond Wrestling, and in 1997 he was the ring announcer for my first ever independent show, Eastern Wrestling Alliance in Auburn, Maine. In 2003 he had a try out as a backstage correspondent for the WWE.

Some of his favorite moments include announcing the 10th Annual ECWA Super 8 tournament on April 8, 2006 in Newark, Delaware featuring Davey Richards and Charlie Haas in the finals. On March 13, 2010 he announced the Ring of Honor 8th Anniversary Show at the Manhattan Center in New York City where Tyler Black defeated Austin Aries for the ROH World Championship. Rich Palladino is one of the finest ring announcers in wrestling today becoming the voice of New England wrestling with nearly 30 years in the business. He has been inducted into the Chaotic Wrestling and New England Pro Wrestling Hall of Fames.

Rich made his Limitless debut at their third show *Under Fire* featuring Zack Sabre Jr. vs. Chris Hero in the main event. Randy Carver had provided ring announcing duties for the first two Limitless shows however on the day of *Under Fire* Randy was suffering from pneumonia and called in Rich to host and he has done so at almost every show since.

Ethan Scott

Limitless Debut: February 25, 2017 ***Do What You Love, Fuck The Rest-Fest*** American Legion Post 84 Orono

Scott got his start in wrestling in 2014 with IWE: Independent Wrestling Entertainment working on the ring crew and running the sound equipment. When Limitless Wrestling debuted, he ran the sound equipment for them as well. He first tried his hand at ring announcing in 2017, not just for Limitless Wrestling but for their sister promotion ¡Let's Wrestle! and other promotions such as the NAWA: North Atlantic Wrestling Association. He states his favorite moment in wrestling is as a fan when Kevin Owens debuted on NXT, "Hearing the crowd erupt as he walked through the curtain gave me goosebumps."

The Referees of Limitless Wrestling

Eric Greenleaf

Limitless debut: September 12, 2015 *Stage One* City Side Restaurant Brewer

Eric began his journey to become a wrestler not a referee. He was training with the Maine based IWE: Independent Wrestling Entertainment however a series of injuries derailed his dreams. Not to be deterred from being involved in professional wrestling he started down the track to becoming a referee. He turned to Joey Gleitz and Eric Johnson for guidance in his early years. This first match he officiated was for IWE in 2013 featuring Johnny Primer vs. Crash Landing. He has also officiated for Blitzkrieg Pro, Northeast Championship Wrestling, Revival Pro Wrestling and ¡Let's Wrestle! His favorite matches he has refereed include Matt Sydal vs. Ricochet at Hysteria and when Anthony Green defeated MJF for the Limitless Wrestling World Championship at Know Your Enemy.

Joey Gleitz

Limitless debut: September 12, 2015 *Stage One* City Side Restaurant Brewer

Joey was born September 28, 1978 in Corydon, Indiana. He began his path to pro wrestling when he contacted City Side Restaurant in Brewer about booking the venue to run a hardcore wrestling show. City Side put him in contact with Eric Johnson the owner and promoter of IWE: Independent Wrestling Entertainment who ran monthly shows at the venue. After a discussion with Johnson Gleitz began his training in 2009 to become a wrestler. A nagging ankle injury prevented him continuing down that road detouring him into the striped shirt. Along with Eric, Chris Berry aided in training Gleitz as a referee. He officiated his first match in mid-2009 and over the years has worked for almost every promotion in Maine. He had the distinction of officiating the first ever match in Limitless Wrestling history at *Stage One* a Fatal Four Way tag team match where The Influence: Mike Montero & Jason Devine defeated The M1nute Men: Devin Blaze & Tommy Trainwreck, The Cute n' Brute Connection: Owen Brody & BA Tatum and The Falcon Corps: Adam Falcon & Joe Quick. In 2019 Gleitz began living his dream wrestling on smaller shows under a mask as Fireball Foreman, he would of course officiate other matches on the card as well. Sadly, Joey passed away at his home September 24, 2020, he refereed his last match just a few days prior on September 19th, a North Atlantic Wrestling Association show at Skip's Bar in Buxton, Maine.

Tony P

Limitless Debut: January 27, 2017 *Unreal* Westbrook Armory

Tony P's journey to the ring began in 2013 training with JT Dunn at his school in Providence, Rhode Island. The first matches he officiated was in February 2014.

His favorite match he officiated in Limitless Wrestling was at *Unreal*, January 17, 2017, calling it right down the middle between JT Dunn and Cody Rhodes.

Will Dojan

Limitless Debut: March 17, 2017 ***Hysteria*** Westbrook Armory

Began training in 2009 with Aaron Morrison, Chris Camaro, and Kevin Landry. His favorite match that he has refereed to date was on March 25, 2017 in Enfield, Connecticut for Blitzkrieg Pro at the Enrico Fermi High School. That night he had the honor of officiating the match that saw Donovan Dijak defeat the "American Nightmare" Cody Rhodes. In Limitless his favorite match was Anthony Greene vs. Paul London at Problematic on May 13, 2017 at the Westbrook Armory.

Kevin Quinn

Limitless Debut: September 22, 2017 ***Question The Answers*** Westbrook Armory

Quinn began his training with Jason Rumble and Beau Douglas at the Bell Time Club Training Center in 2011 after meeting Rumble at a local gym. He then trained under Brian Fury at the New England Pro Wrestling Academy. His favorite match that he has refereed was for NEW: North East Wrestling at WrestleFest XXI at Crosby High School in Waterbury, Connecticut on March 3, 2017 when Cody Rhodes defeated Kurt Angle inside a Steel Cage. In Limitless Wrestling he has officiated some of the biggest matches including the crowning of the first Limitless Wrestling World Champion at *Welcome to the Dance* and the infamous Steel Cage match at *2019 Vacationland Cup*.

Bryce Remsburg

Limitless Debut May 11, 2018 *Feed The Need* Portland Club

A CHIKARA original he appeared on their first show *The Renaissance Dawns* May 25, 2002 in Allentown, Pennsylvania. He got his start training with Mike Quackenbush and Reckless Youth as the WrestleFactory. Aside from refereeing duties Bryce also worked a ring announcer for a time and provided color commentary from 2005 - 2019. He worked for the promotion until it closed along with their sister Wrestling Is… promotions. On December 3, 2005 at the IWC: International Wrestling Cartel *Winter Bash 2005* in Oil City, Pennsylvania he defeated "Sweet & Sour" Larry Sweeney for the ICW/ICWA Tex-Arkana Television Championship. He would lose the title back to Sweeney that same day. On April 5, 2019 he officiated The Invisible Man vs. Invisible Stan *at Joey Janela's Spring Break Part 1* in Jersey City, New Jersey. In Mid 2019 he signed full time with All Elite Wrestling. *Feed the Need* was his only Limitless Wrestling show.

Derek Douglas

Limitless debut: September 08, 2018 *2018 Litchfield Fair*

"I got into referring because I've always wanted to be a part of pro wrestling since I was five or six years old." Watching Tony P in person was a big influence into taking the step towards putting on

the stripes himself. He was also inspired by Bryce Remsburg and Aubrey Edwards as they made being referring feel like an important part of the action. "Kevin Smith often talks about how with art you either consume or create and eventually you have to ask yourself if you're going to consume or contribute." Derek decided to contribute and began training with Limitless Wrestling before the days of the Limitless Dojo, in November 2016. He referred his first matches in September 2018 also for Limitless Wrestling, Alexander Lee vs. Rob Marsh and Ashley Vox vs. Davienne. He has also officiated matches for ¡Let's Wrestle! and Victory Championship Wrestling Can-Am. His favorite match that he has been the third man in the ring for was at Limitless Wrestling *Practice What You Preach* when he officiated the IWTV

Championship match when Warhorse successfully defended against Rip Byson.

Gina Monti

Limitless Debut January 24, 2020 *Flirtin' With Disaster* AMVets Hall Yarmouth

Gina trained with Slyck Wagner Brown and Bobby Ocean at the Test of Strength Wrestling School in 2018. When she started her journey in wrestling it was as a manager, but after participating in practice matches the art of refereeing called to her and she stuck with it ever since. She officiated her first bouts in East Hartford, Connecticut on September 15, 2018 at Test of Strength Fight For Your Dreams. Her first match was between El' Jabroni and Ryan Fraust. Since then she has also officiated matches for Paradise Alley Pro, Blitzkrieg Pro, Wrestle Party, Zero 1 USA Northeast, CHIKARA, Camp Leapfrog, Beyond, and Game Changer Wrestling. Her favorite match to date that she was the third person in the ring for was on January 25, 2020 between Kris Statlander and TJ Crawford at Beyond Please Come Back 2020.

Nate Speckman

September 19 & 20, 2020 *The Road Season 2* American Legion Post 84 Orono

Speckman, a Maine native, moved to Chicago in 2015. He trained to be a referee in Dayton, Ohio with Sami Callihan. He worked for several mid-west promotion including AAW Pro, Warrior Wrestling, Pro Wrestling Revolver and other, until moving home in September 2020. Even though his first matches that he officiated were on *The Road* Season 2, while home on vacation he attended *Pretenders Beware* and helped put behind the scenes at *Know Your Enemy*. When asked about his favorite moment in wrestling he responded, "Even just stepping in the ring to do one match was incredibly fulfilling for me." He also stated being trusted to officiate a company's main championship is an incredible honor. The first time he had the opportunity was when Pro Wrestling Revolver held a tournament to crown their first ever champion on December 28, 2018 in Des Moines, Iowa. That night Matt Palmer defeated Larry D, Shane Strickland, and Trey Miguel to win the title.

Other referee's that have worked for Limitless Wrestling during this time period include Manny Sousa and Chris Berry.

Limitless Wrestling World Championship

When Randy Carver started Limitless Wrestling, he never wanted to create a championship. His reasoning? He felt there were enough championships in wrestling already. At the end of 2018 he began to reconsider. On episode 30 of the Limitless Wrestling podcast, released January 17, 2019, he stated "We are at a point now where it feels that we have to decide who is at the top of the mountains, who is the best in Limitless Wrestling." At the end of *Snakebitten* with the implosion of both Take Me Home Tonight: Anthony Greene & Ace Romero and The Kings: JT Dunn & MJF Randy got in the ring and announced the fatal four way to crown the first Limitless Wrestling Champion.

Limitless Wrestling Championship History

Maxwell Jacob Freidman - 181 Days
March 9, 2019 - September 6, 2019

Anthony Greene - 397 Days
September 6, 2016 - October 7, 2020

Vacant - 73 days
October 7, 2020 - December 19, 2020

Christian Casanova - 90 Days
December 19, 2020 – March 19, 2021

Daniel Garcia
March 19, 2021 – current champion

Limitless Wrestling Championship Matches

March 09, 2019 **Limitless Wrestling** *Welcome to the Dance* The Armory Westbrook, Maine

Fatal Four Way: MJF: Maxwell Jacob Freidman defeated Ace Romero, Anthony Greene, & JT Dunn to become the inaugural champion

Notes from my blog The Wrestling Insomniac: These four guys showed why they deserved to be in the main event fighting for this title. For the beginning of the match it was primarily The Kings staying together, until Dunn hit Death by Elbow on Ace and MJF threw Dunn to the floor to steal a pin attempt. The match went to the floor and around the ring. They went through the crowd to the lockers, this time Greene and Dunn climbed on top, with Greene falling off and then Dunn jumping on everyone.
Back in the ring the finish came when Dunn hit everyone with Death by Elbow, the last being MJF which caused Dunn to fall out

of the ring and MJF to fall back on top of Greene for the three count. There was a huge pop when MJF won the championship, I think part excitement and part disbelief. I myself was rooting for Anthony Greene to pick up the win. In my opinion he has been the true ace of Limitless Wrestling over the years. Post-match Ashley Vox came out challenging MJF for a title match and he accepted.

March 17, 2019 **IPW:UK** *Live in London* Resistance Gallery, London, England

Champion: MJF defeated "Superbad" Kip Sabian

This match represents the reason it's called the title is called a World Championship. Just eight days after winning it MJF's first defense came at an International Pro Wrestling: United Kingdom event.

May 10, 2019 **Limitless Wrestling** *Hooked on a Friedman* The Armory Westbrook, Maine

Champion: MJF defeated "Reel Catch" Ashley Vox

Notes from my blog The Wrestling Insomniac: Dunn came out with MJF but a few minutes into the match was ejected from ringside. MJF opened with a scathing promo putting down Vox and women in general generating a lot of hate and discontent from the crowd. Mikey mentioned he's surprised that no one has attacked him yet, I'd have to agree with Mikey as MJF gets that old-school white-hot heat. Ashley would take a tremendous beating repeatedly in this match but each time she would battle back with some high impact offense much to the delight of the crowd. I was excited to see MJF bust out both a bear hug and torture rack style back breaker in the match.

Late in the match while on the floor MJF pressed Ashley over his head and just threw her into the crowd on both sides of the ring. Probably would have been nice if they would have tried to catch her, but it was a fantastic visual! A few moments later while MJF was on the floor Ashley dove at him three times sending MJF crashing back into Mikey and me. As a front row fan, I know that at times wrestlers are going to crash and land on us, I've accepted it. I'm not one to dive out of the way every time they come near us though unless the wrestlers yell at us to move. If either one of them would have said move, we would have.

Back in the ring the ref was knocked down and MJF got the title belt, Vox said that she would kiss his boot as he demanded at the beginning of the match, but she hit him in the junk instead. Then she hit MJF with the belt and locked on her finisher. MJF tapped out but the ref didn't see it. Eventually the ref came around again and Vox locked her reel catch back on, MJF then violently bit down hard on her finger covering her hand and his mouth with blood. It was vicious! He then drove her into the mat with Cross Rhodes for the pin.

Post-match JT Dunn celebrated in the ring with MJF as the fans threw trash at him which MJF encouraged. He cut a promo saying we were trash and that JT Dunn was going to win the Vacationland Cup and forfeit his title match. Dunn hit MJF with Death by Elbow and cut a promo saying he was going to take the title from MJF.

September 06, 2019 **Limitless Wrestling *Know Your Enemy*** The Expo, Portland, Maine

Anthony Greene defeated Champion: MJF to win the title

Notes from my blog The Wrestling Insomniac: This was a very anticipated match and the perfect finish to the Limitless Wrestling four-year anniversary event. About two minutes into the match MJF hit Greene with a deliberate low blow for which the referee called for the bell. Randy Carver, Limitless owner, restarted the match declaring it no DQ. The match quickly went to the floor and around ringside. This match was not as crazy as the MSP vs. Brandon Kirk & Alexander Lee street fight from earlier in the evening, but they did their fair share of damage to each other. Finish came right in the center of the ring after a so much prettier by Greene on MJF. Biggest pop of the night the referee hit the three count. Every person in the building was on their feet! We all wanted this bad for AG. Post-match MJF shook AG's hand and quickly raised his arm before exiting to the back.

October 25, 2019 **Limitless Wrestling** *Fresh Blood* AMVets Hall Yarmouth

Champion: Anthony Greene defeated Josh Briggs

From my live report on The Wrestling Insomniac Blog: Solid main event Glad to see Briggs back, it's been a long time since he was last in Limitless since his hip injury. These two guys brought it for a solid match that saw Greene retain with his super so much prettier.

November 17, 2019 **Zero1 USA Northeast** *November Reign*, Eagles Club Gardner, Massachusetts

Champion: Anthony Greene defeated Brian Pillman Jr.

January 11, 2020 **¡Let's Wrestle!** *¡Let's Wrestle! Rumble* American Legion, Orono, Maine

Champion: Anthony Greene defeated Ava Everette

From my live report on The Wrestling Insomniac Blog: It's Ava's birthday and the open challenge was answered by her boyfriend AG who gifted her a cake that said It Is Your Birthday and a title shot for the Limitless Wrestling World Championship. Ava used every dirty trick that she could use and cheated as much as she could, but it wasn't enough for her to win the championship as AG retained with his corner pull up piledriver.

January 24, 2020 **Limitless Wrestling** *Flirtin' With Disaster* AMVets Hall Yarmouth

Triple Threat Match: Champion: Anthony Greene defeated Ace Romero and "Top Talent" Christian Casanova

Notes from my blog The Wrestling Insomniac: The world championship match closed out the show, as it should. Before and throughout the match dueling chants were busted out for Casanova and Acey Baby with Greene being left out of the adulation. I tried to get the chant going for him, but my lone voice wasn't enough. Scary moment right near the beginning of the match when Ace went to powerbomb Casanova on the ring apron but only the back of Casanova's head made contact. The crowd was silent while the referee attended to Casanova. It was a legit unsettling moment. This match was very hard hitting and high impact. One moment saw Greene trying to suplex Casanova off the top rope and Ace powerbombing Greene at the same time. It was wicked. Greene stole the pin after Casanova hit his ax kick on Ace from the top rope and Greene tossed Casanova out of the ring pinning Ace. Post-match Casanova and Greene brawled with Casanova demanding another match against Greene. Again, this match was fantastic, lots of action and some great offense from everyone. Casanova will be champion someday, just not while Greene is holding onto the gold.

February 22, 2020 **Limitless Wrestling** *Practice What You Preach* AMVets Hall Yarmouth

Champion: Anthony Greene defeated "Dirty Daddy" Chris Dickinson

Notes from my blog The Wrestling Insomniac: The Dirty Daddy jump started this match when he nailed AG with a missile dropkick during his entrance. It looked like Dickinson was going to win the Championship, but AG reversed a lateral press into one of his own for a quick three count. Post-match Dickinson hits AG with the Pazuzu Bomb and Kris Stat cut a promo on AG about challenging him for the championship next month.

March 30, 2020 **Pandemic At The Dojo** *Episode 1* Brewer, Maine

Open Challenge: Champion: Anthony Greene defeated Davienne

AG got in the ring and laid out an open challenge, surprisingly it took a moment for anyone to respond when Davienne jumped in the ring. This was a great match, very hard fought, excellent back and forth action.

May 5, 2020 **Pandemic At The Dojo** *Episode 6* Brewer, Maine

Champion: Anthony Greene defeated Rip Byson

Byson had defeated DL Hurst in Episode 4 to become the number one contender for the Limitless Wrestling World Championship. An excellent match between these two that was very hard hitting. They spent 11 minutes beating the tar out of each other with Greene getting the pin with So Much Prettier.

Aired October 07, 2020 **The Road** *Episode 11* American Legion Post 84, Orono

Champion: "Retro" Anthony Greene pinned "Reel Catch" Ashley Vox

In the season 1 finale Greene defended the title against a very game Ashley Vox. This was an excellent match that went back and forth with Greene reversing Vox's reel catch finish into the pin fall to retain his title.

December 19, 2020 **Limitless Wrestling** *Vacationland Cup 2020* AMVets Hall Yarmouth

Vacationland Cup Finals: Fatal Four Way Elimination Match: "Top Talent" Christian Casanova outlasted "Red Death" Daniel Garcia, "The Prize" Alec Price, and JD Drake to capture the vacant Limitless Wrestling World Championship.

Prize pinned Drake, Garcia eliminated Price via referee stoppage, and Casanova pinned Garcia.

March 19, 2021 **Limitless Wrestling** *Double Vision* AMVets Hall Yarmouth

"Red Death" Daniel Garcia pinned Champion: "Top Talent" Christian Casanova to win the championship

Title Matches in Limitless Wrestling

The first ever championship that was defended in Limitless Wrestling was at the promotions third show *Under Fire*, January 30, 2016. However, it was for the House of Glory Tag Team Championships not the Limitless Wrestling World Championship. That title was still over three years away from being crowned. Over the years though Limitless Wrestling has hosted sanctioned championship matches from other promotions as an added attraction to the already stacked cards.

House of Glory Wrestling
Based out of Ridgewood, New York House of Glory wrestling was founded in 2012 by The Amazing Red and Brian XL. Their first card was on May 5, 2012 and most recent on December 7, 2019.

HOG Tag Team Championship

January 30, 2016 *Under Fire* Legion Post 84 Orono
Fatal Four Way: Champions: Private Party: Isiah Kassidy & Marq Quen defeated Cuban Rum Crisis: "Top Shelf" Troy Nelson & JGeorge, Alexander Lee & DangerKid and Herbal Corps: Adam Falcon & Rembrandt Lewis.

From my live report on The Wrestling Insomniac Blog: The Fatal Four Way match for the House of Glory Tag Team Championships was my favorite kind, an elimination match with Lucha Rules. Alexander Lee was forced to team with Danger Kid and after being eliminated first Lee blamed Kid and the two battled to the back. No doubt we will see a singles match between them in the future. Next eliminated was the Herbal Corps. In a very impressive move JGeorge nailed a swinging full nelson, I love it when someone busts out classic never seen moves. Private Party retained, Isiah Kassidy is young and is wicked good, can't wait to see more of him.

The House of Glory Tag Team Champions were first crowned on November 15, 2013 when The Young Bucks: Matt & Nick Jackson defeated Homicide & Hernandez in a tournament final. The current champions are The Lucha Brothers: Rey Fenix & Pentagon Jr. who won the titles on June 8, 2019 defeating Santana & Ortiz.

Private Party were the 5th HOG Tag Team Champions holding the titles for 252 days, winning them on December 11, 2015 defeating Santana & Ortiz and losing them on August 19, 2016 to the Hardys: Matt & Jeff.

HOG Elite Championship

January 30, 2016 *Under Fire* Legion Post 84 Orono
Champion: "The Rogue" Anthony Gangone defeated Sonya Strong

From my live report on The Wrestling Insomniac Blog: House of Glory Elite Champion Anthony Gangone successfully defended his championship against a very game Sonya Strong. This is only the second time I have seen Sonya and not only is she fantastic, but she is one tough lady. Gangone won with what looked a combination of a cobra clutch and cattle mutilation, the referee stopped the match after Sonya's had dropped 3 times.

July 23, 2016 ***Hook, Line, & Sinker*** Legion Post 84 Orono
Triple Threat Match: Champion: "The Rogue" Anthony Gangone defeated Ric King and Mike Graca.

The House of Glory Elite Championship was first crowned on December 11, 2015 when Brian XL awarded the title to Ken Broadway. The current champion is TJ Perkins who won the title on November 16, 2019 defeating Mantequilla. On September 24, 2016 the name of the championship was changed, and it is currently known as the Crown Jewel Championship.

Anthony Gangone was the 2nd & 5th champion holding it for a combined 342 days. These matches took place during his first reign which began on December 11, 2015 and lasted for 252 days when he defeated Ken Broadway, Joey Janela, and JT Dunn in a Fatal Four Way match. His reign came to an end on August 19, 2016 when he lost the championship back to Ken Broadway.

Create-A-Pro Wrestling Academy
Based out of Hicksville, New York it was founded in 2014 by Pat Buck and Brian Myers. They ran their first show on February 13, 2015 and most recent show on February 1, 2020.

CAP Championship

June 24, 2017 ***La Kermesse Festival Night 2*** St. Louis Field Biddeford
Champion: "Smart" Mark Sterling defeated Bear Bronson
Bronson had won the opening match battle royal to earn a shot for the championship in the main event against Sterling.

The CAP Championship was first crowned on December 20, 2015 when Max Caster defeated Alex Reynolds in the finals of a tournament. The current champion is VSK who won a six-way scramble defeating Bear Bronson, Johnny Clash, Mark Sterling, Max Caster, and Champion: Pat Buck on August 23, 2019.

"Smart" Mark Sterling is the 4th champion holding the title for 280 days. He defeated Max Caster on January 20, 2017 and was defeated by Johnny Clash on October 27, 2017.

Xtreme Wrestling Alliance
Based out of Johnston, Rhode Island, XWA began promoting shows in 2001. Each year they hold the Xtreme Rumble and Wrestlution.

XWA Heavyweight Championship

July 21, 2017 *Nothing Gold Can Stay* Westbrook Armory
XWA Champion: Anthony Henry submitted Flip Gordon

I can't find the complete history of this championship. Sometime between January 2017 and July 16, 2017 he defeated Mike Bennett to win the title. He held both the XWA Tag Team & Heavyweight championships at the same time.

The Wrestling Revolver
Based out of Des Moines, Iowa, the promotion was founded in 2016 by Sami Callihan under the name Pro Wrestling Revolver before changing to The Wrestling Revolver in 2017. Their first show was June 10, 2016 and the most recent show was February 14, 2020.

Open Invite Scramble Championship

September 21, 2018 *Pretenders Beware* Westbrook Armory
Champion: Ace Austin defeated Sami Callihan, Jessicka Havok, Matt Cross, Mick Moretti, and "Red Death" Daniel Garcia

From my live report on The Wrestling Insomniac Blog: The sixth competitor was a surprise, Bret Domino came out but was ushered to the back by officials, it was hilarious. Then Matt Cross came out as the actual surprise entrant. This was the fifth match of the night and it too was tremendous. It was my first-time seeing Daniel Garcia and he was one I would love to see Limitless bring back. Initially he didn't seem to have much of a personality but as the match went on it really came to the forefront, he's an asshole. I genuinely thought for sure he was going to win the championship. Some great moments in the match with Callihan demanding a kiss from Havok and she punched him in the mouth. Jessicka Havok asking Matt Cross if he was Son of Havok (his gimmick in Lucha Underground) which led to a mother/son reunion mid ring, never mind the fact that Cross is a half dozen years older than Havok. Garcia hit Havok from behind to which Cross yelled, "don't hit my mom!"

Garcia had Moretti in a Texas cloverleaf and ate some kicks from Callihan that had no effect. They then traded blows in the center of the ring, it was awesome. Prior to that Garcia nailed a devastating backbreaker on Moretti setting up the cloverleaf. Austin pinned Callihan to retain.

The first Open Invite Scramble Champion was crowned April 1, 2017 at the first Pancakes & Piledrivers event. Jason Cade defeated AR Fox, Arik Cannon, Caleb Konley, Davey Vega, Joey Janela, Lio Rush, Serpentico, Trevor Lee, Trey Miguel, and Zachary Wentz in the AR Fox Invitational Match to win the title. The current champion is John Skyler who won the title on December 27, 2019 defeating Champion: Clayton Gainz, Air Wolf, Crash Jaxon, JT Energy, & The Yellow Dog.

Ace Austin is the 7th champion holding the title for 78 days. He defeated Champion: Rich Swan, Aaron Williams, Ace Romero, Austin Manix, Clayton Gainz, Dan Maff, Jaxon Stone, Jeremiah, Kimber Lee, Larry D, Mik Drake, Pat Monix, Ron Mathis, Samantha Heights, & Shigehiro Irie on August 3, 2018. He lost the title on October 20, 2018 when Caleb Konley defeated Austin, Andy Dalton, Chainsaw King, Clayton Gainz, Lil N8, Madman Fulton, Pat Monix, Ron Mathis, Steve Manders, and Thomas Shire

¡Let's Wrestle!
Based out of Orono, Maine the promotion was founded in 2018 by Randy Carver, Kalvin Strange, Alexander Lee, Aiden Aggro and DangerKid. Their first show was July 6, 2018 and their most recent show was March 7, 2020. It acts as a developmental promotion of sorts for Limitless Wrestling.

¡Let's Wrestle! Championship

June 23, 2019 *La Kermesse Festival Night 2* St. Louis Field Biddeford
Street Fight: Champion: Kalvin Strange defeated CJ Cruz

The first ¡Let's Wrestle! champion was crowned January 19, 2019 when Davienne won the 30 person ¡Let's Wrestle! Rumble last eliminating Kalvin Strange. The current champion is "Mass Hole"

Mike McCarthy who defeated Kalvin Strange in a fans bring the weapons match on January 11, 2020.

"Classic" Kalvin Strange is the 2nd champion holding the title for 226 days. He defeated Davienne on May 31, 2019 and was defeated by "Mass Hole" Mike McCarthy on January 11, 2020.

IndependentWrestling.TV

Based out of Pennsylvania it was founded in 2017 by Vince Gerard and Adam Lash under the name Powerbomb.TV. In 2018 Adam Lash left the company and in 2019 it was rebranded as IndependentWrestling.TV. IWTV is a wrestling streaming service that provides both live wrestling cards and video on demand services for wrestling promotions from around the world.

Independent Wrestling Championship

November 29, 2019 *Twilight Zone* AMVets Hall Yarmouth
Champion: Warhorse defeated John Silver

From my live report on The Wrestling Insomniac Blog: Decent opening match, this was Warhorse's 15th title defense and I like the fact that they made a point to announce that. It gives importance to the championship and proves he is a fighting champion. Good back and forth match, there was a split crowd with Silver being a Limitless regular. Warhorse retained his title with a double foot stomp off the top rope.

February 22, 2020 *Practice What You Preach* AMVets Hall Yarmouth
Champion: Warhorse defeated Rip Byson

From my live report on The Wrestling Insomniac Blog: This was Warhorse's 34th title defense. I recall first seeing Rip as Tomahawk, who I enjoyed, but Rip Byson is somehow tremendously better. This was a hard-hitting competitive match but, in the end, Warhorse retained his championship extending his reign.

The first Independent Wrestling Champion was crowned on October 22, 2017 when Jonathan Gresham with Stokely Hathaway defeated Joey Lynch with Matt Lynch in a tournament final at a Powerbomb.TV promoted show in Old Forge, Pennsylvania.

Warhorse is the 7th champion having won the championship at a Black Label Pro show defeating Erick Stevens on September 21, 2019 in Summit, Illinois. He lost the title to Lee Moriarty on March 6, 2021 at New South Pro Wrestling in Hanceville, Alabama. Warhorse was champion for 532 days.

Limitless Wrestling Year End Awards

2016

Wrestler of the Year: Ace Romero

Romero finished 2016 with a record of 7 - 1 with victories over AR Fox, JT Dunn, Team Pazuzu, Donovan Dijak, Anthony Gangone, Adam Booker, & Brian Fury. His only loss in 2016, which was also his first loss in a Limitless Ring, was an Anything Goes Match with AR Fox.

Match of the Year: Anything Goes: Ace Romero vs. AR Fox

From *Past Your Bedtime*, September 24, 2016 at the American Legion Post 84 in Orono, Maine. This was their second in 2016 with Romero getting the win at the January 30th *Under Fire* event. On this night AR Fox got the win over Ace in a hard-fought match.

Best Special Guest of the Year: Zack Sabre Jr. at *Under Fire*

ZSJ made the United States his base of operations in 2016 traveling around the US Indies with tours in Germany and the UK. When I spoke to him on April 4, 2019 in New York City at WrestleCon he told me that going to Orono was his favorite road trip while he was living in the United States.

Show of the Year: *Under Fire* January 30, 2016

On a stormy January night at the American Legion Post 84 in Orono, Maine Limitless Wrestling presented *Under Fire*. A card stacked from top to bottom opening with AR Fox vs. Ace Romero, Main Evented by Zack Sabre Jr. vs. Chris Hero with Private Party,

Danger Kid, Alexander Lee, Anthony Gangone and others filling out the middle of the card. The Main Event delivered as these two put on a 25-minute clinic that was appreciated by those in attendance.

Breakout Star of the Year: "All Good" Anthony Greene

Greene finished 2016 with a flawless 8 - 0 record picking up wins over Team Pazuzu, Warbeard Hanson, JT Dunn, Xavier Bell, Tyler Nitro, Slyck Wagner Brown, Champ Mathews and "All Ego" Ethan Page.

Tag Team of the Year: Maine State Posse

A very interesting journey for the Maine State Posse in 2016. Danger Kid started his year teaming with Alexander Lee, Lee then turned on Kid bringing in Aggro as his new protege. MSP faced off against each other twice, once in a tag match and then in a singles encounter with Kid pinning Aggro. Their first time teaming together came in September at Past Your Bedtime. As a team they would go 1 - 3 dropping matches to Brick Mastone & Christian Casanova, JT Dunn & Mike Graca, and Scott Wild & Johnny Torres. Their only win against Sass & Fury: Jeremy Leary & Skylar.

2017

I was unable to locate the 2017-year end awards results, even Randy couldn't find where he had recorded these save the Match of the Year winner. If anyone has this information, please contact us and let us know.

Match of the Year: Take Me Home Tonight: Anthony Greene & Ace Romero vs. American Destroyers: Donovan Dijak & Mikey Webb

This match took place at Unreal on January 27, 2017 in Westbrook, Maine. It was the biggest show in Limitless history at that time with Cody Rhodes headlining. These four men collectively tore it down that night but, in the end, Take Me Home Tonight picked up the win when Anthony Greene pinned Donovan Dijak.

2018

Male Wrestler of the Year: Anthony Greene

Greene went 3 - 3 in 2018 however he was involved in some of the biggest matches and moments as voted by the Limitless fans. He was involved in both the Match and Moment of the year coming up short in both. His other loss was to Colt Cabana. He picked up some big wins including a fatal four way over Dunn, Romero, & Briggs, as well as singles victories over Martin Stone and a Street Fight over JT Dunn.

Female Wrestler of the Year: Ashley Vox

Vox compiled a winning 5- 2 record in her first full year in Limitless Wrestling. She started the year with a trios match with Allie Kat & Kris Statlander defeating the Maine State Posse, winning a fatal four way, and singles victories over Rachel Ellering & Davienne. She lost a tag match being pinned by Kris Statlander and was eliminated from the *Vacationland Cup* by Christian Casanova. In her biggest win, voted match of the year, she submitted Anthony Greene at *No Control* in Portland, Maine.

Moment of the Year: Limitless Fans Holding Up the Cage at *2018 Vacationland Cup*

July 27, 2018 in Westbrook, the Main Event of the *2018 Vacationland Cup* was to feature a grudge match between former tag team partners and now bitter rivals. Shortly into the beginning of the match the unthinkable happened as one side of the cage became detached and fell. The match wasn't over though, as the Limitless faithful held the cage up to allow AG & Ace to finish the match.

Match of the Year: Anthony Greene vs. Ashley Vox

The final show of the year for Limitless Wrestling was *No Control*, November 30, 2018 at the Portland Club. The main event that night saw Santana & Ortiz defeat JT Dunn & Brody King, however the third match on the card stole the show and was voted as the match of the year. AG came to the ring in full pomp and circumstance with his Platinum Hunnies, and even though they interfered several times on AG's behalf Vox still got the submission victory.

Scramble of the Year: Wrestling Revolver Scramble Championship: Ace Austin vs. Daniel Garcia vs. Jessicka Havok vs. Matt Cross vs. Mick Moretti vs. Sami Callihan

A staple of the Limitless Wrestling shows, this year saw the first Scramble Match of the Year award category. September 21, 2018, *Pretenders Beware* at the Westbrook Armory. Matt Cross was a surprise entrant into the match

Show of the Year: *2018 Vacationland Cup*

July 27, 2018 in Westbrook the *2018 Vacationland Cup* was an explosive introduction for the cup. Outside the competitors in the tournament we had PCO vs. Chris Dickinson, an outrageous scramble match, Jordynne Grace fall to Allie Kate, Free to Think best Whiskey Dick and the Moment of the Year Cage match. In the four opening rounds matches DangerKid, JT Dunn, Christian Casanova, & Josh Briggs punched their tickets to the finals that saw JT Dunn walk away with the honor and the trophy.

Biggest P.O.S. (Most Hated): MJF

Maxwell Jacob Freidman only wrestled in two matches in 2018 for Limitless Wrestling winning both matches. In January at *The World is Ours* he submitted Matt Cross and in March at only fools are satisfied he defeated Darby Allin. After defeating Allin he insulted the crowd, his opponent, Randy Carver, and members of the Limitless locker room. He said wasn't going to be here next month and may never come back. Six months later at *Pretenders Beware* after Ace Romero defeated JT Dunn, MJF made a surprise return literally driving into the Westbrook Armory where Dunn attacked Romero from behind. MJF would break his elbow in November keeping him out of the ring the rest of the year, however he seconded Dunn & Brody King at ringside for the final Limitless show of 2018.

Breakout Star of the Year: Christian Casanova

Casanova is a Limitless original competing on the first three shows however did not compete in a Limitless ring for over a year. Casanova's 2018 saw Top Talent amass a 4 - 3 record. A member of Stokely Hathaway's Dream Team, his victories in singles and multiman matches are over Brody King, The Rascalz, The Workhorsemen, Ashley Vox, and Kevin Blackwood. His losses were to Ethan Page & The Thick Boys, DJ Z, and JT Dunn in the finals of the 2018 Vacationland Cup.

Newcomer of the Year (Debut): Brody King

2018 would be the only year that Brody King would wrestle to date in Limitless Wrestling. Randy Carver stated that he was first alerted to Brody King because he is the lead singer to an underground Punk band God's Hate. King would debut in March at *Only Fools Are Satisfied* in a loss to Christian Casanova. He would return in May at *Feed the Need* picking up the only win of his Limitless Tenure defeating Eli Everfly. In September at

Pretenders Beware he would lose to Josh Briggs, and in November teaming with JT Dunn they would lose to Santana & Ortiz. King can move in ways a man his size shouldn't be able to move.

Tag Team of the Year: Maine State Posse

As a team the trio of Alexander Lee, Danger Kid, & Aiden Aggro amassed a record of 3 - 1 with victories over Daniel Garcia & Kevin Blackwood, Free To Think, and Travis Huckabee, Green Ant & Thief Ant. Their only loss as a team came in January to Kris Statlander, Allie Kat, & Ashley Vox. They competed in singles matches and even against each other at the *2018 Vacationland Cup*.

2019
Wrestler of the Year: Anthony Greene

With a 6 - 2 record Greene's 2019 started with two straight losses, first with Ace losing to The Kings, and then he was pinned by MJF in the fatal four way to declare the first Limitless Wrestling World Champion. However, he climbed his way back up the ladder with wins over Mark Sterling, then defeating Shawn Spears & Tommy Dreaming in a triple threat match on his way to the finals of the *2019 Vacationland Cup*. In the finals he defeated Ace Romero, JT Dunn, & Kevin Blackwood guaranteeing himself a shot at the Limitless Wrestling World Championship at *Know Your Enemy* at the Portland Expo. Greene would pin MJF to win the title and then go on and successfully defend it against Josh Briggs at Fresh Blood. Greene would finish the year at *Twilight Zone* the same way he started in teaming with Ace Romero, this time coming out victorious against the Maine State Posse.

Moment of the Year & Match of the Year: MJF becoming the inaugural Limitless Wrestling World Champion

March 9, 2019 at *Welcome to the Dance* in Westbrook, Maine a fatal four way took place to crown the first ever Limitless Wrestling World Champion. All four men involved in the match had been top competitors in Limitless Wrestling, two since the beginning of the promotion. Anthony Greene, Ace Romero, JT Dunn, & MJF gave it their all on this night and MJF was the accidental winner. Dunn hit a tremendous Death by Elbow on Greene putting him down on the canvas, he then knocked Romero to the floor with an elbow, and when MJF turned Dunn around he was hit with DBE and fell backwards onto the prone Greene as Romero pulled Dunn to the floor and referee Eric Greenleaf made the three count.

Debut of the Year: Dan Maff

The 21-year veteran made his Limitless debut at *Know Your Enemy* at the Portland Expo in the biggest way possible, opening the show against Ace Romero. Even in defeat Maff more than earned the respect of the Limitless Faithful that night battling Romero in the hoss fight to end all hoss fights. He returned in October at *Fresh Blood* defeating Matthew Justice in an anything goes match that saw Maff get the pin after a death valley driver through a door.

Show of the Year: 2019 Vacationland Cup

Held at the Portland Club on July 12, 2019 it saw Anthony Greene, Kevin Blackwood, Ace Romero, and JT Dunn win their first-round matches to advance to the finals. Once there, much to the delight of the fans, Anthony Greene last eliminated Ace Romero to win the cup and earn a shot at the Limitless Wrestling World Championship at *Know Your Enemy* at the Portland Expo. In other matches on the card The Maine State Posse defeated the Workhorsemen, Daniel Garcia submitted The Blade Pepper Parks, Ashley Vox won a five-way scramble, Skylar pinned Kris Statlander, and Puf pinned Mark Sterling.

Most Hated Wrestler of the Year: MJF

For the second year in a row MJF was voted on by the fans as the Most Hated Wrestler of the Year. His 2019 Limitless Wrestling record was a winning 3 - 1. With JT Dunn they defeated Ace Romero & Anthony Greene to start the year, he then captured the Limitless Wrestling World Championship in both the Match and Moment of the Year. In May at *Hooked on a Friedman* he defended the title against Ashley Vox and cemented his legacy as Most Hated. While Vox had her finish on MJF he bit her fingers tearing them open and applied Cross Rhodes for the win. During his celebration the fans started pelting MJF with trash. His final appearance in Limitless to date was at *Know Your Enemy* when he lost the World Title to Anthony Greene.

Breakout Star of the Year: Christian Casanova

For the second year in a row Casanova was voted as the Breakout Star of the Year, in 2019 he earned a winning 4 - 3 record. He started his year in January teaming with Austin Theory defeated Pepper Parks & Harlow O'Hara. He lost his next three matches to Kris Statlander, Brad Hollister, & Kevin Blackwood. He then closed out his year with a three-match winning streak defeating Leyla Hirsh at Know Your Enemy, teamed with JT Dun & Josh Bishop defeating Kevin Blackwood and The Butcher & The Blade. He closed out the year with a victory over Myron Reed at *Twilight Zone*. He carried the momentum into 2020 earning a title shot in January at *Flirtin' With Disaster*.

Tag Team of the Year: Maine State Posse

Once again, the Maine State Posse were voted the Limitless Wrestling Tag Team of the Year. It was a rocky road for MSP, but it started well as the trio defeated Thick Boys in January at *Snakebitten* and the Shook Crew in March at *Welcome to the*

Dance. In May at *Hooked on a Friedman* Aggro and Kid fell to the New Hart Foundation of Teddy Hart and Davey Boy Smith Jr. In June at *La Kermesse Festival Night 1* they defeated Sass & Fury. At the *2019 Vacationland Cup* they defeated The Workhorsemen, Alexander Lee turned on them joining forces with Brandon Kirk and Joey Eastman. This led to a street fight at *Know Your Enemy* that saw MSP get the better of Lee and Kirk. At *Fresh Blood* the defeated Violence is Forever and at *Twilight Zone* lost a grueling battle to Take Me Home Tonight. At the end of the year they finished with a record of 6 - 2.

¡Let's Wrestle! MVP: "Masshole" Mike McCarthy

McCarthy started 2019 in ¡Let's Wrestle! At the ¡Let's Wrestle! Rumble on January 19 defeating Mike Montero by referee stoppage. That night he would attack Davienne after she won the ¡Let's Wrestle! Championship leading to their match March 23rd where Davienne would defeat McCarthy. He rebounded in April at Volume 6 defeating Mick Moretti. At Volume 7, May 31st McCarthy accepted the Syndicate Gauntlet Challenge defeating Murdock by Count-Out, BA Tatum by Disqualification before being pinned by Owen Brody. At Volume 10 on October 12th McCarthy returned challenging Kalvin Strange for the ¡Let's Wrestle! Championship coming up short when Strange hit McCarthy with the title belt while the referee was down retaining the title. McCarthy finished the year at Volume 11, December 14th teaming with Brett Ryan Gosselin to defeat Kalvin Strange and Dave Dyer with McCarthy earning another title match at the 2020 ¡Let's Wrestle! on January 11, 2020. McCarthy would defeat Strange that night in a Fans Bring the Weapons Match to capture the ¡Let's Wrestle! Championship.

Top 10 Moments in Limitless Wrestling History

Premiering on October 24, 2020 on YouTube and Facebook, Randy Carver sat down with DangerKid, Aiden Aggro, Jon Alba, and Harry Aaron for a video podcast revealing the top 10 moments in the history of Limitless Wrestling, as voted on by the fans. The video also contained testimonials from wrestlers and fans alike talking about why Limitless Wrestling is important to them.

10: MJF Returns to Limitless and Aligns with JT Dunn at *Pretenders Beware* September 21, 2018 at the Westbrook Armory

9: Fans Bring the Weapons AR Fox vs. Ace Romero at *Problematic* May 13, 2017 Westbrook Armory

8: Zack Sabre Jr. vs. Chris Hero Headlines *Under Fire* January 30, 2016 American Legion Post 84 Orono

7: Cody Rhodes vs. JT Dunn at *Unreal* January 27, 2017 at the Westbrook Armory

6: Alexander Lee Turns His Back On The Maine State Posse at the *2019 Vacationland Cup* July 12, 2019 at the Portland Cup

5: Kevin Blackwood and Daniel Garcia Return After Life-Threatening Car Accident at the *2019 Vacationland Cup* July 12, 2019 at the Portland Club

4: Anthony Greene Defeats MJF For the Limitless Championship at *Know Your Enemy* September 6, 2019 at the Portland Expo

3: The Cage Collapses! Anthony Greene vs Ace Romero at the *2018 Vacationland Cup* July 27, 2018 at the Westbrook Armory

2: Limitless Wrestling Debuts at the Portland Expo at *Know Your Enemy* September 6, 2019

1: MJF Becomes The First Ever Limitless Wrestling Champion at *Welcome to the Dance* March 9, 2019 at the Westbrook Armory

More Limitless Wrestling Results

When compiling the history of Limitless Wrestling there are a series of matches that happened under the Limitless banner that Randy has deemed are not part of the official Limitless Wrestling win/loss records. This section is going to look at those matches.

OPENING PARTY FOR THREE GRACES TATTOO
September 1, 2018 Mason's Brewing Company, Brewer, Maine
Featuring live musical acts, freak show by Baron Von

- Kalvin Strange vs. Aiden Aggro
- Kalvin Strange vs. Alexander Lee

LIMITLESS VS. BLITZKRIEG
December 1, 2018 Banquet Hall, Enfield, Connecticut

- "Retro" Anthony Greene with the Platinum Hunnies defeated DJ Z
- The Maine State Posse: Alexander Lee, DangerKid, & Aiden Aggro defeated Massage NV: Dorian Graves & VSK and CPA
- The Batiri: Kodama & Obariyon defeated Harlow O'Hara & Kevin Blackwood
- Scotty Wild defeated John Silver
- Sass & Fury: Jeremy Leary & Skylar defeated Doom Fly: Delilah Doom & Eli Everfly
- Mark Sterling with Sidney Bakabella defeated Kris Statlander by reverse decision disqualification

- Scramble Match: Ashley Vox defeated Daniel Garcia, Francis Kipland Stevens, Hermit Crab, Kirby Wackerman, Matt Striker, Kid Curry, and Puf
- Anything Goes: Ace Romero defeated Jeff Cannonball with Sidney Bakabella
- Bobby Orlando & Brett Domino with Ms. Susannah defeated Full Blooded Intoxication: Little Guido Maritano & "Top Shelf" Troy Nelson by disqualification
- Elimination Match: Team Blitzkrieg: Jeremy Leary, Kodama, Obariyon, Scotty Wild, & Skylar with Sidney Bakabella defeated Team Limitless: "Retro" Anthony Greene with the Platinum Hunnies, Ashley Vox, and The Maine State Posse: Alexander Lee, DangerKid, & Aiden Aggro

PCO was scheduled to appear on the show and in the early morning hours before the event he signed an exclusive deal with Ring of Honor preventing him from appearing. PCO was replaced by Ace Romero who was not scheduled to appear at this event but missed his flight and couldn't fly out until Sunday. Sidney Bakabella wore a different outfit for each of his three appearances.

Kris Statlander had pinned Mark Sterling and after the referee called for the bell Sidney Bakabella placed a pair of brass knux in the back of Statlander's trunks and told the referee to check her. Upon discovering the foreign object referee Will Dojan reversed his decision disqualifying Statlander.

GLOW VS. GRIT: ROLLER DERBY & WRESTLING!
Saturday May 25, 2019 Cross Insurance Arena, Bangor Maine

When I was a kid, Saturday mornings with my dad consisted of watching a block of candlepin bowling, roller derby, WWF wrestling and monster trucks. So, I was pretty psyched when this event was announced. Now my wife isn't a fan of wrestling, but she is a big fan of the roller derby and this was a perfect outing for the whole family. This would be the first roller derby bout for Canaan & Addison and for Wesley his first time going to the matches. We sat up high for the roller derby bout so we could see the whole floor and then the kids and I moved down closer for the wrestling portion.

Central Maine Roller Derby was hosting the event as their Northwoods Knockouts took on The Inferno of the Androscoggin Fallen Angels Roller Derby League. The bout was very competitive, and the score stayed close, so close that at the end of the first half it was 82 - 80 in favor of the Inferno. At the beginning of the bout the Inferno had jumped out to a lead getting the score up 16 - 0 before the Knockouts came back and took over control. Later in the first half The Inferno were able to catch up taking advantage of a couple power jams.

The second half the Knockouts jumped ahead early and The Inferno just couldn't make the comeback. Both halves featured some very hard-hitting action and some really rough bumps. These girls definitely bring it on the track. There were about 150 people, which is a great turnout, but looks small in this building.

THE DERBY
Central Maine Roller Derby   Northwoods Knockouts (H)
    167
Androscoggin Fallen Angels   The Inferno
    139

The wrestling matches, presented by Limitless Wrestling, started shortly after the derby was over. The majority of the fans moved

in closer to the ring side area including the kids and me. Wrestling is not Kate's thing, so she stayed up in our original seats.
There were only four matches on the card which was perfect because the combination of the two events took just about three hours. After the show was over the wrestlers came back out to sell gimmicks, Addison got some of them to sign her poster. Wesley wanted to meet wrestlers and he did so by walking up to them and staring for a few seconds.

THE MATCHES
- Aiden Aggro pinned "The Prize" Alec Price
- DangerKid pinned CJ Cruz
- Triple Threat: Alexander Lee defeated DL Hurst & Frank Jaeger pinning Jaeger
- Kalvin Strange pinned Mike McCarthy

This show was promoted under the Limitless Wrestling name as you can see in the event poster. However, head boss Randy Carver has deemed that these matches do not count towards the official win/loss records of these competitors.

DL Hurst with a package piledriver, however Lee Stole the pin.

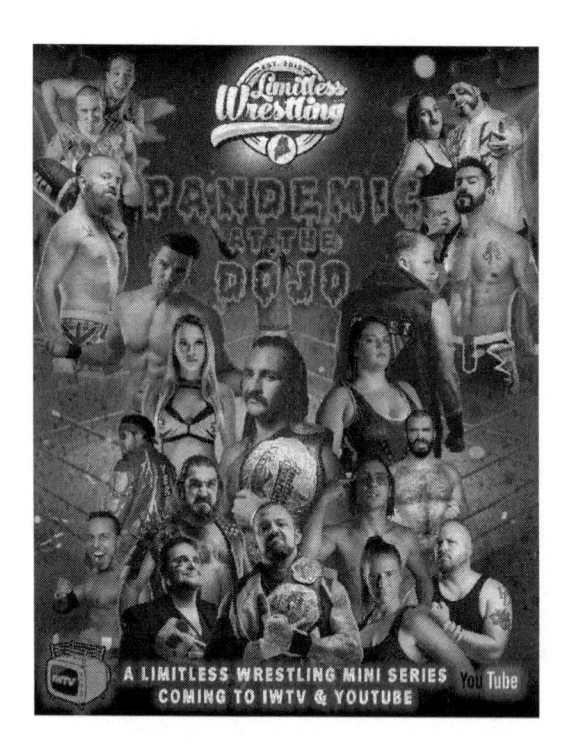

PANDEMIC AT THE DOJO

Due to Covid-19 on March 15th Limitless Wrestling cancelled "Cause for Alarm" which was to take place on March 21st in Yarmouth, Maine. That weekend though talent from Limitless Wrestling, ¡Let's Wrestle!, and new competitors looking to earn future opportunities gathered at the Limitless Dojo for a series of closed set matches. This resulted in a six-episode limited series on IWTV that became known as *Pandemic At The Dojo*. Each episode featured about four matches, promos, and video packages resulting in some very entertaining television.

According to head boss Randy Carver these matches do not count towards the official Limitless Wrestling win-loss record, however I feel for historical purposes the results should be included in this book. All matches took place in Brewer, Maine at the Limitless Dojo with postproduction commentary by Randy Carver.

Episode 1 *Aired March 30, 2020*

- Basic Becca defeated Aiden Aggro
- "The Prize" Alec Price defeated Antoine Nicolas
- Zach Burton defeated Eric Johnson
- Open Challenge: Limitless Wrestling World Champion: Anthony Greene pinned Davienne

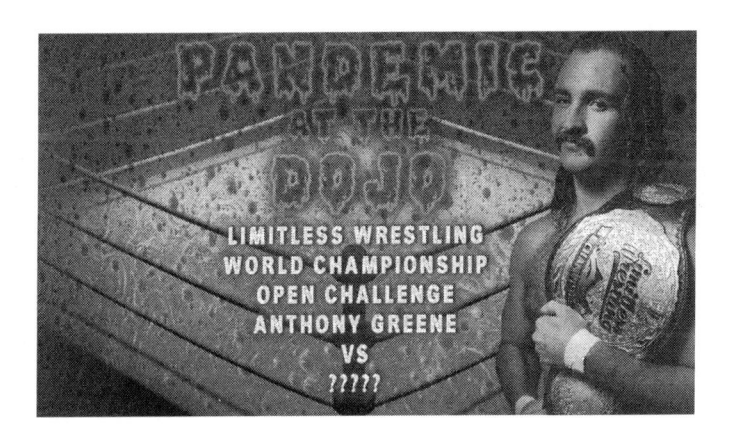

Episode 2 *Aired April 7, 2020*

- DangerKid pinned Ava Everett
- KenneLee: Alexander Lee & Kennedi Copeland defeated Even Stevens: Stephen Azure & Steve Somerset
- DL Hurst defeated Love Doug
- Rip Byson destroyed Frank Jaeger
- Non-Title Match: Limitless Wrestling World Champion: Anthony Greene pinned Basic Becca

Episode 3 *Aired April 14, 2020*

- Mike Law defeated Mac Daniels
- Even Stevens: Stephen Azure & Steve Somerset defeated Waves and Curls: Jaylen Bradyn & Traevon Jordan
- Eric Johnson pinned Dylan Nix
- "The Prize" Alec Price pinned Kennedi Copeland

Episode 4 *Aired April 21, 2020*

- Armani Kayos & Love Doug defeated Waves and Curls: Jaylen Bradyn & Traevon Jordan
- Mike Law defeated Frank Jaeger
- Dick Lane defeated Nick Stapp
- Rip Byson defeated DL Hurst to become the number one contender to the Limitless Wrestling World Championship

Episode 5 *Aired April 27, 2020*

- Antoine Nicolas defeated Armani Kayos
- Eric Johnson pinned Frank Jaeger
- Nick Stapp defeated Love Doug
- The Girls Room: Davienne & Ava Everett defeated Even Stevens: Stephen Azure & Steve Somerset

Episode 6 *Aired May 5, 2020*

- Nick Stapp defeated "The Prize" Alec Price
- Triple Threat: Tom Billington defeated Pimp Daddy Apple Cinnamon and Tim Kilgore
- Eric Johnson defeated Zach Burton
- Limitless Wrestling World Champion: Anthony Greene pinned Rip Byson

The Breakdown:
29 wrestlers competed in 25 matches; three matches were taped that didn't make it to air. One of those matches was Eric Johnson vs. Jacob Drifter, which was released on the Limitless Wrestling YouTube channel. Another was Alexander Lee vs. Zach Burton vs. Jacob Drifter in a triple threat anything goes match.

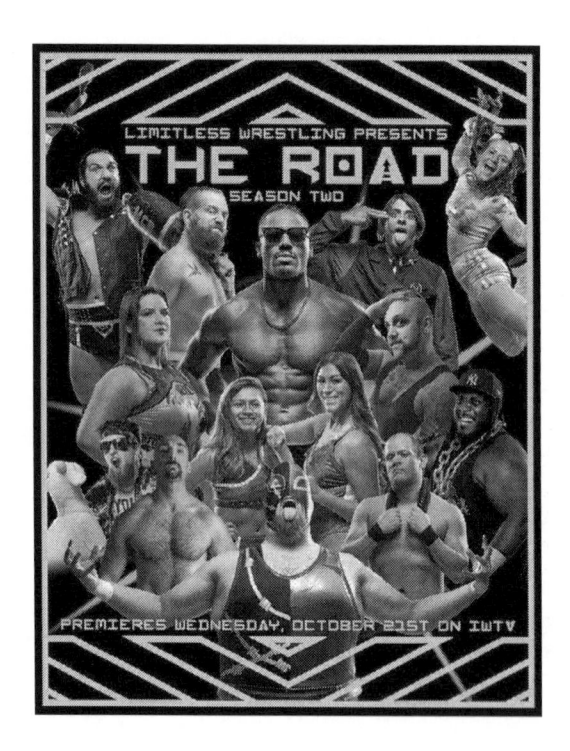

The Road: Season 2

The weekend of September 19 & 20, 2020 the talent from Limitless Wrestling, ¡Let's Wrestle!, and new competitors looking to earn future opportunities gathered at the American Legion Hall in Orono, Maine for another round of closed set tapings. The Road: Season 2 debuted on IWTV on Wednesday October 21, 2020 at 7pm and ran for 16 episodes concluding on February 3, 2021.

Episode 1 *Aired October 21, 2020*

- Ashley Vox pinned Basic Becca
- Channing Thomas defeated Swilly O'Brien
- Alexander Lee defeated BA Tatum
- Christian Casanova pinned Rip Byson

Episode 2 *Aired October 28, 2020*

- Brett Ryan Gosselin pinned Zach Burton
- Davienne pinned Love Doug
- Apostles of Chaos: Chris Beene & Logan Black defeated Shawn Phoenix & Andrew Palace when Black pinned Phoenix
- "The Prize" Alec Price defeated Tyree Taylor

Episode 3 *Aired November 4, 2020*

- Eric Johnson pinned Mike Gamble
- Mac Daniels pinned Kennedi Copeland
- Zachary Pierre Beaulieu defeated Elias Markopoulos
- Christian Casanova defeated Davienne

Episode 4 *Aired November 11, 2020*

- Blitzkrieg Pro: Bedlam Champion: Bobby Orlando defeated Chris Beene, Hermit Crab, & Shawn Phoenix pinning Beene
- DangerKid defeated Jessie Nolan - Nolan's pro-debut match
- Kaiju Grand Championship: American Beetle defeated Perry Von Vicious
- "Iron" Rip Byson pinned Zachary Pierre Beaulieu

Episode 5 *Aired November 18, 2020*

- Traevon Jordan defeated Steve Somerset
- Dylan Nix & Konnor Hex defeated The Competition: Champ Mathews & Connor Murphy
- Eric Johnson pinned Elijah Six
- Kennedi Copeland defeated Logan Black

Episode 6 *Aired November 25, 2020*

- Elias Markopoulos defeated Brett Ryan Gosselin
- Kaiju Grand Champion: American Beetle, Perry Von Vicious, & Powa Ranjuru defeated Bear Ranger, Big Callux, & Double Unicorn Dark
- Kirby Wackerman wrestled "Baby Girl" Nick Stapp to a no contest
- Slade pinned Bobby Orlando

Episode 7 *Aired December 2, 2020*

- Big Callux with The Hive defeated DangerKid
- Katie Arquette defeated Little Mean Kathleen
- Eric Johnson pinned Konnor Hex with Dylan Nix
- "The Prize" Alex Price pinned Elias Markopoulos

Episode 8 *Aired December 9, 2020*

- Basic Becca pinned Paris Van Dale
- Kirby Wackerman defeated Hermit Crab with the Hive
- Owen Brody pinned Dylan Nix
- No Rules: Alexander Lee defeated Slade

Episode 9 *Aired December 16, 2020*

- Boomer Hatfield with the Hive defeated "Baby Girl" Nick Stapp
- Channing Thomas defeated Little Mean Kathleen
- Eric Johnson pinned Love Doug
- Christian Casanova defeated "The Prize" Alec Price

Episode 10 *Aired December 23, 2020*

- Andrew Palace defeated Channing Thomas
- Sean William O'Brien pinned Love Doug
- Jeremy Leary with the Hive defeated Jacob Drifter
- The Higher Society: Armani Kayos & Paris Van Dale defeated The Sea Stars: Delmi Exo & Ashley Vox

Episode 11 *Aired December 30, 2020*

- TJ Crawford defeated Zachary Pierre Beaulieu
- Anything Goes: Nick Stapp defeated Jeremy Leary
- The Competition: Champ Mathews & Connor Murphy defeated Apostles of Chaos: Chris Beene & Logan Black
- Davienne defeated Travis Huckabee with The Hive

Episode 12 *Aired January 6, 2021*

- Delmi Exo defeating Channing Thomas
- Davienne defeated Katie Arquette
- Adam Booker pinned Owen Brody
- Travis Huckabee with Jeremy Leary defeated Perry Von Vicious

Episode 13 *Aired January 13, 2021*

- Rip Byson fought Perry Von Vicious to a no contest
- Traevon Jordan defeated Brandino Davis
- Loser Eats Dog Food: Jacob Drifter with Doug Wyzer defeated Dave Dyer
- Ricky Archer defeated CJ Cruz

Episode 14 *Aired January 20, 2021*

- The Hive: Big Callux & Boomer Hatfield with Travis Huckabee defeated The Syndicate: Owen Brody & BA Tatum
- Armani Kayos defeated Mike Gamble
- Traevon Jordan defeated TJ Crawford
- Ricky Archer defeated Mac Daniels

Episode 15 *Aired January 27, 2021*

- Street Fight: Mutually Assured Destruction: Rip Byson & Perry Von Vicious defeated The Apostles of Chaos: Chris Beene & Logan Black
- Travis Huckabee with Jeremy Leary defeated Ashley Vox
- "The Prize" Alec Price defeated Davienne
- DangerKid battled Tyree Taylor to a no-contest

Episode 16 *Aired February 3, 2021*

- Basic Becca vs Delmi Exo ended in a no contest after a double pin

- Mike Gamble pinned Love Doug
- The Hive: Big Callux, Boomer Hatfield, Leary, Hermit Crab, & Travis Huckabee defeated Team Limitless: DangerKid, Johnny Miyagi, Kirby Wackerman, Nick Stapp, & Tyree Taylor

The Breakdown:
63 wrestlers competed in 63 matches. Two matches that were filmed that didn't make it to air on season two, both involving the Higher Society: Armani Kayos & Paris Van Dale. One match was them against Little Mean Kathleen & Swilly O'Brien. The other was Higher Society against Even Stevens: Steve Somerset & Stephen Azure, early in the match Armani Kayos slapped Azure in the face breaking his jaw and halting the contest.

The Road: Season 3

The weekend of January 30 & 31, 2021 the talent from Limitless Wrestling, ¡Let's Wrestle!, and new competitors looking to earn future opportunities gathered at the American Legion Hall in Orono, Maine for a third round of closed set tapings. The Road: Season 3 debuted on IWTV on Wednesday February 24, 2021 at 7pm. This season featured a new weekly segment *Maine's Pro Wrestling History* hosted by Michael Labbe.

These results are not complete, these are the episodes that have aired to date at the time of publication.

Episode 1 *Aired February 24, 2021*

- Tyree Taylor pinned Mac Daniels

- Bobby Slam Challenge: Mike Gamble slammed Bobby Orlando
- The Competition: Champ Mathews & Conner Murphy defeated The Prestige: Brett Ryan Gosselin & Channing Thomas
- Davienne pinned TJ Crawford

Episode 2 *Aired March 03, 2021*

- Maine State Posse: DangerKid & Aiden Aggro vs. CJ Cruz & Ricky Archer went to a no-contest when The Competition ran in and attack all four men
- Rip Byson pinned Love Doug
- Alexander Lee defeated Jessie Nolan
- Masha Slamovich pinned Travis Huckabee

Episode 3 *Aired March 10, 2021*

- Jaylen Brandyn pinned Love Doug
- Alexander Lee pinned Konnor Hex
- Basic Becca defeated Delmi Exo
- Richard Holliday pinned TJ Crawford

Episode 4 *Aired March 17, 2021*

- Conner Murphy pinned Love Doug
- Alexander Lee pinned Dylan Nix
- Nick Stapp defeated Armani Kayos
- Davienne pinned Alex Price

Episode 5 *Aired March 24, 2021*

- The Kids: CJ Cruz & Ricky Archer defeated The Prestige: Brett Ryan Gosselin & Channing Thomas
- Tyree Taylor pinned Dylan Nix
- TJ Crawford defeated Nick Stapp
- Dog Collar Match: Rip Byson pinned Alexander Lee

Episode 6 *Aired March 31, 2021*

- Tyree Taylor defeated BA Tatum
- Ava Everett submitted Little Mean Kathleen
- Zachary Pierre Beaulieu defeated Kirby Wackerman
- Masha Slamovich pinned Becca

Episode 7 Aired *April 7, 2021*

- "The Prize" Alec Price pinned TJ Crawford
- Zachary Pierre Beaulieu pinned Delmi Exo
- Ava Everett vs. Jessie Nolan ended in a no-contest when Davienne interfered
- Maine State Posse: Aiden Aggro & DangerKid defeated the Competition: Champ Mathews & Conner Murphy

DOUBLE VISION
March 19, 2020 AMVets Yarmouth, Maine

Pre-Show
- "Main Attraction" Mac Daniels with Jon Alba pinned Love Doug

Main Card
- "The Prize" Alec Price defeated Myron Reed
- Triple Threat: Kevin Blackwood defeated Ken Broadway and Charles Mason when he submitted Broadway
- Becca pinned Ashley Vox
- Big Beef defeated Tyree Taylor
- Rip Byson pinned Rob Killjoy
- Ava Everette defeated Davienne

- Triple Threat: The Competition: Champ Mathews & Conner Murphy defeated The Kids: CJ Cruz & Ricky Archer and Maine State Posse: Aiden Aggro & DangerKid
- Daniel Garcia defeated Limitless Wrestling World Champion: Christian Casanova to win the championship

This show featured the debut of Rob Killjoy and Charles Mason and the return of Ken Broadway who had no appeared on a Limitless event since *Under Fire* January 30, 2016. Originally Rip Byson was going to have a return match with Warhorse, however Warhorse was not able to make it to the show. Rob Killjoy was removed from the Fatal Four Way, now Triple Threat Match, and placed as Byson's opponent.

Author's Note: I watched this event live on IWTV when it first aired. It was a very solid night of wrestling with some fantastic matches and one tremendous upset. Alec Price and Myron Reed showed up and showed out in the opening match of the main card. Charles Mason was very impressive; the finish of the Triple Threat was disturbing as Blackwood had Broadway locked in a submission and instead of breaking the match up, he simple watched Broadway fade away and appeared to get great joy out of it. We got three very hard-hitting matches in a row with Big Beef vs. Taylor, Byson & Killjoy, and Ava vs. Davienne.

The competition came out victorious in their tag team match, but we need them one on one, if you will, with the Maine State Posse. The main event was a World Title caliber match with both men giving everything they had for over 20 minutes until Garcia captured the title.

Alternate Poster Art

Epilogue

I love professional wrestling, with a passion that I cannot fully articulate. I don't have a memory of when I first fell in love with wrestling, my dad was a fan and because he watched it, I watched it. My dad would rent all the wrestling tapes that came out, at first, we even had to rent a VCR to watch them. We would watch all the wrestling on TV, even setting my alarm on Saturday Nights to get up to watch *Saturday Night's Main Event*.
I do remember the first big show I watched live on pay-per-view, it was *WrestleMania IV*, and I was eight years old. My Dad would normally bring me to my mother's house, instead we went to his friend's house and down in the basement, among all my Dad's work friends was an empty seat directly in front of the television for me.
I went to my first live wrestling even just before my 10th birthday on June 4, 1989 at the Cumberland County Civic Center in Portland, Maine to see the WWF. "Macho Man" Randy Savage beat the WWF Champion Hulk Hogan by count-out in the main event. I went to my first independent show an Eastern Wrestling Alliance event on March 16, 1997 in Auburn, Maine. I have list of every wrestling show I have ever been too and the results of those shows. I know many have been to more, but I have been to 256 shows in two countries and sixteen different states. I have been to some of the biggest shows, WrestleMania XXIV, and the smallest, a show where I was the only person sitting on my side of the ring. Before Limitless wrestling I would go to an Indie event and if I got one good match for my $10, I was happy for it. With Limitless Wrestling I always feel the quality of the matches far exceeds the value of my ticket. Limitless has made Maine a destination for independent wrestlers and fans alike. I feel fortunate to have Limitless as my hometown promotion.

Photo Credits

Page 1	Harry Aaron – Randy Carver ring announcing
Page 3 & 4	Randy Carver – Emerge Wrestling concept art
Page 4	Randy Carver – Carver with Lee in ring
Page 5	Harry Aaron – Randy Carver with Ace & AG
Page 6	Randy Carver – Anthony Greene Stage One victory
Page 11	Randy Carver – The crowd for Stage One
Page 13	Michael J. Labbe – Tim Donst tying up Alex Mason
Page 14	Michael J. Labbe – AG locking up with Canaan
Page 17	Ethan Scrutchfield – Zack Sabre Jr. shaking hands with Chris Hero
Page 18	Michael J. Labbe – Sabre tying Hero up with his legs
Page 18	Still from Video – Bradford hitting elbows with Chris Hero
Page 20	Randy Carver – Team New England
Page 21	Randy Carver – Chris Dickinson twisting Donovan Dijak
Page 23	Harry Aaron – EYFBO with moonsault on Private Party
Page 25	Harry Aaron – Legion Crowd
Page 27	Harry Aaron – Flip Gordon vs. Lince Dorado
Page 28	Harry Aaron – AR Fox vs. Ace Romero anything goes
Page 32	Michael J. Labbe – Brian Fury submitting Brian Cage
Page 33	Michael J. Labbe – Tenacious Two vs. Maine State Posse
Page 35	Randy Carver – Big Baddy Beluga lap dance for Davienne
Page 36	Jeremy Leary – Sass & Fury
Page 38	Ethan Scrutchfield – Cody Rhodes vs. JT Dunn

Page 39	Harry Aaron – JT Dunn with death by elbow on Cody Rhodes
Page 43	Harry Aaron – Troy Nelson headstand
Page 44	Michael J. Labbe – Swoggle in win
Page 44	Harry Aaron – Swoggle victorious
Page 45	Harry Aaron – Matt Sydal & Ricochet
Page 47	Randy Carver – Crowd at Portland Club
Page 50	Michael J. Labbe – Paul London singing his entrance music
Page 51	Harry Aaron – Fox with guitar hero
Page 52	Harry Aaron – Ace through a table
Page 53	Shane @jodocow – AR Fox flying off the top rope
Page 53	Shane @jodocow – Ace standing tall in the corner
Page 54	Michael J. Labbe – Ace Romero & AR Fox showing the battle wounds of the match
Page 56	Randy Carver – Skylar jumps off moving truck
Page 59	Michael J. Labbe – Sami Callihan with stretch muffler on MJF
Page 60	Harry Aaron – Tabarnak de Team entrance
Page 60	Harry Aaron – TDT interacting with the crowd
Page 61	Michael J. Labbe – Rey Fenix Moonsault & AR Fenix victorious
Page 63	Harry Aaron – Maine State Posse
Page 64	Randy Carver – Crowd at Westbrook Armory
Page 66	Michael J. Labbe – Dickinson Pazuzu Bomb on Zagami
Page 67	Michael J. Labbe – Greene & Dunn double count out
Page 69	Michael J. Labbe – Ethan Page with broken rope
Page 70	Michael J. Labbe – Suplex onto chairs
Page 71	Michael J. Labbe – Teddy Hart issues challenge
Page 75	Harry Aaron – Ashley Vox vs. Rachel Ellering
Page 76	Still from Video – Anthony Greene falling towards table

Page 78	Harry Aaron – JT Dunn with 2018 Vacationland Cup trophy
Page 79	Harry Aaron – The Cage falling
Page 81	Jason Worthing – Kris Statlander defeats Delmi Exo
Page 81	Jason Worthing – Brett Domino
Page 83	Jason Worthing – Alexander Lee & DangerKid entrance
Page 83	Jason Worthing – Brandino Davis in the crowd
Page 85	Michael J. Labbe – MJF returns to Limitless
Page 86	Harry Aaron – MJF leaving the chaos he created
Page 87	Anthony Greene – Anthony Greene & The Platinum Hunnies
Page 89	Michael J. Labbe – Delilah Doom
Page 90	Sunny D Photography – Ashley Vox submits Anthony Greene
Page 92	Doug Wyzer – Randy Carver announcing the Limitless Wrestling Championship
Page 94	Michael J. Labbe – Teddy Hart has Darby Allin set for a move
Page 95	Michael J. Labbe – Tommy Dreamer with Piledriver on Chris Dickinson
Page 96	Sunny D Photography – A surprised MJF crowned as first Limitless Champion
Page 98	Michael J. Labbe – Kris Statlander & Pat Buck
Page 99	Michael J. Labbe – Victoria with Muta Lock on Skylar
Page 100	Michael J. Labbe – MJF biting Ashley Vox
Page 101	Michael J. Labbe – MJF in a trash littered ring
Page 105	Sunny D Photography – Daniel Garcia with sharpshooter on Pepper Parks
Page 106	Sunny D Photography – Alexander Lee turns on the MSP

Page 106	Sunny D Photography – Anthony Greene with 2019 Vacationland Cup trophy
Page 108	Randy Carver – Portland Expo sign
Page 109	Randy Carver – Portland Expo crowd
Page 110	Sunny D Photography – Dan Maff with burning hammer on Ace Romero
Page 111	Sunny D Photography – Jeremy Leary getting his hair cut
Page 112	Sunny D Photography – Anthony Greene is your new Champion
Page 113	Sunny D Photography – DangerKid flies onto Alexander Lee
Page 113	Sunny D Photography –The Butcher and the Blade
Page 115	Sunny D Photography – Dan Maff driving Mathew Justice through a door
Page 116	Sunny D Photography – Kris Statlander and Ashley Vox
Page 119	Michael J. Labbe – Last Creature Standing
Page 120	Michael J. Labbe – Last Creature Standing
Page 122	Michael J. Labbe – Brandon Kirk about to skewer Alexander Lee
Page 123	Doug Wyzer – The Crowd before the main event at Flirtin' With Disaster
Page 126	Michael J. Labbe – Trevor Murdoch with the win
Page 127	Michael J. Labbe – Kris Statlander vertical suplex on Jody Threat
Page 135	Harry Aaron – 2020 Vacationland Cup Final 4
Page 138	AG & Ava – There matching WrestleProm gear
Page 145	Shane @jodocow – JT Dunn vs. Anthony Greene
Page 147	Harry Aaron – Ace Romero vs. JT Dunn
Page 148	Super No Vacancy – Ace Romero vs. Anthony Greene
Page 150	Randy Carver – Alexander Lee vs. Danger Kid

Page 151	Sunny D Photography – Ashley vs. Kris Statlander
Page 154	Wrestlebrook Photo – Ace Romero
Page 156	Michael J. Labbe – Ace Romero and others
Page 157	IWE – Ace Romero IWE promo
Page 160	Wrestlebrook Photo – Alec Price
Page 163	Jessie Nolan – Alexander Lee
Page 165	Michael J. Labbe – Scotty "By God" Vegas
Page 166	Michael J. Labbe – Scotty "By God" Vegas vs. Robbie Ellis
Page 167	Wrestlebrook Photo – Alexander Lee
Page 172	Wrestlebrook Photo – Anthony Greene
Page 174	Harry Aaron – Anthony Greene
Page 175	Jason Worthing – Anthony Greene & The Platinum Hunnies
Page 179	Wrestlebrook Photo – Ashley Vox
Page 182	Harry Aaron – Ava Everette
Page 188	Michael J. Labbe – Brandon Kirk
Page 198	Michael J. Labbe – Champ Mathews
Page 200	Wrestlebrook Photo – Chris Dickinson
Page 203	Wrestlebrook Photo – Christian Casanova
Page 205	Wrestlebrook Photo – CJ Cruz
Page 206	Jason Worthing – Colt Cabana
Page 207	Harry Aaron - Conner Murphy
Page 212	Wrestlebrook Photo – Daniel Garcia
Page 218	Harry Aaron – Delmi Exo
Page 222	Wrestlebrook Photo – DL Hurst
Page 227	Harry Aaron – Eric Johnson
Page 240	Wrestlebrook Photo – JD Drake
Page 243	Sunny D Photography – Jeremy Leary
Page 246	Wrestlebrook Photo – Jody Threat
Page 249	Wrestlebrook Photo – John Silver
Page 254	Harry Aaron – JT Dunn
Page 256	Super No Vacancy – JT Dunn

Page 261	Wrestlebrook Photo – Kevin Blackwood
Page 263	Harry Aaron – Kimber Lee
Page 265	Sunny D Photography – Kris Statlander
Page 267	Wrestlebrook Photo – Leyla Hirsch
Page 272	Harry Aaron – Mac Daniels
Page 274	Harry Aaron – Maine State Posse
Page 276	Wrestlebrook Photo – DangerKid
Page 278	Harry Aaron – Maine State Posse
Page 279	Wrestlebrook Photo – Aiden Aggro
Page 292	Sunny D Photography - MJF
Page 293	Wrestlebrook Photo – MJF
Page 308	Wrestlebrook Photo – Rip Byson
Page 309	Wrestlebrook Photo – Rip Byson, Perry Von Vicious, Scott Wild
Page 311	Michael J. Labbe – Sami Callihan
Page 313	Michael J. Labbe – LAX, or EYFBO, or Santana & Ortiz
Page 320	Wrestlebrook Photo – Skylar
Page 326	Harry Aaron – Tabarnak de Team
Page 336	Harry Aaron – Troy Nelson
Page 341	Wrestlebrook Photo – Warhorse
Page 344	Harry Aaron – Xavier Bell
Page 347	Zack Sabre Jr. – ZSJ with Moose Statue
Page 349	Harry Aaron - Sidney Bakabella
Page 350	Sofie Vasquez – Jon Alba with Mac Daniels
Page 352	Harry Aaron – Joey Eastman
Page 353	Harry Aaron – Stokely Hathaway
Page 354	Jason Worthing – Rich Palladino
Page 356	Harry Aaron – Ethan Scott
Page 357	Sunny D Photography – Eric Greenleaf
Page 358	Randy Carver – Joey Gleitz
Page 359	Harry Aaron – Tony P giving the business
Page 360	Sunny D Photography – Kevin Quinn & MSP

Page 362	Jason Worthing – Derek Douglas and Alec Price
Page 363	Harry Aaron - Nate Speckman
Page 365	Randy Carver – Limitless Wrestling World Championship
Page 367	MJF – MFJ vs. Kip Sabian
Page 368	Michael J. Labbe – MJF vs. Ashely Vox torture rack
Page 370	Anthony Greene – AG vs. Brian Pilman Jr.
Page 372	Megan Nielsen – AG and Davienne
Page 374	Sofie Vasquez – Daniel Garcia defeated Christian Casanova
Page 376	Michael J. Labbe – Anthony Gangone vs. Sonya Strong
Page 379	Michael J. Labbe – Daniel Garcia with Texas cloverleaf
Page 382	Wrestlebrook Photo – IWTV Champion: Warhorse vs. Rip Byson
Page 394	Wrestlebrook Photo – Kalvin Strange
Page 398	Michael J. Labbe – Roller Derby track and wrestling ring
Page 399	Michael J. Labbe – DL Hurt with package piledriver on Frank Jaeger
Page 414	Sofie Vasquez – Ava Everette vs. Davienne
Rear Cover	Harry Aaron – all three photos

All poster art courteous of Randy Carver

Printed in Great Britain
by Amazon